CURRICULUM

21 Essential Education for a Changing World

Edited by

HEIDI HAYES JACOBS

Alexandria, Virginia USA

ASCD®

1703 N. Beauregard St. • Alexandria, VA 22311-1714 USA
Phone: 800-933-2723 or 703-578-9600 • Fax: 703-575-5400
Web site: www.ascd.org • E-mail: member@ascd.org
Author guidelines: www.ascd.org/write

Gene R. Carter, *Executive Director;* Nancy Modrak, *Publisher;* Scott Willis, *Director, Book Acquisitions & Development;* Julie Houtz, *Director, Book Editing & Production;* Darcie Russell, *Editor;* Catherine Guyer, *Senior Graphic Designer;* Mike Kalyan, *Production Manager;* Valerie Younkin, *Desktop Publishing Specialist*

Printed in the United States of America. Cover art © 2010 by ASCD. ASCD publications present a variety of viewpoints. The views expressed or implied in this book should not be interpreted as official positions of the Association.

All Web links in this book are correct as of the publication date below but may have become inactive or otherwise modified since that time. If you notice a deactivated or changed link, please e-mail books@ascd.org with the words "Link Update" in the subject line. In your message, please specify the Web link, the book title, and the page number on which the link appears.

ASCD Member Book, No. FY10-4 (Jan. 2010, PSI+). ASCD Member Books mail to Premium (P), Select (S), and Institutional Plus (I+) members on this schedule: Jan., PSI+; Feb., P; Apr., PSI+; May, P; July, PSI+; Aug., P; Sept., PSI+; Nov., PSI+; Dec., P. Select membership was formerly known as Comprehensive membership.

PAPERBACK ISBN: 978-1-4166-0940-7   ASCD product #109008

Also available as an e-book (see Books in Print for the ISBNs)

Quantity discounts for the paperback edition only: 10–49 copies, 10%; 50+ copies, 15%; for 1,000 or more copies, call 800-933-2723, ext. 5634, or 703-575-5634. For desk copies: member@ascd.org.

Library of Congress Cataloging-in-Publication Data
Curriculum 21 : essential education for a changing world / edited by Heidi Hayes Jacobs.
     p. cm.
  Includes bibliographical references and index.
  ISBN 978-1-4166-0940-7 (pbk. : alk. paper)   1. Curriculum planning.   2. Educational technology.   I. Jacobs, Heidi Hayes.   II. Title: Curriculum twenty one.
  LB2806.15.C6915 2009
  375′.0010973--dc22
                                                                                          2009035423

20 19 18 17 16 15 14 13 12 11 10   1 2 3 4 5 6 7 8 9 10 11 12

In memory of Richard Strong

Fierce and stunning intelligence

Hearty laughter and warmth

Having read everything, he was a university

Fearless about the future

A commanding public learner

Richard was my teacher

CURRICULUM 21
Essential Education for a Changing World

ACKNOWLEDGMENTS

To encourage means to give courage. I thank the 10 authors who have contributed to this book by sharing their convictions and bold thinking. They are a virtual team spanning diverse places, but with a singular belief that growth is essential in education. I continue to learn from each of them.

I feel deep appreciation for the personal encouragement (and prodding) from specific colleagues who have been with me relentlessly at every turn: Betsi Shays, Ann Johnson, Valerie Truesdale, Earl Nicholas, Greg Lind, Beth Beckwith, Janet Hale, Jeanne Tribuzzi, and Brandon Wiley. Thanks to Nicki Newton for our collaboration over the years at Columbia University's Teachers College. I value the devotion and steadfastness of Kathy Scoli who has worked with me for almost 20 years. My communication with Kathy feels like a comforting shorthand.

Perspective means to see meaningful relationships from a range of angles. On this one I am sincerely grateful to Vivian Goldstein, Jay McTighe, Giselle Martin-Kniep, and Brian Cory. ASCD has played a pivotal role in my work over many years. Praise to the astute and insightful editorial eye of Scott Willis and Darcie Russell. They have made this book a better one. And, a special thanks to Kathleen Burke for giving me the opportunity to make a special presentation at the ASCD conference held in San Francisco in 2003 on the seed ideas that eventually grew into this book. It was a turning point for me.

For both encouragement and perspective, I thank my husband Jeffrey, and our adult children, Rebecca and Matt. They help me clarify what matters every day. I rely on their honest and aware views of the world.

Over many years, I have had the opportunity to meet many educators in many parts of the world. I have been fortunate to be a learner and I thank you. Ultimately this book is to help all of us prepare our learners for their future.

INTRODUCTION

....

Heidi Hayes Jacobs

What year are you preparing your students for? 1973? 1995?

Can you honestly say that your school's curriculum and the program you use are preparing your students for 2015 or 2020? Are you even preparing them for today?

Johnny might not even know that his classroom experiences are not providing him the tools to enter a global economy that changes exponentially. Maria's gap in knowledge about the last 50 years of history is not helping her make sense of the contemporary world she lives in. Is your curriculum replacing older methodologies with new tools for communicating and sharing? Or is the use of technology an "event"? Are your students learning world languages that will be dominant and influential when they are adults? Or are you primarily, and painfully, focused on the next state test based on textbooks from the 1950s? It is no wonder that we are behind other nations in international comparisons of academic achievement when our school structures are fundamentally based on an antiquated system established in the late 1800s.

The contention of this book is that we need to overhaul, update, and inject life into our curriculum and dramatically alter the format of what schools look like to match the times in which we live. Our responsibility is to prepare the learners in our care for their world and their future. There is rising concern about 21st century skills and tools for our learners, although it is noteworthy that as of the writing of this book, almost 10 percent of the 21st century has already passed.

Our questions will be straightforward: What do we cut? What do we keep? What do we create? Ironically, we will find many of our answers by looking to the past. For example, in Latin, *curriculum* means "a path to run in small steps." We negotiate and choose that path, but ultimately it is the students who determine how they will, or if they can, take steps on the path with each class, each teacher, and each day. And if the path is going to 1973 and they know it, then their will and desire to engage are diminished.

To exemplify the imagination, courage, and practicality of 21st century learning, I have invited 10 educators to share their work with you. Certainly there are progressive and practical innovations going on in the United States and other nations that are well worth examining, and obviously the limitation of space afforded by print limits the number that can be included in this book. I have invited these colleagues to elaborate on particularly inventive and timely projects to stimulate like-minded practice.

Stephen Wilmarth has a fine grasp on two critical points that I ask the reader to consider in this book. First, he has articulated how technology is altering the very nature of pedagogy. In short, we cannot expect to "think the same" about teaching when the act of teaching is shifting dramatically as a result of technology tools and access to information. Second, he has created an enormously successful program for bringing together technology innovation, international exchange, and future-oriented work skills. Students in Connecticut work with students in China through his 21st century learning project.

Globalizing the curriculum is the driving force behind the brilliant work of **Vivien Stewart,** vice president of the Asia Society in charge of education. Not only does she pointedly reveal the necessity for a thorough reconceptualizing of what global education should look like, but also she is acting on her vision with research and creativity. Her perspective and pragmatism make her one of the leading world authorities on this dynamic next chapter in curriculum design.

Tim Tyson is one of my school heroes. His remarkable work as a building principal at Mabry Middle School in Cobb County, Georgia, should inspire any 21st century leader to look at how school improvement efforts need to shift the culture to one that "makes learning irresistible," as Tim did at Mabry. Winning the Intel and Scholastic School of Distinction award, the Mabry faculty and student population—with Tim's leadership—show us how to replace the old with the best of the new.

Frank W. Baker is a highly experienced television journalist who has been developing curriculum tools for teaching media literacy for the past 10 years. It is shocking to me that the one medium that is without doubt the most potent in terms of its effects on children and youth—television—is not mentioned formally in state standards. How can we help learners become critical consumers of media if we do not work with them on media literacy? This is not just the purview of the family, for we educators certainly do not restrict ourselves to print literacy. Frank's approach is tested and solid.

David Niguidula is the pioneering developer of the digital student portfolio, which is revolutionizing how we access learning and how students view their learning. The state of Rhode Island now requires that each learner develop a digital portfolio showing readiness to graduate. Each learner becomes the navigator of her own work. The ultimate accountability is for learners to take responsibility for their work. The portfolio includes a full array of assessment types. Not only will traditional testing scores and results be linked, but classroom projects, writing collections, and digital film clips of performances are part of the picture compiled by the learner. For me, David represents the best of the diligent scientist-teacher. His work is beginning to revolutionize assessment.

Jaimie Cloud has devoted her career to building curriculum that supports sustainability and global understanding. The Cloud Institute for Sustainability Education, based in New York City, has produced powerful and user-friendly curriculum for adaptation in any classroom. Her travels and work in underdeveloped countries and with her innovative team infuse this curriculum project with reality and passion.

Alan November has always been ahead of his time. My first encounter with him was around 1992 at a national conference on curriculum integration where he was touting the advent of technology. It is hard to remember that terms like *Internet* or *BlackBerry* did not come up in regular conversations at that time. Alan could see the train coming, and he wanted to ride in the engine. He still does. With humor and insight, he shares his views on how schools need to be reengineered.

Beginning with his classroom experience as a high school physics teacher in South Carolina, **Bill Sheskey** starts from the point of view of the tech-savvy student. With extraordinary energy and creativity, Bill has developed straightforward strategies to help fellow teachers employ digital tools with students, who often know more than the adults. Bill is asking us to follow the lead of the students, and he suggests that many of the resources that can help classroom teachers are readily available as open-source software and tools. Our students are familiar with many of those very tools and might be our instructors if we give them the lead.

What mental dispositions and attitudes will help us enter new times that bring new challenges? Our quest requires that our most human, psychological, and spiritual aspects be considered as we look into the future. With their thoughtful and productive models as revealed in the Habits of Mind, **Bena Kallick** and **Arthur Costa** coach us with years of cumulative wisdom. They advise us not only on traits to engender in our learners, but also on traits we should cultivate in ourselves as curriculum designers.

Our goal as authors is to stimulate specific dialogue, specific debate, and specific actions for your consideration at all levels—the school setting, the district board, and the state office of education. We share our various perspectives with sincerity and experience. Our purpose is direct. We invite your engagement in Curriculum 21. We believe that educators at the local, community, state, national, and global levels need open discussion and that their actions need to be anchored in a candid response to contemporary challenges. Is the curricular practice and organization of your school program designed to address the best interests of your learners, or is it running on habit? Is your state education department deliberately engaged in long-term strategic planning for learners, or is it committed to old-style gatekeeping? Are global organizations and corporations merely agreeing to broad generalities, or are they finding specific solutions to address worldwide educative concerns?

To assist educators who are serious in their quest for a new kind of school and curriculum, in Chapters 1, 2, and 3, I propose a model for upgrading curriculum. Chapter 1 lays the groundwork for the reasons to make significant changes in our education system. Chapter 2 provides specific steps for short-term revision of assessments and skills in order to directly engage learners with 21st century products and proficiencies. The review process is based on specific phases, considerations for each phase, and corresponding actions. Upgrading content is the focus of Chapter 3, as each subject area is examined to find potential provocations and points for reconsideration and replacement.

Chapter 4 provides a set of considerations to use when planning for long-term versions of a new school. Specifically, I look at four program structures that need to be seriously altered and altered in sync with one another: schedules, the grouping patterns of learners, the configurations of professional personnel, and the use of space (both physical and virtual). The goal is to move the process along realistically and proactively among those groups of teachers, administrators, students, parents, and community members ready and willing to grow. I share new choices and alternatives that will be familiar to some, knowing that readers bring their own ideas to the discussion. It is a new age that requires some new directions and strategic collaborations.

The premise here is that a new curricular approach should begin with specific rethinking and examination of choices based on the tensions between critical points from our past practice and new challenges for the future. Examining this debate is the primary purpose of this book. You will be making choices for the generation you are charged to nurture. You are making these choices now. We invite you and your leadership teams to consider these tensions within each discipline; in interdisciplinary connections; in applications for new career possibilities in the future workforce; in the portals between the school, the community, and the globe; in the individual child's sense of physical and mental well-being; and in the sustainability of our planet. We encourage an active target for a curriculum that marries pertinent ideas and purposeful practice— a curriculum that addresses what is essential for our learners. The new generation of thoughtful leaders in education will carry this torch to new levels. It is to them, ultimately, that we direct this book.

1

A NEW ESSENTIAL CURRICULUM
for a New Time

....

Heidi Hayes Jacobs

I often wonder if many of our students feel like they are time traveling as they walk through the school door each morning. As they cross the threshold, do they feel as if they are entering a simulation of life in the 1980s? Then, at the end of the school day, do they feel that they have returned to the 21st century? As educators, our challenge is to match the needs of our learners to a world that is changing with great rapidity. To meet this challenge, we need to become strategic learners ourselves by deliberately expanding our perspectives and updating our approaches.

In *Understanding by Design* (2005), Wiggins and McTighe reinforce their well-respected axiom that we should determine "what it is we want students to know and be able to do" before we start short-sighted activity writing for the classroom. They are asking us to stop, reflect, and make intelligent choices, and to engage in "backward design" by beginning with the end in mind. They are asking us to be deliberate and forward-thinking as well. *Designing* backward does not mean *going* backward.

What concerns me is that when the crucial step of looking forward is missed, we are restricted by "what we know" and "what we are able to do." In a sense, many schools and leaders compose well-intended but antiquated mission statements reminiscent of the past century. Running schools and using curriculum on a constant *replay* button no longer works. It is critical that we become active researchers and developers of innovations and new directions.

To provide a context for the chapters in this book, I would like to share some problems, themes, and counter-themes regarding the reason we sometimes seem stuck during what should be a dynamic and exciting age in education. I will also touch on a few of the critical points to be discussed by our remarkable team of writers.

The Cavernous Curriculum: Old Habits Run Deep

What are the roots of our school-related habits and dated curriculum? The Committee of Ten, appointed at the meeting of the National Educational Association in 1892, shared their findings at Saratoga Springs, New York, on December 4, 1893. (The report is available at http://tmh. floonet.net/books/commoften/mainrpt.html.) With the move away from agriculture and the advent of the industrial revolution, more children were going to school. By the late 1800s, educators across the United States had identified a need for educational standardization.

It was a contentious time, with competing viewpoints, pedagogies, and approaches regarding how school should be organized and the nature of the curriculum. Some educators favored critical thinking, whereas others preferred rote memorization. One philosophy considered high schools in the United States solely as institutions that would, from the start, divide students into college-bound and working-trades groups (sometimes based on race or ethnic background). This preference was in contrast with another viewpoint that attempted to provide standardized courses for all students. On the curricular front, debates took place over whether classical Latin and Greek or practical studies should be at the core. All this debate led to the final report from the Committee of Ten that recommended that all students—whether college bound or work oriented—should be taught the same curriculum.

Schooling would take place over 12 years—8 for the elementary grades (in which we now include middle school) and 4 for high school.

The effect of this 19th century committee is seen to this very day. The academic program was predicated on English, history, civics, mathematics, biology, chemistry, and physics on the high school level. In practice, this focus led directly to the decisions made in elementary school as a means of reaching the high school curriculum. This was not a developmental approach. It is noteworthy that famed developmental psychologist Jean Piaget was born in 1896, too late to redirect the committee's notion of who children are and what they can learn.

In fact, schools were not designed for children. Rather, they reflected the factory model of organization resulting from the ascension of industry and economic expansion between 1897 and 1921, which ultimately was applied to education as well as business (Feldman, 1999). With roughly 180 instructional days based on an agrarian calendar and a six-hour day with eight subjects, the standardization took hold. It still holds children, teachers, and communities in a fierce grip.

Although we have had a century of fascinating innovation, experimentation, and exciting ideas since the committee issued its report, the artifacts speak. Simply by picking up a school catalogue or guide, one can see clearly that the Committee of Ten reigns. The concept of what a school is does not need *reform*—it needs *new* forms.

Currently, there are legislative and educative efforts that, on the surface, appear to attack the problem of responsible education for our nation's students. Prominent among them is the standards movement.

Fifty Countries: Which Standards Movement?

In the United States, one dominant influence in schools during the first decade of the 21st century has been the focus on establishing clearly delineated standards as a means of setting high learning targets. I have often heard the catchphrase "standards, not standardization." The implication is that teachers need latitude to help individual learners reach proficiency targets. Yet, in practice, classroom experience too often locks in rigid standardization with an overemphasis on low-level testing and dated standards. The intention may be to help schools reach for targets, but the reality is that often educators feel that teaching to the test is what counts, and the tests are often suspect in terms of value.

A prevailing myth is that the standards movement exists to prepare students for their future. I wonder which particular standards movement we are talking about? There is no national movement for standards in my country; there are, in effect, 50 countries. Imagine that 50 basketball teams are playing, and every court has the basket in a different place and at a different height. How would you rank the teams? How could you even tell the winners from the losers? The disparities between states on the number of standards, the actual standards themselves, and the graduation testing requirements are so vast as to be startling. It often seems that in mathematics, the overwhelming majority of the actual assessment items are reductive copies of what came out of 1950s textbooks as multiple-choice items.

Consider this finding from one of the National Assessment of Education Progress (NAEP) reports, which compared state proficiency standards to the NAEP standards:

> There is a strong negative correlation between the proportions of students meeting the states' proficiency standards and the NAEP score equivalents to those standards, suggesting that the observed heterogeneity in states' reported percents proficient can be largely attributed to differences in the stringency of their standards. (National Center for Education Statistics, 2007, p. iii)

These disparities have direct and mighty repercussions on the testing that emerges.

To be blunt, some states have lower standards than others in order to meet No Child Left Behind (NCLB) expectations. In an article in the *New York Times*, Susan Saulny (2005) points out that the disparities between the NAEP and the individual states are critical: "The comparisons suggest how widely the definition of 'proficient' varies from state to state, as each administers its own exams and sets its own performance standards."

When it comes to education, the United States are not united. The state systems are in parallel universes. But there is a larger question. It is not only the wide-ranging standards that are problematic, but also the focus on highly reductive testing in many of the states. Whereas one state may have archaic approaches in almost every field of study, a neighboring state might have a more contemporary approach. Let's say Johnny has been steeped in three years of learning his state's history when his family moves across the border and he enrolls in a new school, where he will engage in two full years of global studies, learning about political, economic, and historical issues from all parts of the world. Which state will best prepare him for his future?

We need to make choices. Policymakers and education leaders do make choices, and these affect whether Johnny will be a literate, aware, and prepared citizen of his country and his world. As Tony Wagner emphasizes, preparation for future work situations requires teaching learners "to use their minds well" rather than testing them reductively (Wagner, 2008, p. 8). I do not support the notion of one national curriculum, but I do believe there are other possibilities, such as a national array of thoughtful, well-articulated curriculum options. The extraordinary amount of effort and energy that goes into each state's efforts is pointedly redundant.

Signs of Progress

There are some interesting new directions in motion as the Council of Chief State School Officers has commissioned committees to develop potential national standards in reading and mathematics. In addition, a workgroup is developing a set of global competencies for potential adoption by the states. All these groups will produce documents in the next few years that undoubtedly will receive careful review. Nonetheless, as long as the United States views education as a state area of focus, our public schools will find that geography is destiny and that the local school board has exceptional power over the direction an individual school will take. In some ways, it appears that each state education department will ultimately have the greatest influence over school boards and policies in the years ahead. Having established some concerns, it is important to acknowledge some promising signs of state education departments showing 21st century leadership in curricular policy development.

In New Jersey, three specific goals have been set to ensure that the new standards (1) address global perspectives; (2) employ 21st century digital and networking tools; and (3) identify salient interdisciplinary linkages for real-world applications. There has been an impressive emphasis in their rethinking of curriculum frameworks and standards to thoughtfully clarify work based on a range of meaningful principles of practices including enduring understandings, meaningful essential questions, mapped vertical articulation, balanced literacy, formative assessments, and future career proficiencies.

Another example is the state of Rhode Island, with its innovative and forward-thinking portfolio requirement for graduation. Each student develops a digital portfolio of self-selected work that matches standards. The work evolved from the 2003 Board of Regents high school regulations and became standard practice in 2008. This requirement means that before receiving a diploma, each student will have shown that it was earned with work going back to kindergarten. (See Chapter 9 for more about this innovative approach to accountability.)

The Hawaii State Education Department was a leader long before other states in providing all of its schools with a common Internet-based program with the proper infrastructure for communication. In part because of the state's geography, the Internet provided a marvelous alternative to costly air travel for state education meetings. Years before any other state, the Hawaii State Education Department was creating video modules for professional development and videoconferencing "bridges" between the complexes (districts) on all of the islands.

There are certainly other pockets of innovation, but many standards documents seem strikingly dated. Given that the focus of education is local in the United States, this book attempts to charge the debate with specific ideas for consideration as we open the menu of options and approaches for the 21st century.

Upgrading Curriculum and Developing New Versions of School

The word *essential* comes from the Latin *esse*, meaning "to be." When combined with Webster's definition, "to distill to the core," the application to curriculum making is clear. New essential curriculum will need revision—actual replacements of dated content, skills, and assessments with more timely choices.

The steps and strategies presented here can focus a faculty on upgrading specific elements of the existing curriculum with more engaging and powerful selections. It is a nonthreatening approach that can be worked into the school culture gradually. Rather than a change model, it is a growth model. Change in schools can often feel trendy and superficial, whereas growth is positive and deep. All members of a professional learning community should arguably be committed to growth, and the model described in this book has proven to be a useful set of practices to develop a 21st century curriculum.

The Need for New Versions of School

A dynamic look at what needs to be new and essential in curriculum necessitates a corresponding, bold reconsideration of "the place called school." Four key program structures affect curriculum: the schedule (both short and long term); the way we group our learners; personnel configurations; and the use of space (both physical and virtual). Because curriculum is housed in these programmatic structures, they hinder or support implementation as well. Curriculum changes will not be enough. Frustration abounds among educators as some try to amend, adjust, and revise within the tight confines of 19th century structures. These efforts can actually make the problems worse as dissatisfaction arises among teachers and students. Education is about growth, not designed malaise.

If we are attempting to move to a more essential set of choices for curriculum, then we need to make corresponding shifts in these four structural areas. To me, a major change in these structures is the more challenging task. For example, as creatures of habit, we are used to 13 years of school, kindergarten through 12th grade, although I hope to make the case that this structure is dated, inhibiting, even negative. The fact that teachers and students come to school for the same hours every day supports a kind of entrenched monotony. The actual design of the physical space limits the types of learning experiences that students can have as well as how frequently teachers will have opportunities to interact with one another. We know that multi-age groups, accompanied by thoughtfully grouped personnel for our young learners, have proven to be extremely effective, yet we isolate our teachers within self-contained classrooms. Frankly, the phrase itself suggests a kind of narcissistic alcove cordoned off from others (a self-container). We are accustomed to the isolation. It is part of our school habit. And perhaps this isolation from the larger world is why too many of our students drop out and leave school. Many of them who stay in school leave mentally. The old habit of school structures needs to be altered to match the time in which we live.

Form should support function and not lead it. These very forms that we put our curriculum into have a great deal to do with the difficulties curriculum planners have in developing contemporary and riveting opportunities for our learners. We have 1930s schedules, grouping patterns, and spaces; and so the curriculum follows. Form should follow function. And now more than ever, we have genuinely new forms to work with that do not seem to be breaking into and replacing these restricted structures. The very fact that I can access e-mail, curriculum maps, and plans at my convenience from anywhere in the world is astonishing. Yet we still see curriculum binders holding reams of paper on a shelf in a principal's office.

I would ask that we examine some attitudes and assumptions prevalent in our communities and in ourselves as we take on the task of designing new curriculums and new schools.

Myths That Shape Our Operational Visions of School

At our best, we operate on beliefs and values that show in our organizations and clearly in curriculum and instructional practice. I would like to point out three prevailing myths that often prove to be genuine obstacles in creating viable changes in the curriculum and our school programs. In turn, in the following chapters we propose tenets to replace those myths as operational points of departure to take action for the 21st century curriculum.

Myth #1—The good old days are still good enough. Adults tend to have positive memories of school and to feel comfortable re-creating the same setting for each subsequent generation. Perhaps keeping schools in time-check allows us to remember our youth and our childhood. We recall our own experiences, good and bad, and reason that we will know how to prepare our children for school because we have been there before. New kinds of schools and new kinds of curriculum create some insecurity, though I would argue that the real insecurity comes from *not* growing or changing. Schools stay the same, and communities collude. Schools often are mirrors of what a culture values and aspires to. Those communities that have been able to create and sustain engaging innovation want growth, not nostalgia. There are real dangers in glorifying the good old days and clinging to our schools' myths and stories. How can we grow the curriculum if schools are shackled by memories?

I certainly know that rethinking the curriculum, however boldly, will prove insufficient. It is not enough to shape and reshape epistemology. Economics and community views of schooling restrict or enhance possibilities. Education is a practical field, a place where hopes and dreams for the young are realized or lost. Real children with real parents, in real places, with real teachers, real bus schedules, real buildings, and real budgets determine how the curriculum is put into operation. Parents, school board members, business leaders, policymakers, and community members care deeply about their children, and many of them bring a necessary perspective to education concerns. These groups are critical to successful learning and are becoming increasingly involved with breaking out of the shackles that confine genuine progress. There will also be those who hold onto the 20th (if not the 19th) century. I ask only that the mission statements of the latter be altered to reflect their choice. Be honest with the children.

Myth #2—We're better off if we all think alike—and not too much. America has a love/hate relationship with being educated that is also reflected in our schools. There are those who use the word *elite* in a pejorative sense when referring to a well-educated person who has made a significant accomplishment. Societal attitudes of a country and a culture directly affect its education systems. As we consider choices for our learners, we need to think like anthropologists and historians for a moment. We need to consider the attitudes that dominate our systems and our nation.

With fierce intellect and focused passion, Susan Jacoby in *The Age of American Unreason* (2008) dissects the underlying forces that have shifted the original tradition of argument, debate, soaring rhetoric, and vigorous exchange that was the basis for the United States. Countervailing forces breeding narrowness, dogma, and fear of ideas have grown stronger and stronger, with frightening results. For those who want to cultivate a deeper and more reflective view, she points to the fact that the current tendency is to limit ourselves to those with whom we already agree. The greatest American tradition is to deliberately expose ourselves to those with whom we do not agree.

I believe we need a return of the contrarian tradition in our curriculum choices. Our greatest political leaders have been thinkers who could convey direction and provide comfort. But those we venerate the most are those who challenged us to grow and to consider new ideas and possibilities as well as to fight for those notions that needed protection. Whatever one's personal political views, certainly the ideas of Lincoln, Adams, Roosevelt, Jefferson, Stevenson, King, Kennedy, Goldwater, Arendt, and Sontag are worth examining. Start your own professional community list of thinkers whose ideas will provoke innovation and reflection.

In our 21st century, there is still a prevailing attitude that to be intellectual is to be effete. Jacoby makes the stark point that the tradition of the rugged individual who makes it on his own is more widely regarded if that person is not educated. Intellects are scoffed at in the United States. They are viewed as snobs or outsiders in the worst type of stereotyping. The fact that our founding fathers were brilliant intellects has had its obvious benefits. A genuine and engaging emphasis on ideas is necessary in determining the curriculum. We should be fearless about ideas and openly engage in discussion and debate about what should matter in the subject matter.

Myth #3—Too much creativity is dangerous—and the arts are frills. In his book *A Whole New Mind*, Daniel H. Pink (2006) contends that our collective futures will depend on the right-brained thinker:

> We are entering a new age. It is an age animated by a different form of thinking and a new approach to life—one that prizes aptitudes that I call "high concept" and "high touch." High concept involves the capacity to detect patterns and opportunities, to create artistic and emotional beauty, to craft a satisfying narrative, and to combine seemingly unrelated ideas into something new. High touch involves the ability to empathize with others, to understand the subtleties of human interaction, to find joy in one's self and to elicit it in others, and to stretch beyond the quotidian in pursuit of purpose and meaning. (p. 2)

Curriculum should not only focus on the tools necessary to develop reasoned and logical construction of new knowledge in our various fields of study, but also should aggressively cultivate a culture that nurtures creativity in all of our learners. This point seems particularly important as the institutions of school are so difficult to change; the fierce grip of the staid holds back learning and the lives of children. Out-of-the-box—or no-box—thinkers should be valued as we begin drafting creative designs for our curriculum and our schools.

In particular, the arts curriculum is still put on the back seat in our schools, and thus we leave many of our learners there as well. Ultimately, we all lose. An ambivalence and a resentment toward artists prevails as well unless they achieve exceptional monetary success. As Maxine Greene notes, "Artists are for disclosing the extraordinary in the ordinary" (Greene, 1989, p. 215). We need to go out of our way to encourage learners to take risks both in artistic expression and in the realm of creating ideas. That is what intellects do as well. An intellect is a creative thinker and an idea shaper, just as a sculptor throws clay on the table and experiments with forms and materials.

It is not only the children we need to cultivate, but also the responsible adults in our midst who have bold ideas and new directions to consider. In our work to improve education, we need to be bold advocates for creative ideas that are actionable, rational, and constructive.

2

UPGRADING THE CURRICULUM:
21st Century Assessment Types and Skills

Heidi Hayes Jacobs

It is a late October afternoon in the Hudson River Valley in upstate New York. The scene is a K–12 teacher workshop, and I am facilitating a discussion with faculty members on the topic of digital tools for the classroom. Mr. Eldridge, a middle-aged man in the back of the library, earnestly says, "I am a history teacher. I understand the need for modernizing our work. I do. The kids really must think that a lot of what goes on in school seems backwards. I think most of us in this room are willing, but we feel pressure to meet the guidelines and the testing cycle. It seems overwhelming to drop what we are used to. So, where do we start?"

His question goes to the heart of the issue. He is not resisting new approaches; he just wants to do it "right."

The way to modernize our work is not to use a computer instead of a typewriter and call it innovative. It is to *replace existing practices.* I believe that a practical route is to start with assessments, then work on revising content and skills. The impetus for the approach advocated in this chapter is a direct response to Mr. Eldridge's question. The model for "upgrading" emerged from that visit to Mr. Eldridge's rural school district as he and his colleagues attempted to "integrate technology into the curriculum." I had heard that phrase for years, often used with good intentions by instructional technology staff. I had often interpreted it as code for "our teachers view computers as something separate from what they do, and we have to help them see what is possible." But Mr. Eldridge, the history teacher in the back of the library, wanted more— and he just wanted to do it right.

What seemed clear to me when addressing the problem was the sequence of key points to address with the faculty. Rather than introducing the wonders and possibilities of hardware and software, it might be more effective if we started with what teachers are familiar with: their curriculum. If the emphasis shifted from the technology to formally examining each curriculum area in light of critical review questions, people might be more likely to examine potential connections.

Curriculum Mapping Software as the Vehicle

Fortunately, Mr. Eldridge's school district was using curriculum mapping software, which provided the vehicle for examining the curriculum. Because curriculum mapping uses electronic means of communicating, it is a natural way to attack the problem of segregating modern technologies from our classroom planning. The process for curricular revision comes directly from the seven-phase curriculum mapping review model that I developed in *Mapping the Big Picture: Integrating Curriculum and Assessment K–12* (Jacobs, 1997). Using the procedures in this model, groups of teachers examine maps for discrete and specific purposes, with the goal of improving what they teach and how they teach it. Because the maps are electronic and Web based, all teachers have immediate access to them throughout their school, their state, and the globe. Curriculum mapping software is a 21st century means for generating ideas as well as reviewing current curricular practice.

We began working on this shift in this rural school district by going to department meetings at the high school with the IT group and asking all the teachers to look at the map of their curriculum and try to find a place to "integrate technology." In truth, the effort felt rather pedestrian, the kind of "going through the motions" staff development that we all dread. It was during a session with the English department that I had a curricular epiphany. We were using the wrong words to help colleagues, and we were not specific enough about what to do. We needed to use the word *replace*, not *integrate*, and we needed something concrete to offer as a replacement. And given how overwhelming it might seem to change an entrenched curriculum, we needed a reasonable place to commence *upgrading*. As a lifelong student of curriculum, I am aware that curriculum has three basic elements: content, skills, and assessment. Each element needs to be revised for timeliness and aligned for coherence.

And so to answer the question from Mr. Eldridge, I suggested that we start small, we start focused, and we start with assessments. My work with his district led to the idea that targeting assessment types first and replacing them gradually, thoughtfully, and strategically is the most direct way to engage the staff in their own growth. Our discussion led to a joint resolution, an agreement to move ahead with an organized and focused procedure. The work in this school ultimately produced a pledge that I have shared with educators in workshops throughout the world (see Figure 2.1, pp. 22–23). I have found that starting with assessments has proven to be the most successful portal to moving school faculty and administrators into 21st century teaching and learning.

The upgrade model begins with consideration of assessment types, moves to content reviews and replacements, and then links both of these to upgraded skills and proficiencies. Ultimately we zoom in on each of the elements, with the goal of aligning them in the curriculum map. My experience is that starting with assessment types is a strong and provocative move because it forces educators to confront the very work assignments that are required of our learners. These are friendly confrontations, as we look at past practice and recognize that we all have something to learn.

This active and deliberate examination of the curriculum is the essence of mapping. *Mapping* is a verb, an action to be carried out by faculties as they breathe life into the curriculum. The goal is to formally upgrade all three fundamental elements of the curriculum and reconsider the essential questions that bind and focus them. Mapping allows us to zoom into each element and have the simultaneous capability to take a wide-angle view. With these various views, educators can see how each element ties to the others within a classroom and aligns to larger schoolwide, community, national, and global perspectives. The ultimate zoom-in is on the individual child. Curriculum maps provide an easy-to-use tool for differentiating instruction to match the needs of Johnny, Maria, Abdul, and Rachel, who are advancing into the next decades of the 21st century.

Upgrading Assessment Types: A Model for Short-Term Revision

Most teachers want to improve their professional practice in the classroom. We like the idea of becoming 21st century teachers. We just don't know what to do differently. As my colleagues and I advocate in this book, there is a need for a formal, collective, systemic review. For your consideration, I offer a series of specific steps as a model for upgrading the curriculum.

From the onset, I wish to stress that upgrading each component of the curriculum requires a different approach. Discussions related to upgrading assessment types are related to but different from the types of discussions required to upgrade content.

First, let us clarify the term *assessment type*, which is the actual form of the product or performance selected to demonstrate student learning. An assessment is a form used as evidence of learning reflecting progress or regress. The word *assessment* is a noun. It is the name of what a student produces to show knowledge and insight into content, skills, and proficiencies. Some assessments, such as multiple-choice tests or short-sentence constructed responses to a prompt, tend to be mundane and yet necessary routines on a relatively low level in terms of revealing knowledge and skill. Often when teachers are gathering evidence of more dynamic thinking skills, they use generic words such as *project* to represent a more active classroom experience that will reflect displays of work. But in practice, a *project* can range from creating a diorama in a shoebox to setting up a community service program in which students

Figure 2.1 | A 21st Century Pledge:
A Curricular Commitment from Each Teacher

A Rationale: 21st century tools benefit learners by ...
- Providing a visual and organizational tool that enables them to make meaning in "concrete" ways that they can also control with immediate access.
- Developing a different kind of "thinking tool" helps them develop their critical thinking in far more ways.
  - Enables them to make choices and selections more efficiently.
  - Stimulates visual reflection through a highly visual profile.
  - Develops their verbal expression in response to visual stimuli; they exhibit less hesitation when visual is first, in contrast to processing verbal/linguistic approaches (for specific groups of students).
- Increasing engagement because of immediate excitement, control, and interactivity.
- Allowing transfer of engagement and interaction into other aspects of the curriculum, especially when deliberately planned by the teacher.
- Increasing classroom teaching and learning time when intrusive routines can be minimized.
- Increasing the likelihood of completion of academic work during out-of-school time.

What the commitment is *not*:
- The limited and immediate use of a technological tool.
  - Using an LCD projector versus an overhead.
  - Using a computer versus a typewriter.
  - Using an interactive whiteboard versus an LCD projector.

What the commitment *is*:
- An integrated use of technology that enhances content.
- An application to a specific unit of study.
- Evidenced directly in student products and performances.

Each teacher commits to ...
- Review all current available technological resources in the district.
  - Online resources: video streaming; Internet Web sites and subscriptions; WebQuest creation; Webcasting through laptop.
  - Hardware resources: videoconferencing; laptop labs; digital cameras; digital recording studio.
  - Creative software: Movie Maker; MediaPlayer; video clips via digital cameras.
- Identify at least one specific unit to revise.
- Plan to replace a specific content, skill, and assessment practice with a 21st century upgrade within the unit.
- Share the proposed change with colleagues.
- Learn to use the tool that will be requisite to replace the current unit design with the new practice.
- Revise the unit and begin implementation with students.
- Tolerate a certain degree of frustration.
- Celebrate the victories.
- Review and share 21st century learning openly with colleagues at targeted work sessions through the school year.

Figure 2.1 | *Continued*

Administrators commit to ...
- Review, monitor, and provide feedback to teachers on individual curricular pledges to update.
- Identify at least one specific staff development or administrative task to revise.
- Plan to replace a specific content, skill, and assessment practice with a 21st century upgrade.
- Share the proposed change with colleagues.
- Learn to use the tool that will be requisite to replace the current unit design with the new practice.
- Revise the task and begin implementation with teachers.
- Tolerate a certain degree of frustration.
- Celebrate the victories.
- Review and share 21st century learning openly with colleagues at targeted work sessions through the school year.
- Document and share on Web site.
- Conduct formal reviews of resources for cross-disciplinary connections.

read to senior citizens. Precision in communication is critical because it clarifies what skills are being addressed in the assessment. Portfolios of work reflect collections of writing and also need clarification in terms of the precise types of writing. Different skills are being assessed in the portfolio work, whether it is an essay to dissuade versus persuade, a collection of sonnets, or a collection of interviews. Each of these broad generic types has inherent limits and can potentially be viable and valid forms of showing how our learners are learning, but the main point is that they are limited as 19th and 20th century forms and need expansion to reflect our times.

Step 1: Develop a pool of assessment replacements. Once you are clear about the definitions of assessment types, I suggest that you begin with a targeted group of teachers and ask them to brainstorm, to research, and to list the types of products and performances contemporary professionals use in a range of subjects that they teach. For example, 21st century social scientists, scientists, mathematicians, artists, writers, language specialists, musicians, and business men and women might produce the following:

Documentaries	Films
Podcasts	Online courses
CAD projections	Video podcasts
Web sites	Screenplays
E-mail exchanges	Quarterly e-reports
Digital music compositions	Video conferences
Webcasts from live sites	Second Life simulations
Online journals	Blogs

Step 2: Teachers, working with IT members, identify the *existing* types of software, hardware, and Internet-based capabilities in their school, district, or regional service center. When these tools and resources are identified, the implications for dynamic staff development are increased. As individuals, we bring the possibilities and limits of our personal knowledge and skill base to instructional approaches in the classroom. I would encourage teachers to stretch themselves and commit to becoming comfortable with at least one new tool per semester or school year. Obviously, many faculty members will be comfortable with an array of these, but others will not. I espouse differentiated staff development (Jacobs, 2004, p. 133) to organize and provide precise support to staff members. For example, a school might have the following resources available to teachers:

Interactive whiteboards	Moodle
Webcams	E-interviews
Laptop computers	Wikipedia
E-mail accounts	Electronic field trips
Digital cameras	Twitter
iPods	E-games
Web simulations	Blogs
Photoshop	Online courses
Flip cameras	Web design tools
WebQuests	Video conferencing
Wordle	Web 2.0 sites

Sometimes we do not know what is available in our electronic back-yard. William Sheskey of the Oconee School District in South Carolina (and author of Chapter 12) gave a presentation with a colleague, Mary Isenberg, at the national Curriculum Mapping Institute several years ago about engaging faculty members with Classroom 2.0. The evaluations were enthusiastic because the presentation focused on using what was already available. Sheskey now presents at workshops about Web sites, open-source software, and resources that are free for teacher use (see www.sheskeylearning.com). One of his innovative ideas was purchasing in bulk an inexpensive MP3 player for each participant to take home. With that hardware, each participant was compelled to make and then post a podcast.

Step 3: Replace a dated assessment with a modern one. This step is key. I propose that each teacher commit to a replacement and then deliberately upgrade at least one assessment type per semester. By this I mean that if an 11th grade English teacher is asking students to write a short story, she replaces that outcome with a screenplay. If a 4th grade teacher is asking students to make a chart of the exports and imports of Peru, he replaces that with a WebQuest regarding Peru. We should aggressively go out of our way to search for better ways to help our learn-ers demonstrate learning with the types of products and performances that match our times. If we do not do this, then we should change our mission statements to reflect the desire to hold onto the past.

One could argue that making one revision each semester is not enough. Frankly, I feel that way personally. But we all need time to make transitions, and inviting at a minimum one alteration is a step. Rather than seeking a complete overhaul, there is some wisdom in making small moves.

Step 4: Share the assessment upgrades formally with colleagues and students. When these replacements are identified, the curriculum maps are changed accordingly, to be reviewed and shared with other colleagues. It can be daunting to develop alternative ways of creating assessment types, because we are all limited by our own experience. Thus collaborative brainstorming is essential across and within disciplines. In addition, we often overlook students as a potential fount of ideas for curriculum planning. Any teachers willing to improve and to revise their work do well to let their students know about it. The greatest type of modeling is when teachers show that they, too, are learners.

The sharing should be done both electronically in the maps and formally in planning sessions. I recommend that the original version of the map be shown compared to the "new and improved" draft.

Step 5: Insert ongoing sessions for skill and assessment upgrades into the school calendar. It seems a contradiction in terms to make changes for the future only when time happens to be available. A formal work session to review upgrades can replace the old-style "staff development day." The notion of teachers meeting once or twice a year is equivalent to having an annual "student development day." Rethinking the current use of professional development days should be considered not only to ensure that the map is kept current, but also to move toward active instructional and curricular reviews. If teachers knew that there was a built-in, recurring time set aside to update their curriculum and to meet and discuss current practice, they would be more likely to upgrade their curriculum and expand their instructional repertoire.

Partnership for 21st Century Skills: Going Deeper

Integrated directly into this review cycle is the natural tendency to include 21st century skills. This motivation is valid, but there are cautions. The generic 21st century skills endorsed by many state departments of education, national organizations, and businesses often refer to those espoused by the Partnership for 21st Century Skills (see www.21stcenturyskills.org). The fact that a wide-ranging group of business, political, and education organizations could come to the table and agree on goals for U.S. students is admirable if not remarkable. The partnership's model is broad and inclusive, reflecting the type of language that is seen in mission statements. It is a tool that has become a common reference point for many organizations. As a general organizing framework, it does not purport to provide the specificity necessary for direct applications in a school, and for this it has been roundly criticized as well. Jay Mathews (2009), education columnist for the *Washington Post*, referring to the sweeping nature of the mission statement, writes, "This is the all-at-once syndrome, a common failing of reform movements. They [the partnership] say changes must be made all at once, or else. In this democracy, we never make changes all at once.... So please don't tell us we have to." His concern reflects a concern shared by others when he says, "But I see little guidance for classroom teachers in 21st-century skills materials. How are millions of students still struggling to acquire 19th-century skills in reading, writing and math supposed to learn this stuff?"

The partnership does provide links and resources that directly relate to the general skills in place, such as creativity and innovation, critical thinking and problem solving, communication and collaboration (see www.21stcenturyskills.org). In truth, except for specific media skills, the entries do not look significantly different from skills that might have been proposed 30 or 40 years ago, or as Mathews notes, perhaps even earlier: "It calls for students to learn to think and work creatively and collaboratively. There is nothing wrong with that. Young Plato and his classmates did the same thing in ancient Greece." What has changed is the knowledge base, which has grown, and the tools for communicating and sharing what students are learning as they cultivate these skills in a new world. These tools have given students new forms to convey their ideas, changing the immediacy and range of input that is possible. Most of us would agree with Mathews on the through-line of critical thought and collaborative action espoused by Plato, but I would argue that new forms open the possibility of new ways of thinking. Just as the Greeks are credited with refining the process of how we perceive the world, the fact that we assimilate immediate time-and-space communications requires new skills for processing and sorting that information. Just as Euripides and his fellow dramatists gave the world a new form with theater, new forms give us new platforms for thinking. What has also changed is that business, political, and cultural institutions are partners with schools in emphasizing the importance of these shared proficiencies. If educators work only with the general skills and do not revise and focus them, it is difficult to apply them to real-world practice.

To make the 21st century skills meaningful to specific learners, the key is to translate them into highly discrete classroom applications connected to the assessment types and to the curriculum content. Integrating these skills when deep into the curriculum mapping process is a natural way to ensure their genuine development in the classroom.

Teachers are familiar with various assessment types within their lesson plans that will stimulate direct engagement in the upgrade process. Here is an example of how this match between skill and assessment might transpire in an initial draft of a lesson plan:

> Let us take one of the 21st Century Partnership skills and attach it to one of the assessment types from our brainstormed list of alternatives.
>
> Here is a skill directly from the chart under #2 regarding Critical Thinking and Problem Solving: *Identify and ask significant questions that clarify various points of view and lead to better solutions.*
>
> Mr. Eldridge, our high school social studies teacher, is working on an economics unit on Issues and Realities—Sustainability, a contemporary content issue. He has posed the following content questions: How can we design a solar collector to run our high school? What points of view and considerations will we need to take into account?

If the means of sharing findings is a video podcast based on interviews from community members, and the means of presenting the plan is through a computer-aided design (CAD) program, then we begin to see how curriculum design can be upgraded to match the needs of our learners.

Mr. Eldridge Revisited

At the beginning of this chapter, Mr. Eldridge wanted to know where to start in his desire to become a teacher who uses 21st century tools that students can relate to. He was willing to learn. In this chapter, I have attempted to make a case for straightforward revision of curriculum and accompanying lesson plans to replace dated assessment types with newer forms of expression. When students are engaged in the types of products and performances that are ongoing in the larger contemporary world, they are more motivated to respond to those forms and to create them as well. The deliberate and formal work of identifying new options and working to target replacements is a sensible place for a faculty to begin. We also considered the importance of applying both past and present-day skills with precision. Many groups and organizations are posing important policies and frameworks to assist us in engaging our learners to develop proficiencies. I believe that Mr. Eldridge and his colleagues will do best when they zoom into their actual classrooms and align those skills to the critical content they wish to explore with students and the assessment types that students will produce as evidence of their learning.

Yet changing our assessments and skills is a different type of upgrade than altering content. They are codependent elements when designing curriculum, but very different. Wrestling with content decisions will demand deliberate debate and discussion.

3

UPGRADING CONTENT:

Provocation, Invigoration, and Replacement

Heidi Hayes Jacobs

Upgrading content requires deliberate provocation. Active and vibrant discussion and debate formally planned at each school site, at each district office, and at each state, provincial, or national education office should engage key players around three questions: *What content should be kept? What content should be cut? What content should be created?*

Content replacements require us to carefully articulate what is timely and timeless and to concurrently find what we can let go. For our purposes, content is the selected subject matter either taught by the teacher or self-taught by the learner; it is knowledge we wish to impart and to investigate within the time available. Content is a central element in curriculum design and can be organized within disciplines or through interdisciplinary designs. The decision on what knowledge to present and share with learners is most often predetermined by professional educators, but in some schools and settings, content is selected and constructed by the student. A best practice in planning is organizing content around central concepts supported by selected facts and information (Ericksen, 2002; Jacobs & Johnson, 2009; Wiggins & McTighe, 2005).

To provoke thoughtful reconsideration of these concepts, selected facts, and knowledge in an upgrading review cycle, fundamental questions need to be asked: *What is essential and timeless? What is not essential or dated? What should be created that is evident and necessary?* A knowledge-updating review process is daunting to maintain and cultivate in any field of study, yet it is the bedrock of learning. The ongoing process of challenging accepted knowledge and the cycle of replacing it are the signs of cultural maturation.

Tenets for Purposeful Debate Leading to Content Upgrades

Members of Curriculum 21 review or inquiry teams need to carefully consider each discipline or, if they choose, multiple disciplines in their curriculum maps from a K–12 perspective. In the Curriculum Mapping Review Model (Jacobs, 1997, 2004), school teams regularly review maps vertically or across grade levels to solve a problem and research potential places for revision, which may be focused on gap analysis, eliminating redundancies, or aligning with standards. In this case, the Curriculum 21 team reviews the content entries on maps specifically to address these tenets for upgrading:

• A global perspective is developed and presented in the content area, where natural and viable.

• A personal and local perspective is cultivated so that each student can create relevant links to the content.

• The whole child's academic, emotional, physical, and mental development is thoughtfully considered in content choices.

• The possibilities for future career and work options are developed with an eye to creative and imaginative directions.

• The disciplines are viewed dynamically and rigorously as growing and integrating in real-world practice.

• Technology and media are used to expand possible sources of content so that active as well as static materials are included.

• The complexity of the content is developmentally matched to the age and stage of the learner.

Mapping review teams are site-specific in their composition, depending on the size of a school or organization. Some schools have ongoing curriculum councils that review maps, but more often mapping review teams function as a task force. The key is to begin with motivated and engaged educators reflecting a cross-section of the school or setting. The focus for a Curriculum 21 content review team is to question, to raise specific challenges, and to generate provocations, with the goal of upgrading and targeting content replacements based on strong principles and tenets.

To move out of the content rut, deliberate debate and discussion must continue, with the goal of replacing dated content with dynamic and current material. I wish to reinforce that eventually all faculty and administrative members of a school should become part of a review. Stimulating thought and review by the staff in a school is at the heart of teaching and learning. Direct engagement by our instructors increases their investment in the curriculum that they teach. I recommend that students also be part of the review team and contribute, if possible. Each individual brings a unique perspective and voice to critiquing curriculum. Active contributions from a team of professionals models and stimulates the very inquiry we want our learners to cultivate.

Some specific considerations are required in examining each discipline, even as there is a need for rigorous inquiry into finding meaningful interdisciplinary connections. We cannot simply lean on what we are accustomed to teaching.

Examining the Disciplines

The upgrading process is not a passive discipline review. Rather, it is a quest to modernize and to pose constant and active queries. A Curriculum 21 review team should challenge prevailing practice with vigorous intellectual, rational, and forward thinking. The goal of discussion is to open up the content menu, which seems so constricted by past practice and the devotion to testing.

To encourage, prompt, and add to active debate and discussion, this chapter offers some specific alterations. I identify traditional topics that I believe should be cut and offer corresponding replacements as a means of modeling the review process and offering samples for consideration. Moving through the disciplines will bring us to interdisciplinary possibilities. The fundamental continuum between discipline-based and interdisciplinary curriculum has been an ongoing epistemological tenet in my work, raised first in *Interdisciplinary Curriculum: Design and Implementation* (Jacobs, 1989). In a 21st century review, these connections seem even timelier.

The thoughtful review of curriculum maps to actively replace and upgrade content is central to learning, both on the individual classroom level and the institutional level. We cannot update every lesson plan at every moment, but we can address and adjust some glaring problems. We need to formally review specific areas in each discipline and share openly (even bravely) with our colleagues our inquiry mantra of questions. Genuine exchanges between colleagues, even when difficult, are necessary to the lifeblood of an institution, providing more curricular space in the planning process.

Epistemological questions about the design of knowledge and the relationship between the disciplines should be active and ongoing (Jacobs, 1989, 2006). Certainly we might enter into a review from other angles, but the general familiarity with content areas allows us a point of entry and a way to reconceive the connections between fields of knowledge.

In determining the sequence of disciplines to review, there is no implicit order in terms of importance and power. Each discipline has unique characteristics, and there are natural junctures and overlaps that are suitable for integrated curricular investigations. Given that most readers will be wrestling with the disciplines as they consider standards and material, I begin here with them. The key is to grapple with content choices by challenging the status quo.

Guiding Questions

The following questions can provide a framework for challenging the status quo in the disciplines:

- *Within the discipline being reviewed, what content choices are dated and nonessential?* Some of these may prove to be difficult to relinquish because of curricular habits or even because we simply enjoy teaching a particular topic. We need to shed unnecessary studies because they ultimately limit the possibilities for viable curriculum building. Coming to the review table prepared with investigative work regarding recent developments, breakthroughs, or international practice in a field of study is a strong way to begin the discussion. If we examine curriculum without new ideas and perspectives, we tend to simply reinforce the familiar.

- *What choices for topics, issues, problems, themes, and case studies are timely and necessary for our learners within disciplines?* This area is where a rich dialogue, debate, and professional discussion should ensue. I advocate research and development task force groups to investigate the range and possibilities in both the larger world of education institutions and, more important, in the actual fields in practice (see Chapter 2). What are scientists studying? What are engineers trying to build? What are historians uncovering? What forms are writers generating? What are artists saying in their work?

- *Are the interdisciplinary content choices rich, natural, and rigorous?* When we find links and possibilities for integration between subjects, the focus should be on relevant and dynamic themes for investigation.

Some Provocations and Possible Replacements

I am keenly aware of the limitations of my perspective, and readers will want to amplify specific areas or topics. Undoubtedly you will find points of agreement and disagreement with my analysis of what should be cut, kept, and created for each field. Do counter my ideas with your own; for that is precisely the point—to encourage an active inquiry as opposed to passive acceptance of content. Inquiry is at the heart of our work as educators. *What content should be kept? What content should be cut? What content should be created?* I would simply like to add the following ideas to your curriculum planning table.

Social Studies as Perspectives on Humanity

I have deliberately chosen to begin with social studies, in part because standards for social studies are often one of the last sets of standards approved. The arguments get personal because the discipline is, indeed, social: *Whose history will we leave out? Which communities should we study in depth?* Social studies may have been given short shrift in some of our states, because it is not assessed with regularity or at all. Yet when we look at this century's themes of global awareness, changing economies, communications, shared technologies, and planetary survival, social studies is fundamental. It is ultimately the study of ourselves as human beings that is the basis for addressing contemporary issues.

A critical area for reconsideration is the divisive nature of the traditional social studies model. Too often the discipline has been sharply divided into its subdisciplines: geography, history, anthropology, sociology, economics, and political science. If we combine any of these six subheads into pairs, triads, or combine all of them, the results can be immediately richer, more complex, and relevant. Consider a few of these fusions: political economics, economic anthropology, historical sociology, historical geography, and anthropological politics.

If we go a step further and begin to attach specific and contemporary issues, topics, and problems to these fusions, our learners can start becoming actual social scientists. Consider the possibilities that might emerge from questions such as these: *Is geography inevitably destiny in the political life of the Middle East? How does cultural anthropology shed light on the economy of resource-rich Brazil? How do the limited resources of the island nation of Japan affect its social mores and economic relationships? Why do people in my neighborhood want to buy the things they want to buy?*

Some fundamentals in social studies need reconsideration and replacement. For example, geography should be cut as a snapshot unit and replaced with an integrated approach continuously woven into the academic year. Rather than the token "let's start off the school year with our classic unit on geography," the curriculum should include an ongoing injection and use of geography and a full range of maps. When schools do not use maps of all kinds with regularity in a range of classes (English, science, art), our students do not get to apply geography in a meaningful way. It is as absurd as a 1st grade teacher saying, "I am posting the alphabet but will take it down after a month." Knowing where places are, where people live, where we are in the solar system, where our neighborhood is—this knowledge is the basis of reality. What is even more alarming is that most of our students are using a 16th century map of the world for the basis of a geographic context.

Maps of the World as Political Statements: Too Much Mercator

Beyond the need for more constant use of and exposure to geography, students need exposure to multiple maps and projections. Most U.S. students are familiar with the Mercator map (see Figure 3.1) developed in 1569. Unfortunately, the Mercator projection distorts the size and shape of large objects (bodies of water and continents) so that the scale increases from the equator to the poles. When the Gall-Peters Projection map was published in 1974 by Arno Peters, it was a source of controversy. It displays all areas—whether oceans, countries, or continents—according to actual size, making comparisons accurate and possible. Figure 3.2 shows a cylindrical equal-area projection oblique case map.

To be sure, a full range of projections should be compared and considered. Our U.S. Geological Survey (www.usgs.gov) provides a detailed analysis of map projections, as does the Web site at www.progonos.com/furuti/MapProj/Normal/TOC/cartTOC.html. And the Goddard Space Flight Center provides tools for examining global perspectives at its site, www.giss.nasa.gov/tools/gprojector/.

Our students should be examining a myriad of maps to garner information and insight. For example, the projection in Figure 3.2 is used by the CIA in its *World Factbook* (2008). Students of various ages look at this map with utter fascination because it provides another perspective on the size of our oceans and the proximities of the continents to Antarctica.

Figure 3.1 | Comparison of Mercator and Gall-Peters Map Projections

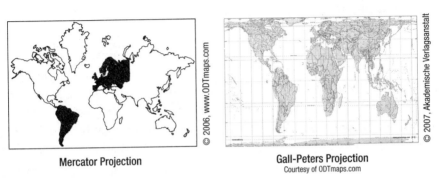

Mercator Projection   Gall-Peters Projection
                                                 Courtesy of ODTmaps.com

Peters map link: http://odtmaps.com/peters-equal-area-maps.46.0.0.1.htm
Mercator map comparisons: http://odtmaps.com/detail.asp Q product id E STM-2-BK

Google Earth (www.earth.google.com) also offers students and adults an exceptional roving view of Earth and the relationship between landforms. If we are seeking to globalize the curriculum, as Vivien Stewart

Figure 3.2 | Map Projection from the CIA *World Factbook*

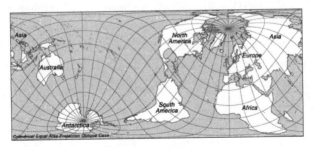

Source: Central Intelligence Agency, *The World Factbook* [online].
Available: https://www.cia.gov/library/publications/the-world-factbook/geos/xx.html

argues for so elegantly in Chapter 6, it is critical that we actively bring a view of the globe into each subject at every level. Whether it is an English teacher anchoring a plot, a science teacher explaining the movement of landforms and the composition of our planet, or a physical education teacher describing the history of the Olympics, geography is ultimately interdisciplinary.

Not Just Global Studies: The Study of a New World Era

In his brilliant book *The Post-American World* (2008), Fareed Zakaria introduces the reader to a very new time frame as he writes, "This is not a book about the decline of America, but rather about the rise of everyone else" (p. 1). Emerging economies from Brazil to India and from Russia to China are on a steady pace to shift and diversify the full range of economic power points. He points out how the tallest buildings, the largest dams, the most widely seen movies, the most innovative cars, and the latest communication devices are being designed and built outside the United States. The obvious interdependence of global production sites and the ease of communication have moved us rapidly into a new era without the parameters of the past. Zakaria is suggesting that the United States should use its characteristic adaptability and energy to re-create its role in this new time and to thrive. Whether one agrees with Zakaria or not, the fact remains that economic realities are changing. The devastating losses beginning in 2008 due to the floundering economic markets are a case in point. The question is, are we preparing our learners for this time? State and local education standards would do well to take a hard look at the proficiencies and concepts valued in their statements and replace them with an updated set based on contemporary and possible future capacities. Are the students in the United States being prepared for the present and the future or for an Eisenhower-era view of politics and the economy?

A forward-thinking working paper that I have found regarding the shift needed to prepare our learners for their poli-economic future is available through the Australian Curriculum Studies Association (www.acsa.edu.au). The Curriculum Standing Committee of National

Education Professional Associations (CSCNEPA), a group of leaders from a wide range of professional organizations throughout Australia, crafted this progressive and engaging document to provide a basis for reflecting on and generating possible curricular solutions for Australian learners. In particular, I was struck with the openness of the document and the language that was selected to describe the necessary global perspective for all future curriculum planning. The authors use fresh and realistic phrases such as "globalisation of economies ... centred more on China and India"; "insecurity of nations"; "likely environmental degradation"; "internationalisation of employment" (CSCNEPA, 2007, p. 4).

One of the phrases in the text is "school leavers," a powerful phrase evoking the image of the child becoming a young adult. The Australian paper asks if the country's learners are prepared to leave school and function independently in the actual world they will encounter.

America's Story:
Replacing Redundancy with the Contemporary

When I consider the traditional social studies curriculum, what strikes me is that it is rare for a high school graduate to have studied the past 50 years of history. Standard upper-elementary curriculums in the United States often allow for a redundant examination of the seeds of U.S. government and the remarkable, tumultuous beginnings of the American Revolution at the expense of studying recent history. I propose that the Revolutionary period become a realistic study of the many conflicting ideas in play for the future of the colonists, which makes the ultimate coalition of strikingly different colonies into a single country all the more remarkable. In short, the question is this: *As historians, what is essential for our learners to know as they look at a range of perspectives on our country's beginnings?* We are who we are because of where we have come from. But it isn't realistic for the social studies curriculum to spend the same amount of time on all 300 years of U.S. history. An introduction to the nation's story can begin as it often does in the upper-elementary grades, but I believe that the next iterations should examine our roots and their relationship to present-day realities.

Moving from State History to Case Studies of the States

Where do we find the time to teach global studies and take a fuller look at contemporary America? We find the time by deemphasizing state history. According to the U.S. Census, not only do we have high numbers of legal immigrants accepted annually into the United States, we also have high rates of domestic migration (2009). Four metropolitan areas added 100,000 to their populations from 2007 to 2008: Dallas–Fort Worth, Houston, Phoenix, and Atlanta. This means that there is the real possibility that a student in your district might move to another state. If your student studies Nebraska's history and then moves to Maine, that student would have benefited more from understanding Nebraska's role in the American story within a context for understanding global connections than spending 36 weeks on Nebraska in isolation. I suggest replacing the traditional practice of teaching state history with three curricular practices: (1) focus your state's history on its role in the larger American history narrative; (2) make the state's perspective more personal by using a case-study model and the Internet to interview students in other parts of the state; and (3) keep an ongoing view of global connections and relationships as a constant in both local and national history. Since there is a trend toward urban living, I believe all students should learn about new directions in 21st century cities with resources such as livable streets and streets education; see www.streetseducation.org and www. livablestreets.com.

One upgrade would be a seminar for high school students in which they investigate the state of the world in relation to key events and patterns. Working backward from each news story, they answer the question: How did we get here today? Researcher William Daggett (2005) suggests using rigor and relevance in our curriculum. If we follow his ideas, we'd use rigor to examine varying perspectives on the past and pose critical questions; relevance requires that students study immediate situations anchored in the relevant lessons of the past. New York has made this commitment with a two-year course on global studies for freshmen and sophomores.

The Sciences in Action:
Layers and Breakthroughs

Every Tuesday, the *New York Times* publishes the Science Times section, with articles on recent scientific breakthroughs and discoveries. As I peruse this section, I often note an incredible array of specialty prefixes: *micro*biology; *eco*chemistry; *geo*astronomy. The old way of laying out the sciences was to package them in the tidy categories of earth science, space science, life science, and physical science. It's not quite so easy anymore. To inject excitement and practice into science for our students, we need to organize the curriculum around problems rather than relying solely on the traditional and rigid approach to separating the sciences. In this regard, Princeton University has adopted an integrated approach. Its introductory program for science students integrates two or more of the classical disciplines (see www.princeton.edu/integratedscience).

In the same spirit, the New Zealand national curriculum is organized around one overarching unifying strand, the Nature of Science, which embraces scientific reasoning and the methodology of how scientists work. Of particular interest are the four subset strands: the Living World, which integrates biological and environmental studies; the Planet Earth and Beyond, which engages students in the integrated study of astronomy and the geology of the universe, our solar system, and Earth; the Physical World, which considers physics, technology, and real-world application; and the Material World, which connects sources of energy, chemistry, and sustainability to social and everyday needs.

Supported by the National Center for Research Resources, a part of the National Institutes of Health, the Science Education Partnership Awards (www.ncrrsepa.org/) provide for university and research institutions to work directly with schools and other educative settings to find out how to cultivate potential scientists as well as a better-educated general population. The partnerships consistently base their work on an opportunity for each student to be a scientist by carrying out active research.

In the same vein, Curriculum 21 review teams can examine the curriculum to ensure that our students are able to investigate and pose their own problems in science instead of following a scripted lab experiment. Original science "composition" is as critical as students writing creatively in an English class. Students from New York state win and are semifinalists in disproportionate numbers (ranging from 40 to 45 percent) in the Intel Scholarship Program (Berger, 2008; Koppel, 2005). I submit that this is due in part to the prominence of the state's Science Research Program, which is available to high school freshmen. Students commit to an original research study to be carried out for three full years before the final presentation of findings.

If we invest in promising talent, then we will get results. Many of our schools invest in outstanding athletic programs supporting great talent to get results. I argue that promising science students need the same consideration earlier in their schooling as well. As evidenced in New York, results will follow.

A problem-based approach has always been and will continue to be the core of science instruction, but if the problems are of no immediate and long-term importance, the students may not be as motivated in their work. A Curriculum 21 review team effort to base science instruction on critical and timely problems is more likely to provide a fascinating vehicle for our learners' engagement. As Jaimie Cloud proposes in Chapter 10, sustainability education is a natural interdisciplinary link forged at the core of applied science. Our need to find alternative energy sources and use them productively should be a key organizing proposition of the science curriculum. For example, rather than a physics unit based on a particular topic, science investigations should be wrapped around applied questions, such as these: How does the construction of air-tight apartments in Germany make it possible to avoid heating them altogether? Is it possible to make similar adjustments in our own housing?

Neglected Areas of Science

One of the most fascinating areas of science that is often neglected in terms of in-depth study is astronomy. Astronomy does not get proportional attention in the science curriculum despite easy access to inexpensive or free resources. For example, it could become common practice for schools to build a Dobsonian telescope (for about $200) that would enable students to see the stars and appreciate the universe and our place in it (for more information, see www.telescopepictures.com). Other options abound. Students can visit an observatory via an e-seminar. Using public access, a middle school science student can download footage from the Jet Propulsion Lab. As described in Chapter 4, the Virtual Learning Magnet developed by Tom Welch with the cooperation of the Council of Chief State School Officers and NASA goes to the heart of this gap in our astronomy curriculum.

We also find tendencies at different levels to favor specific areas in science. For example, I've encountered elementary schools that emphasize the life sciences at the expense of the physical sciences. As one elementary principal put it, "There are too many mammal reports in our primary program." I encourage elementary and middle school teachers to use programs developed by some of our premier national science organizations. Engaging and practical, *Active Physics* is a course developed by Dr. Arthur Eisenkraft with the support of the American Association of Physics Teachers and the American Institute of Physics. This course, and *MATH Connections*, funded by the National Science Foundation and *EarthComm*, can be reviewed at the Its About Time Web site: www.its-about-time.com/.

Moral Dilemmas in Science

Perhaps because of fear of controversy, schools sometimes avoid examining moral dilemmas in science. A direct and reasoned approach to ethical dilemmas in modern science should be fostered in a Curriculum 21 review.

The question of the relationship between religion and science might emerge when schools review their curriculum maps. On this issue, I support letting science be science and religion be religion. Many issues facing our society, such as genetic engineering or space exploration, prompt ethical and moral dilemmas. Individuals' beliefs directly affect their views on such questions. But when proponents of intelligent design claim some inner track to knowledge about the evolution of life based on a particular story or belief, a critical line is crossed. Of the many views and explanations regarding creation from a range of religions and cultures throughout the world and history, which ones will be left out? To be an educated person requires some background knowledge of religion and its role. Arguably the social sciences are a natural place to look at how beliefs affect how people choose to live. Curriculum bringing empirical science to the classroom is based on procedure, method, and rationalism. The intersections between moral beliefs and scientific investigation have always been and will always be inevitable. They should not be avoided but handled directly and respectfully.

Organizing Science Around Ideas That Have Changed the World

A few months before he died, author and educator Richard Strong gave me a book, *Ideas That Changed the World*, by Felipe Fernandez-Armesto (2003). Beyond the visual feast of photographs, it was the elegance and power of Fernandez-Armesto's thesis caught Strong's attention and resonates with me as a viable direction for science education. The book is arranged chronologically and focuses on 175 pivotal ideas that have altered the way the world works. To be clear, these are not concrete inventions, historical movements, or specific people; rather, they are "mental events" that "constitute new ways of envisioning humankind or the cosmos" (p. 7). All of science, including the development of inventions or models for making sense of Earth and beyond, starts with the human mind and an idea. I believe that one of the reasons Strong wanted me to see this book was that it offers another angle on the challenge of finding ways to bring all learners into academic areas of study. Certainly it is a challenge to find ways to organize the study of the sciences to engage students in understanding the context of scientific models, laws, and tenets in ways they will remember. Engaging them in a lab is the "hands-on" part of our work, and I constantly hear from science instructors that "minds-on" is the greater challenge.

Consider sample chapter titles from Fernandez-Armesto's book. He develops the idea in the chapter:

- Here Comes the Sun: The IDEA of a Sun-Centered Universe
- No Dice: The IDEA of an Orderly Universe
- Invisible Powers: The IDEA of Harnessing Natural Energy
- Tooth and Claw: The IDEA of Natural Selection
- Calculating Machine: The IDEA of Artificial Intelligence
- Time's Arrow: The IDEA of Linear Progression

I would suggest to classroom teachers the possibility of examining the full list of themes for a series of courses and units to invigorate and focus their students.

Scientists are detectives and solution makers. They are curious, inquisitive, focused, skeptical, creative, and observant—and a strong science curriculum should dynamically cultivate these attributes in learners. One key method for approaching the sciences is to emphasize that our learners are scientists and are learning to refine their problem-solving and field-testing approaches. The youngest children should learn to make observations and organize those findings objectively, activities that can lead to fundamental experiments and deductions. As our children mature, we can cultivate the concurrent traits of curiosity and precision in the scientific mind. The challenge is to rethink how we can integrate scientific knowledge more effectively into the curriculum and couple that integration with ongoing experiences for students to practice as scientists.

Educating the Person: Health and Physical Education

The most personal subjects, health and physical education, are often bonded in school curriculums. In certain ways, some of the most revolutionary work in upgrading curriculum has taken place in these areas of study. Schools of education in some universities have changed the name of their physical education department to Department of Movement Science, with a stronger emphasis on the human anatomy. In the past, the athletic dimension of learning was almost always about learning how to play a sport with some warm-ups in class. Now it is common for students to be studying personal hygiene, nutrition, issues of substance abuse, the human anatomy, safety issues, metabolic rates, mental and emotional health, and lifelong fitness, as well as basic sports skills. The question is how to bring these areas together effectively in a curriculum.

One of the most promising, well-organized approaches I have seen was developed by a group of physical education teachers and educators in Spokane, Washington, called Focused Fitness (accessible at www.focusedfitness.com). They have created a sensible approach that spirals around five components ("Five for Life," consisting of cardio-respiratory endurance, muscular strength, muscular endurance, flexibility, and body composition) to give learners the skills to gain control over their bodies, their choices, and their physical and mental health. The curriculum is predicated on the belief that all students should graduate from high school with the knowledge, skills, and behaviors to be fit, healthy, and active for life. The program is a K–12, activity-based program designed to teach the principles of health and fitness while continually improving the fitness levels of students. The goal is to build a fascination with how habits and choices can have a direct and observable effect both physically and mentally. With an emphasis on vocabulary building, students are empowered not only to monitor their well-being but also to become scientists while doing so. As the program advances from primary grades through high school, students develop correspondingly more sophisticated skill sets that prepare them for a lifetime of healthy habits and practical knowledge about their unique physique and identity.

Coupled with the study of personal health in most schools is the study of specific sports, which are often categorized in the curriculum as team sports and individual sports. Often the choice of sports that schools concentrate on reflects the climate, the cultural context, and the values of a community. Ector County, Texas, loves its football. In Bangor, Maine, students slap their hockey sticks. Lacrosse sticks fly in Westchester County, New York. In Honolulu, high school students paddle canoes and kayaks competitively. In Utah and Colorado, students ski slalom courses. Indiana worships the hoops. What is exciting is the recent expansion of sports choices, which allows more students to participate in a sport that might better suit their interest and natural skill set. In the United States, one of the most striking signs of global awareness is the rise of soccer in schools over the past 30 years. Conversely, the National Basketball Association claims over 30 million more viewers per week in China than in the United States (Cody, 2006). Given that access to and awareness about specific sports are growing, it seems that this very notion of the pairing of localism and globalism should be part of the curriculum and not simply emphasized by events such as the Olympics or the World Cup.

Contemporary English Language and Literature

Regarding upgrades to the English curriculum, let us consider two fundamental points: those dealing with the fundamentals of building language capacity and those related to the expansion of genre studies. Let me begin with some reflections on the first point.

Several years ago, in a book entitled *Active Literacy Across the Curriculum: Strategies for Reading, Writing, Speaking, and Listening* (Jacobs, 2006), I recommended specific strategies to be implemented schoolwide as a means of improving student engagement and performance. Given the significant gaps in curriculum K–12 between grade levels and across content areas in some of the most fundamental skills, it should not surprise us that we see corresponding problems in student achievement. The book suggests specific adjustments in such areas as vocabulary development (high-frequency words, specialized terminology, and embellishments); creative note taking and note making; and strategies and policies for editing and revising. For our purposes, the area that I would like to highlight here is the striking lack of attention to a specific modality in language capacity building—that is, speech.

Teaching English as a Foreign Language to Native English Speakers

At the root of all performance is a student's capacity in four language modalities: reading, writing, speaking, and listening. Language development in our curriculum assists the learner in cultivating the sound-symbol relationship in English and grasping the nature and logic of language structures that connect reading, writing, speaking, and listening in the individual. When individuals have acquired a level of competence in these capacities, they become functionally literate. Thus literate students can engage in the fundamental purpose and structure of learning English: (1) making meaning of ideas and information through exposure and critical response to literature and nonfiction text; and (2) creating meaning for themselves and others. What is noteworthy is that these two modes are the same for all language instruction. To this end, the teaching of the English language or the dominant language in one's own country would be improved by emulating the best tactics used by world language teachers. Upon reviewing curriculum, I usually find a fundamental mode missing: a formal and consistent emphasis on speech.

When reviewing the K–12 language arts curriculum, I recommend an increased and sustained emphasis on speech, with ongoing and required use of both video and audio podcasting as evidenced in a digital portfolio project (see Chapter 9). With the same clarity of purpose that they devote to developing a young writer's talent in specific genres, English teachers should seek to develop the talent of the young speaker. Curriculum plans need to include an emphasis on various speaking genres. Here are a few forums to consider: podcasts, video conferences, YouTube, documentary voice-overs, e-comments, feedback, forums, electronic roundtables, debates, speeches to persuade or dissuade, town meetings, comedy forums, folklore stories, interviews, lectures, docent work, oral defense, and facilitating and teaching situations. A critical life skill for our learners is the ability to use speech effectively in academic, professional, and personal communication. In particular, consider upgrading the English curriculum to more clearly reflect the formal study of a full range of forms of speech and more daily practice, as a world language teacher would routinely do.

Expansion of Modern Genres

Certainly many English teachers will rightfully claim that they use contemporary genre and Web-based tools to enhance the classroom experience. What is missing in English content is targeted and *guaranteed* exposure to contemporary genres from school entry to graduation. As Frank Baker argues in Chapter 8, modern media formats are strikingly nonexistent in most of our schools. If students read and wrote screenplays, documentaries, and podcasts, they would be more inclined to use the appropriate grammatical constructions necessary for high-quality communication. The implications here are that the 21st century English curriculum needs to include content related to the actual forms of these various genres as an integral part of instruction, just as the structure of a short story is assumed to be part of the instruction for the school year. Using sources such as the Public Broadcasting Service (PBS), Discovery Channel, Nova, and lists of award-winning productions (such as the Oscar-winning films *Spellbound* and *An Inconvenient Truth*), documentary study should be part of any contemporary K–12 English/language arts curriculum.

Similarly, in the study of narrative fiction films, it is presently common practice for English teachers to use a work of cinema as an enrichment experience and possibly link it with the social studies curriculum, whether it is Steinbeck's *Grapes of Wrath* in conjunction with a history unit on the 1930s and the Dust Bowl, or Harper Lee's *To Kill a Mockingbird.* I am recommending that we go further, that starting in the upper-elementary grades, students should have at least one experience a year in which the genre of film is studied, with formal exposure to exceptional works. At least once, our high school students should have a unit of study in their English curriculum called "Book to Film" in which, for example, after reading Shakespeare's *Richard the Third*, they might view the film version directed by Richard Loncraine and starring Sir Ian McKellen and compare the challenges faced in the film version versus print versus stage production. In a similar way, younger students who have read Natalie Babbitt's classic work *Tuck Everlasting* would not just view Jay Russell's film rendition passively but would question whether a book with such a strong author's voice can be translated to film. What is lost? What is gained? Discussion and instruction should always include focus on the filmmaking itself, not only the content of the films.

Expanding genres is easier today than in the past given the vast array of free and open Web sites and materials available to teachers of literature.

Students can enter into classic works with greater involvement, using, for example, Google Lit-Trips (www.googlelittrips.org).

More important, students can and do create their own WebQuest sites as part of their exploration of literature at all grade levels. I would recommend that the review team scour the English curriculum and find places to include international perspectives in our genre studies. To some extent this happens when students study folktales from other countries at the primary level or an occasional international author at the secondary level. What might be of interest is for students to see how works of literature written by favorite American authors are viewed by students in other countries. Envision a book study of *To Kill a Mockingbird* with students from the United States and other countries.

Given modern technology, students can contact some of their favorite writers through an author's personal Web site. One of the most influential and widely read authors of adolescent literature is Judy Blume; students may find it fun to visit her Web site, read her blog entries, and peruse the guest book blog entries from across the world at www.judyblume.com. Similarly, younger children might enjoy connecting with Eric Carle by going to www.eric-carle.com.

Many of our students are fascinated with the word play and social messages conveyed through rap, which certainly is a form of modern lyrical poetry. Recently I received a video podcast of a group of students in the Bronx having a poetry slam filled with heartfelt, powerful, and moving words. The teachers told me that many students who have fled from poetry, resisting it as a viable form of expression, find that they can begin to appreciate poetry using rap as the starting point. These teachers are going to the students' forms of poetry to begin. As in any poetic form, some examples will display better-quality writing than others, and selections should be age appropriate. But rap has been a form of music since 1979, and it has not gone away. Perhaps it will be through *The Cool* album by Lupe Fiasco or the work of another composer, but we owe it to our students to examine newer forms as assuredly as we have them study the sonnet, the elegy, blank verse, satire, and haiku.

Learning Languages

The New Zealand curriculum guide (Ministry of Education, 2007) lists three official languages: Te Reo Maori, New Zealand Sign Language (NZSL), and English. They are all taught in New Zealand public schools because the government recognizes the inherent importance of knowing one's own culture and language, as well as the need to communicate with and understand others, despite differences in languages, cultures, and abilities.

If we are committed to a greater degree of global understanding, I encourage the expansion of language instruction to include a more dynamic view. Within the United States, we do support native languages in Hawaii, where there are public schools committed to maintaining the rich tradition of the native language and culture in a program called Papahana Kaiapuni Hawai'i (Public School Hawaiian Immersion Program). According to Kamana and Wilson (1996), the Hawaiian language was banned in all private and public schools in 1896. Through the efforts of lobbyists, this ban was overturned in 1986. In 1987, parents and administrators from the Punana Leo preschools persuaded the state board of education to open two kindergarten–1st grade combination classes to serve Hawaiian-speaking children.

The learning of other languages does alter perspectives. Along with expanding our native language, we should consistently support the learning of at least one additional world or indigenous language, with American Sign Language among the options for consideration.

World Language Instruction

As we often hear, the country with the largest English-speaking population will soon be China. I usually hear two vastly different responses to that fact: one is the desire to motivate and raise awareness regarding the need for more world language instruction, and the other is a verbal shrug suggesting that this observation is a relief because now "we won't have to learn any additional languages since the rest of the world is going our way." To function successfully in the future workforce of a global economy, in the political realm of negotiation where nuance in language is critical, in the virtual classroom, and amid the flux of immigrant movement worldwide, knowledge of world languages is critical.

If you were born in Amsterdam, you studied at least three languages in order to have opportunities to thrive in a multilingual society on the European continent. In the past, because of the geographical isolation of the United States, the need for a second language had a distinctively different function. Twenty or thirty years ago, the requirement to take French had nothing to do with our need to communicate with neighbors from Quebec. Rather, the requirement reflected a respect and appreciation for a great language used by writers and diplomats of an influential world power.

But it is different now. Now the question is not only which languages will be of greatest value to our 21st century learners, but also how critical language instruction is as a direct means of connecting with the culture of others. There is arguably no more direct route for understanding another country or understanding someone else's perspective than working at using their language. When one learns a language, one literally has to use the muscles in the face in a different way and make sounds that are new while also learning about new places and people. As Vivien Stewart points out in Chapter 6, global connectivity is one of the most commonly acknowledged needs to consider in revising curriculum. World language instruction is at one with this goal.

The key question is, which languages? The response is not simply "as many as we can support." Instead, we need a savvy examination of which languages are emerging as necessary for political, economic, and social interaction on the world stage. Consider using the CIA *World Factbook* as an up-to-date source of clear, concise information. According to the *Factbook* (Central Intelligence Agency, 2008), the most frequently spoken languages in the world are Mandarin Chinese (13.22 percent), Spanish (4.88 percent), English (4.68 percent), and Arabic (3.12 percent).

From a practical and economic perspective, the Committee for Economic Development, consisting of leaders from business and higher education, endorsed the recommendations of the 2006 report, *Education for Global Leadership*, that called for an expansion and improvement of foreign language education in the United States. The committee warned,

> In order to confront the twenty-first century challenges to our economy and national security, our education system must be strengthened to increase the foreign language skills and cultural awareness of our students. America's continued role as a global leader will depend on our students' abilities to interact with the world community both inside and outside our borders. (Committee for Economic Development, 2006)

We must consider multiple approaches to the question of world language instruction. The fundamental question is a policy decision as to whether language study should be a requirement or an elective, and the array of options reflects directly on what a culture or community values for its learners. The policy of a school and its directors reflects how they wish to prepare students for connection with people who use different words to communicate.

Teaching Mathematics as a Language

In the area of mathematics, 4th and 8th graders in the United States score below other countries on the TIMSS (Trends in Mathematics and Science Study) in international comparison, yet we reject successful global practices in our curriculum. What can we learn as we revise our curriculum plans? (TIMSS, 2008; www.nced.ed.gov/timss/results07_math07.asp).

Mathematics and music are our most abstract disciplines, based on nonverbal symbol systems, hence presenting children and teachers with particular challenges. I believe that our problems in mathematics are attributable to three key reasons, and that an upgrading review can address all three of these. The reasons are as follows:

Mathematics in the United States focuses on memorization instead of reasoning. A conspicuous difference between the United States and the countries that produce much stronger results on comparative measures is that the other countries work to ensure that a student can explain precisely what is behind the concept being addressed. In basic terms, if students cannot tell us what they are doing, they don't know what they are doing. Do our students know what addition is, or only what it looks like?

Understanding mathematics requires language capacity on the part of the learner. If students do not comprehend the teacher's oral explanations in math and struggle through reading a math textbook, then they do not have the necessary language capacity to do well in math.

American culture does not visibly and aggressively support mathematical genius. According to a University of Wisconsin study (Mertz, Andreescu, Gallian, & Kane, 2008), the United States is failing to develop the math skills of both girls and boys. Furthermore, the study finds that those girls who do succeed are almost always the children of immigrants from countries where mathematics is highly valued. In a *New York Times* interview (Rimer, 2008), the study's lead author, Professor Janet E. Mertz, asserts, "Kids in high school, where social interactions are really important, think, 'If I'm not Asian or a nerd, I'd better not be on the math team.' Kids are self-selecting. For social reasons, they're not even trying."

Putting these three points together, it makes sense that the highest, most consistent results in mathematics come from countries where mathematical genius, talent, and persistence are valued, where the mathematics curriculum is predicated on reasoning, and where math literacy is coupled with an active focus on language-based assessments.

We need to overcome the stigma regarding math prowess. Thus an upgrade review in math should not be about interesting technology only; it should be about a fundamental shift in attitude requiring commitment and action.

Consider the increase in adoptions of Singapore Math. For example, the Scarsdale Public School District made a thoughtful commitment to Singapore Math in October 2008. This is the first public school system in the state of New York to formally adopt the program. The 30-member review team examined programs and researched why Singapore is consistently number one on all international forms of mathematical assessment. Their investigation found that the perception that math instruction in the United States is a mile wide and an inch deep is true, whereas in Singapore, math instruction is a steady, well-organized spiral of learning.

Like science instruction, the study of mathematics requires regular opportunities for inquiry and application. An area that can readily be laced throughout the math curriculum is economics and culture, which can be part of a more interdisciplinary emphasis throughout the curriculum from kindergarten through graduation. The goal is to foster financial literacy, entrepreneurialism, an understanding of global and local career interdependence, and knowledge of budget design. Students should be responsible for monitoring classroom and personal budgets; graphing local, national, and global economic trends; and making ethical monetary choices and linking them to the practical realities of work. Given the remarkable changes, genuine challenges, and obvious interconnectedness of the global economy, it is only rational to sustain and to assist our learners with fundamentals of economics on a regular, ongoing basis in their mathematics instruction. Too often, economics is an elective left for senior year, as opposed to being an essential component in our curriculum maps K–12.

The Arts

Central to becoming an educated person is the cultivation of an aesthetic sensibility and the capacity to give form to ideas and emotion. It is startling that arts programs still must often seek justification, given the research on how the brain works (Jensen, 2005), the universal demand for creative innovation, and the exemplary student work from arts programs.

Two fundamental forces are at work when designing arts curriculum: (1) cultivating instruction that fosters the ability to take in and receive meaning and insight from artwork and performance, and (2) the ability to express and generate meaning and insight through artwork and performance. Upgrading arts content translates into the inclusion of new, modern forms in all areas of the arts and adding a global component. This upgrade involves not only the use of technical and digital tools for communicating artistically, but also new ways of perceiving the artistic experience. By accessing art, performances, and events through the Internet, our students can have virtual aesthetic encounters. Art forms are expanding to include multimedia forms and fusion between them— whether filmmaking, or visual or performing arts—which means students have more expansive opportunities to express themselves. With the advent of Second Life technologies, students can create active virtual worlds to dramatize scripts and the impromptu. Global links between students can contribute to joint performance art projects. The particular challenge of an arts curriculum is to sustain the great classical traditions of these fields while inviting learners to use modern tools to express the human condition in their time. In that spirit, I recommend that sometimes the simplest tools can be particularly effective.

Let me make a case for a pencil and plain white paper. I am reminded of a visit to London years ago. I was strolling through the National Gallery and kept running across school groups of students about 11 or 12 years old splayed across the floor with sketch pads, sitting for long periods in front of various great works by the masters. When I asked the teacher of one of these classes what the assignment was, she replied, "Oh, it's a requirement in most of our schools that at least once all students must sit for over an hour, slow down, sketch a great work of their choice, and then comment in depth about what the painter is saying to them through the painting. We want them to be artistically literate, very much like reading a great work of literature." I was startled by the simplicity of this task. Our major cities make many great works available, from New York City's Metropolitan Museum of Art to Atlanta's High Museum of Art, the Art Institute in Chicago, the Wichita Art Museum, the Getty in Los Angeles, and the Seattle Art Museum. Great art is also available for any student who has access to a computer and can "visit" a full array of museums around the world. Cézanne can live on your desktop.

Too often our arts curriculums have gaps in exposure to and experience with an array of art forms. Technology can at least bridge some of those gaps. In the same way that the students in London concentrated on a specific work of art, our learners need an opportunity to slow down and concentrate on specific works from an array of both classical traditions and new directions, with periodic "arts literacy benchmark tasks." Whether it is viewing the choreography of Balanchine, Robbins, or Tharp from great performances, or comparing an aria from *Nixon in China* to one from *La Bohème,* digital video archives now make access easy and immediate. In addition to viewing masterworks, we can take advantage of the dynamic Web sites with classroom materials and supportive lesson plans available through the Kennedy Center's ArtsEdge (http://artsedge.kennedy-center.org/) or through specific museums or arts groups.

As previously noted, the curriculum needs to account for both making meaning from existing works of art and also generating and performing works of art. Consider the Lakewood Project, developed by Beth Hankins, an innovative and imaginative teacher and music director in the Lakewood district in metropolitan Cleveland, Ohio. Hankins found that many talented students in the secondary program were not trying out for "regular" orchestra because they played electronic instruments. In 2002, Hankins created an electronic orchestra with electric Viper violins and cellos custom-designed by Trans-Siberian Orchestra string master Mark Wood, along with rock drums, electric bass and guitar, synthesizer, and a full acoustic string section. As reviewer Thomas Mulready said on the Cool Cleveland Web site (www.coolcleveland.com) after a concert before an audience of 5,000, "The huge ensemble floats like a flutter-bye and stings like a snake with a repertoire that whipsaws from The Who's *Tommy* to Vivaldi's *Winter.*" With participants putting together their own musical arrangements, the project has presented at the Rock and Roll Hall of Fame and has created CDs. Everyone wins here. This is a 21st century music program that respects and builds on the rich traditions of classical music and acknowledges new forms of expression. It was Hankins's vision and determination to learn with her students, the support of district leadership, and the willingness of students to step up and innovate that created such a dynamic program.

A strong arts curriculum is essential for 21st century learners. Such a curriculum exposes them in greater depth to encounters with specific works and performances from a full array of the various arts fields while incorporating contemporary tools in the expression, creation, and sharing of individual works. Given the fundamental need for imaginative thinkers, any review team updating its curriculum maps should be vigilant for opportunities to develop a viable 21st century arts curriculum.

Targeting Content for Strategic Replacements

As researchers, Curriculum 21 inquiry teams identify specific points in the K–12 curriculum for reconsideration and replacement. If the vast majority of the faculty has taken responsibility for engaging in genuine academic inquiry, students will be in an active professional learning culture.

When touring through traditional, discipline-based curriculum guides, there is often the sense of "I have been here before." No doubt, you have. The element of content in curriculum design is particularly susceptible to staying static because as teachers we tend to share what we know well and are comfortable with. It is also difficult to stay on top of a field of knowledge when enormous breakthroughs and new learning occur daily. Yet we also live in a time when cybertools make it easier to stay current.

In our Curriculum 21 inquiry teams, we can walk through maps entered on Internet-based software and make replacements that lead to significant changes in instruction. For example, a 2nd grade teacher replaces her unit on Communities Around the World with one called Interviews with Children Around the World. Students in another class review computer-generated models that look at the variables that should have been considered and that might have averted the collapse of the I-35W bridge in Minneapolis in 2007. The local high school launches its annual film festival with entries in a range of categories, including documentaries and narratives. New language options of Mandarin Chinese, Korean, and American Sign Language are offered to students from elementary school through high school, with supporting instruction offered via webcasts.

Furthermore, the district's professional development team also displays the same spirit of progressivism. Teachers attend video conferences, employ curriculum mapping software, and share their thinking on a Ning with a national study group. As part of professional development, just like their students, teachers create podcasts on new work in a content area, produce and view documentaries on instructional practice, and attend webinars with global professional learning communities. In their individual fields, they have assimilated new knowledge and breakthroughs from psychological, physiological, and pedagogical perspectives, and over the years this information finds its way into workshop programs.

But staff development initiatives should also move to looking at current breakthroughs in the full range of subjects that we teach. If we do not upgrade content, then we are accepting slippage into the past. Updates in curriculum content should be at the heart of our work for our learners and our own professional development.

The Peters Projection World Map was produced with the support of the United Nations Development Programme. For maps and other related teaching materials, contact ODTMaps. com, Box 134, Amherst, MA 01004 USA. Phone: 800-736-1293. Fax: 412-549-3503. E-mail: odtstore@odt.org. Web site: www.ODTmaps.com

Aerial distortion on Mercator's Projection. From *Seeing Through Maps* by Wood, Kaiser, & Abramms, p. 7. Available from ODT Maps (above).

Peters map link: http://odtmaps.com/peters-equal-area-maps.46.0.0.1.htm
Mercator map comparisons: http://odtmaps.com/detail.asp Q product id E STM-2-BK

4

NEW SCHOOL VERSIONS:

Reinventing and Reuniting School Program Structures

Heidi Hayes Jacobs

Imagine James, a new graduate 100 years from now, thinking back on his time in "school." Will he become nostalgic for the good old virtual learning magnet program? Will he remember all of the projects that he and his global network buddies produced? Perhaps he will bring out the holographic yearbook to reflect on the good times. What is probable is that the very forms of school life that James knows will have evolved into more liberating, engaging, and exciting possibilities from those we know now.

The United States has seen reform movements in education since the inception of formal education. The intentions behind reform have varied, but it could be argued that many of these reforms have merely taken an existing practice, bent it a bit, and tinkered with it, thus ending up with the same basic form. The proof is the fact that the overwhelming majority of our schools run on the same length of school year and the same daily schedule, with the same rigid grouping of students and the same faculty organization, and fundamentally in the same type of buildings as in the late 1890s.

Our present century has opened up the possibility of new kinds of forms. For example, when software solutions are moved to new versions, the term *platform* is used. The image clearly describes a systematic, interconnected change in all functions rather than one small adjustment. A new version takes all components on the platform and revises them systemically. The new version has all of the elements working in concert. It is for this reason that I use the word *version* when a group of school leaders elect to make significant and concerted changes to their existing school program to improve the lives of their learners in school. The Latin derivation of *version* means "to turn" or "turning." It is easy to construe the verb "versioning" as an active process for education leaders to develop in their attempts to create viable 21st century learning environments.

If we develop a 21st century curriculum and continue to fuel it with innovation and new knowledge, then we must keep turning the platform that we share with our learners to explore that curriculum. As discussed in the previous chapters, we can make worthwhile upgrades in curriculum and assessment practices, but our options are limited by the basic program structures that house our practice. Those structures become the proverbial "box." Ironically, the central purpose of this chapter is to make the case that in order to build a 21st century school reinvention and reform movement, we must put into operation two classical, fundamental tenets: (1) form should always follow function; and (2) the whole is the sum of the parts.

Curricular Destiny: Schedules, Grouping Patterns, and the Use of Space

As noted in Chapter 1, four interlocking structures are fundamental to the options that schools have for implementing dynamic curriculum and instruction:

- Schedule (long term and short term)
- Grouping patterns of learners (institutional and instructional)

- Grouping patterns of professionals (multiple affiliations)
- Space (both physical and virtual)

The interplay between these structures determines how effectively we can upgrade our curriculum.

To move our school structures into more open, fluid, and correspondingly inventive forms, we need *new* forms, not *re*form. The four structures work together and can be separated only for the sake of discussion, but in practice they are, indeed, interdependent. Arguably, a pivotal reason why schools have such difficulty functioning is because decisions regarding any one of these factors are made in separation from the others. We can zoom in and look at the options, but then they are brought together on the drawing board.

For example, in any composition, the composer can closely consider each element in the ultimate design but eventually will need to connect it with other elements. When writers are developing a novel, they will look at the characters and the plot that emerges from who the characters are in a specific setting. Musical composers make choices about the rhythm, melodic pattern, instrument, harmony, or dissonance but, again, weave these elements together to orchestrate an integrated whole. An architect who is aware of various materials can consider them but needs to match them thoughtfully with the selected style, function, and proportion of the building that will be constructed. Similarly, in designing a school environment, we can consider a wide range of options for each component, but then we need to match these program structures with the actual needs of students. As a 5th grader in New Jersey once said to me, "You know, our school is a kind of biosphere."

To think in fresh ways about the shaping of new versions of school, preparation and research are essential. Otherwise we will simply reiterate what we know. The Greeks talked of the prologue as "setting the scene before the action of the play." We need an active prologue stage, when extensive and exciting study commences. I propose a redesign task force for long-term research and development with a goal of creating possible proposals for new versions of school. The first focus should be on viable drafts, sketches, and scenarios for potential action. The essential questions that should govern the programmatic structures we use to support student learning should be as follows:

- What type of both long-term and short-term schedules will best support our specific learners?
- What various ways of grouping our learners will assist them in their learning experiences?
- How should faculty be configured to best serve students and to assist one another?
- In what ways can both physical and virtual space be created and used to support our work?

Depending on the size of your task force, it is certainly possible to have subgroups investigate each of the structures, but it is critical to weave together the possible implications for the various combinations of each structure. With this requirement in mind, I would like to stimulate investigation by posing possible options for each structure as a way to promote a similar process in your setting. I do not presume to have complete answers or even complete questions, but I hope to prompt your inquiry by sharing some thoughts and observations from extensive field experience and travel to schools. To organize this discussion, the following sections present each of the structures, with highlighted provocations for your consideration.

The Structure of Time: Schedules

At the most basic level, curriculum is nested within long- and short-term schedules. Examining current practice versus current possibilities suggests a number of intriguing alternatives.

Against Graduation as We Know It

To focus our discussion of different schedules, let us start with the big-picture question: Why do we need school to run for 13 years, kindergarten through 12th grade, to say that Johnny has graduated? This structure is the ultimate seat-time problem. If Johnny can endure 13 years rather than 10 or 14 and can show up often enough, take tests, and make sure his pulse is beating, then the diploma is his.

Commencement means *beginning,* and we should take that literally so that students can launch into their futures. We need to give our learners the time that they need to grow and to be ready for launch. Many students drop out of school in part because they cannot make a particular deadline in early June at precisely the same time as their peers. What if these students had another year, or even two years, to work toward a meaningful diploma? Consider the students who are sophomores or juniors in our high schools who are ready for higher education yet have to wait. We ask them to tread water because of their maturity or ability. Something is wrong with this picture.

The Rhode Island requirement involving digital portfolios, which David Niguidula details in Chapter 9, provides the basis for a useful alternative. What if students are expected to demonstrate their readiness to graduate with independence? What if it takes whatever time it takes, with reasonable guidelines? The problem of curriculum planning is compounded in the United States by the shortest school year of any industrialized nation.

Time as Currency in Weeks and Days: Periods, Blocks, Modules, Minutes

The school schedule can be broken down into minutes, hours, days, weeks, and months. Rather than jumping directly into the question of block schedules versus traditional schedules, the larger questions should be these: *What type of time frame matches the nature of the task? What kind of time do my learners need to carry out a specific task?* A totally free and flexible schedule would not work for many teachers and learners, where continuity and structure are essential to learning.

Another approach is to have both structured and unstructured time, strategically planned. I have always thought of teaching time as a form of currency. With a $1 bill, I can buy certain things; with a $20 bill, I can buy others. In a similar way, the question that might be asked is what type of classroom activities are possible and well serviced in a 20-minute block of time, in 40 minutes, in two hours, in a half-day, in a day, in a week, and so forth. Currently we have submitted to the concept that the only thing we can do is what the schedule allows. We think, "I only have 40-minute blocks, so I can only do 40-minute types of activities." It is no wonder that a school's schedule becomes the tyrant of boredom. Teachers and students look at the clock as the mechanized referee of an endurance contest. Conversely, parents and teachers have seen children seemingly "lost in time" when absorbed with a task or interest they are fascinated by.

Technology has also changed the way that we consider time. We should never take for granted the convenience of checking our e-mail on our own time frame. I find it difficult to remember how certain phone calls had to be scheduled and how all mail correspondence was on paper with postage. Yet even though we have embraced change in this area, we seem to be relying on the old habits of time and schedules when it comes to our schools. It is not that we should throw all sense of structuring time out the window, but we should consider our planning from a different angle.

I advocate that your strategic planning team begin by matching time frames to tasks. Let function lead form. Consider these "time as currency" questions:

- What kind of time do I need to help my students edit a first draft? Perhaps 20 or 30 minutes.

- How many minutes will my students need to review a draft with a peer? Perhaps 15 to 20 minutes.

- How much time do we need to view a documentary film and then go into small discussion groups? Eighty minutes.

- How many hours do we need for a field trip to a local business to interview employees and the employer? Three hours.

- How many minutes do my students need for me to introduce a math concept at the interactive whiteboard? Twenty minutes.

- How many minutes would help them talk about the new math concept and show their ideas in pictures and words? Twenty minutes.

- How many weeks will my learners need to shadow a professional in an internship model to gain some rudimentary understanding of the world of work? Six weeks.

These are the questions that we as teachers want to ask. Sometimes, in the best of conditions, we *can* ask them. The point is that far too often we don't ask these questions but use reversed thinking and wonder, "What can I stuff into the 40 minutes I have for math?"

I propose a professional instructional schedule that would give adult professionals the opportunity to envision the learning experiences first and then match them with the time configurations available within the limits or possibilities of the school. This approach also suggests that sometimes learning does not have to be structured in the school space but can be handled in virtual space, which is, indeed, one of our four critical programmatic structures in versioning.

When scheduling, we tend to start with a box and create time sections within it. Complaints about a crowded, cramped day, with time blocks that restrict and generate boredom, have long been common. The advent of the block schedule was intended to give teachers more time to carve out variations within the time frame. Certainly some schools claim a block schedule has been helpful, but others have found the set rotation of an A/B day and the larger blocks also tyrannical. The sameness of these schedules forces sameness into curriculum and instruction. The form is leading function, and the old-style schedule has led us into decades of restriction.

Consider other scenarios. What if schools gave classroom teachers and teaching teams the option of three or four full weeks to go into depth on their personal projects, research investigations, creative generation of digital products, and onsite visits? These weeks could be planned throughout the year and would provide an open opportunity to create exciting interactive sessions. What if schools provided a larger canvas of time with built-in variety for teachers to employ that matched the needs of their students?

Heroic School Schedules

Schools that counter all conventional schooling not for the sake of experimentation but out of good sense and for the ultimate clients, the learners, can be called "heroic" schools. The schools in the Metropolitan Regional Career and Technical Center are heroic. Based on the groundbreaking work of Dennis Littky, the Met Center is composed of six small public high schools in Rhode Island (Littky & Grabelle, 2004). More than 50 schools across the country have followed the Met Center approach. The innovative educators at these schools offer a tailored curriculum for each learner, "one student at a time." There are no bells and no 45-minute blocks of time. Part of their work is to examine the real world through internships and projects. With this type of schedule, it is possible for innovative curriculum work and instruction to focus on six basic tenets:

- Learning in the Real World
- Advisory and Assessment
- Applied Academics and Assessment
- College Transition Program
- Health and Wellness
- Travel Opportunities

Thinking and Planning Outside the Scheduling Box: Virtual Space

At 7:00 a.m., a group of American high school students pour into the videoconferencing room at their tech center, yawning, stretching, waking up with coffee and orange juice in hand. They are in the advanced French class at the school. Simultaneously at 1:00 p.m. in Paris, a group of French adolescents file into their videoconferencing room with coffee in hand. They are in the advanced English language class at their school. For the next three hours, the two groups will converse with one another actively, humorously, and vividly. Other than a plane trip and a visit abroad, there is simply nothing that will match the quality of this type of classroom virtual space for an authentic learning experience.

One of the most promising new forms of learning experiences is the Virtual Learning Magnet (VLM), which matches learning time with engaging and purposeful tasks, offers self-selection on the part of the learner and the teacher, and connects cyberspace with physical space. Tom Welch, a dynamic and innovative educator working with the Council of Chief State School Officers (CCSSO), explains that VLMs are highly modularized, dynamically sequenced curricula that are based on performance rather than seat time. They are designed to take advantage of open-source content delivered via individualized instruction based on the highest levels of competencies and standards (www.ccsso.org. projects/virtual_learning_magnet/). The project is at the proof of concept stage, to be field-tested for possible dissemination.

A key feature of the Virtual Learning Magnet is to link our finest cultural and scientific institutions directly to the student in a focused experience using Internet-based tools. The CCSSO has produced a viable and exciting 21st century design that includes "stretch goals for every learner," with a direct connection to possible career and academic goals. Envision the VLM for Space Science and Mathematics designed in collaboration with NASA, which offers opportunities to replace traditional courses. Disseminated to virtual schools for full online experiences with electronic site visits, the program will offer students the possibility for direct coaching. Tom notes that by using game-based environments for teaching complex material, participatory online network environments, and possibilities for active research, students can create unique and exciting problems to investigate as part of a larger community. The VLMs have evolved from online courses to become more dynamic and creative in their use of sources and tools.

Reflecting on the work of Tom and his colleagues at CCSSO, imagine if your school could offer students a virtual curriculum menu. Students could peruse a set of options that they could work on at home on their own time as opposed to using seat time at school. The notion of a virtual school is provocative. It can stimulate excitement and anxiety because it challenges our fundamental sense of place. Has technology eliminated the need for students to congregate in common spaces during regulated time frames? Perhaps the real question is how to maximize and rethink the use of our schools and schedules for children and expand our view of other ways and places (both physical and virtual) where they spend that time.

The Grouping of Students

To the extent possible, we should group students to best suit their needs so that, again, form follows function, in contrast to the common practice of using preexisting grouping patterns to determine how we package our learners. Grouping in school can be thought of in terms of three fundamental categories: institutional, instructional, and independent, with the first two being those that most of us are used to considering.

Institutional grouping involves fundamental choices based on criteria such as these:

- Gender
- Age group—grade level, multi-age
- Developmental spans—primary, elementary, junior high, middle school, upper school, high school
- Function—general program, vocational, charter, magnet, specialty
- Proficiency based—honors, remedial, special needs, varsity sports, advanced placement, arts performance classes, ELL

Instructional grouping involves the teacher's choices in response to the internal needs of a classroom. Here are some examples:

- Skill groupings that are constant
- Skill groupings that change in response to immediate needs
- Cooperative groups
- Competitive groups
- Individualized work

Independent grouping applies to activities that usually take place outside the school day and are voluntary in nature. Here are some examples:

- Clubs
- Online courses
- Internships
- Work experiences
- Travel abroad
- Community service and projects

The tendency for form to lead rather than follow function has far-reaching and often disheartening results when it comes to decisions on grouping students. At their worst, our systems can do damage, even if our intentions are good. For example, the debate regarding homogeneous versus heterogeneous grouping can at times seem specious. Students in any class, whether it is AP physics or basic biology, will *always* display a range of skill levels. In short, to some extent all classes are heterogeneous, and the wrong question is being raised. Rather than asking whether homogeneous or heterogeneous is the best generic grouping, the question should be, "What type of grouping would best support learning for a specific group of students to address specific objectives?" The real issue is what commonality makes sense to support student learning. In short, sometimes grouping patterns are too sweeping and imprecise. Consider some scenarios that might sound familiar.

The moment 5-year-old Amy starts school, she is placed, labeled, and created into a product. She is placed in a grade level that will be coeducational, although it is possible that a multiyear program that groups girls together for some of the math instruction could make all the difference in the world.

Chuck is a 7th grader who struggles in math. His friend Johnny excels in math. The middle school policy gives highly capable math students in 7th grade the option to accelerate their 8th grade year, better enabling honors students to move rapidly through the high school program. This option appears to truly match Johnny's needs, but it has two drawbacks. First, the school offers no counterpart for Chuck and many others to "decelerate." With extra time and the opportunity to work at a different pace, not only would Chuck understand more complex mathematical concepts, he also would have a greater likelihood of success in high school. The second drawback is that 80 percent of the students in the accelerated program are male, which is certainly statistically significant. In this particular school, would segregating the sexes in mathematics in earlier years lessen this disparity?

An extremely motivated and competent high school sophomore, Maria, wants to graduate early and has a genuine interest in pursuing a career in psychology. To graduate, she must complete a full-year series of course requirements, which she could actually complete online, independently, during the summer. She would prefer spending time doing an internship with a community social service agency in the afternoons during the school year.

These examples illustrate the direct link between the schedule of a school day and the grouping of students. Think how different a child's life might be if school planners began with a variation on the question that has run throughout this chapter: *What grouping patterns would best help our learners meet their needs?*

The Grouping of Professionals: The Need for Multiple Affiliations

A programmatic structure that touches the very identity of a teacher is the array of possible professional affiliations. The way teachers are grouped obviously affects whom they work with and see regularly, but it also has direct repercussions on the learners. We are creatures of habit, and day to day, forms and labels can go beyond habit to the realm of rut if not thoughtfully reexamined. Consider how arbitrary and habitual our usual patterns are. In most schools, grouping is currently based on the following:

- Departments
- Grade levels
- Building levels—elementary, primary, middle, high school, or upper school

The standard and isolated nature of these groupings is a large contributor to the gaps in student performance. Curriculum mapping reviews help us consider that if a group of 4th grade teachers does not interact with other teachers, then their decisions are not formally informed by 1st, 2nd, or 3rd grade teachers, let alone the 5th grade teachers who will receive their learners. Reviews remind us that high school students do not advance to one department—they matriculate to a group of teachers who work with them throughout the year. Our old forms of working in isolated departments is almost to the point of those departments becoming self-sustaining colonies.

I would recommend that personnel consider multiple types of affiliations and groupings as well as the duration of such groups to provide variety and perspective in their work. These affiliations should not be random but targeted and strategic.

The Meeting Habit

The wrong people meet regularly in our schools. Instead of meeting by department, what if we were to meet around problems? What if we were to meet strategically with the best people to address a problem? For example, if issues arise related to poor performance on 8th grade math tests regarding balancing an equation, then the group that is most likely to meet are the 8th grade math teachers. A more strategically planned group would be teachers in grades 4, 5, 6, 7, and 8 who would meet virtually to examine curriculum maps and consider the requisite building of skills; furthermore, English teachers should be involved to help determine if, in fact, the test results reflect a reading problem rather than a math problem. What is more, to see if students have a real understanding of an equation, it would make sense to involve a physics teacher who relies on applied mathematics when students demonstrate the application of equations in their study of the laws of force and motion.

Similarly, if curriculum means "a path to run in small steps," then perhaps one of the most logical groupings for ongoing discussion and dialogue would be vertical teams. Yet it is striking how rarely teachers who share a child over time and over years actually meet.

A deliberate personnel policy might eliminate the static nature of professional relationships. The goal of the policy would be to encourage teachers and administrators to join several communities and networks outside their school site as well as inside. Consider expanding the traditional list to add the following groups in your school or district:

- Vertical teams K–12
- Vertical strategic teams, such as K–2, 3–7, or 8–11
- Cross-disciplinary teams
- Internship supervisors
- Task force study groups constructed around issues, books, new directions
- Data analysis teams
- State education network team
- National network team
- Global peer coaching team
- Global network team

The last suggestion should be a network of educators from throughout the nation and the world sharing their curriculum maps to examine a unit of study from global perspectives. This sharing happens now because users of certain curriculum mapping software have access to any classroom teacher who uses the same software. With this type of link, a kindergarten teacher in Milwaukee might have a peer coach from Auckland, New Zealand, sharing points of view on reading readiness. A social studies teacher in El Paso, Texas, might have a peer coach from Doha, Qatar, sharing points of view on examining the role of oil in world economics. This notion is clearly possible now, given the ease of technological access to peers at the state, national, and international levels. Having said this, it is the internal connections and the communication between colleagues within a location that are critical to the development of the individual learner.

Social Learning Frameworks

When I think of education thought leaders, one of our authors, Stephen Wilmarth, always comes to mind. He has shared with me an example that underscores the possibilities of combining new ways of grouping students and personnel, using virtual space, and renegotiating time—the social learning framework. Stephen has described this as "leveraging social production, social networks, new modalities for discovery, media grids, and an organic learning process" (February 7, 2009; personal correspondence).

An example is the Penn LPS Commons, from the University of Pennsylvania's College of Liberal and Professional Studies (see www.sas.upenn.edu/lps/commons). Here is not just the possibility but the reality of an educational platform that encompasses new global faculty relationships, new kinds of student groupings and network relationships, activated curriculum queries, flexible use of time, and virtual space. Will this approach replace the contact time between teacher and student in a room called a classroom? No, but the reverse is true as well. The traditional classroom cannot replace the new forms. Our new versions of school need to reflect the times in which we live and continue to be open to new and dynamic structures.

New Versions of Physical and Virtual Space

Location, location, location. Any historian or anthropologist will tell you that where people live has everything to do with their possibilities in life. It is precisely the same in education. Where a school is located and how it sets up internal structures determine its possibilities. Today we have a new way of discussing how space affects our learners: virtual space. As Prakash Nair states:

> Let's start with the fundamental building block of almost every single school in this country: the classroom. Who seriously believes that locking 25 students in a small room with one adult for several hours each day is the best way for them to be "educated"? In the 21st century, education is about project-based learning, connections with peers around the world, service learning, independent research, design and creativity,

and, more than anything else, critical thinking and challenges to old assumptions. (Nair, 2009)

Most schools were not really built for children, let alone for learning. They tend to be buildings with uniform-sized classrooms, although the students vary in size at different ages. Chances are that the majority of readers of this book work in a place that has restrictions on the use of space. You have inherited a space dictated by a mind-set about school design that is highly limited. However, there are genuine ways to rethink any space more effectively. One way to provoke discussion in your redesign task force is to consider how existing school space might be used differently. I would invite your students to take an architectural walking tour of the school and suggest different ways to use traditional classrooms as well as ancillary locations. Younger sets of eyes help us see in new ways, and students bring the perspective of actual users of the building.

Over the years, I have enjoyed perusing the school designs of award-winning architects from around the globe at DesignShare (www.designshare.com), one of the most exciting sources for ideas on improving the quality of life and space for learners. With a truly global reach, architects, educators, planners, and designers visit the site for inspiration regarding their work for all levels of education, nursery through university. DesignShare has partnerships with leading organizations and initiatives such as Edutopia, the National Clearinghouse for Educational Facilities, Great Schools by Design, and the United Kingdom's School 4 Life. Annually they present awards to dynamic designs that match the needs of students in specific settings with a remarkably imaginative range of architectural solutions. Many of the winners do not have large budgets, but they focus on *how to best support engagement on the part of their learners*. Some have effectively used light and space to promote a more soothing place to think and to play. Sometimes the transformations are small, such as a window seat being expanded to become a reading alcove; or, in a school in an underdeveloped nation, lowering the blackboard so it can be easily viewed by children sitting on a floor in a space without chairs and desks. Sometimes the design involves reconceptualization of large spaces so that a whole campus flows with the environment. The positioning of balconies and walkways can connect students to classroom activity rather than separate them. The boldness and the power of the solutions are inspiring and striking. I encourage you to see the remarkable International Award School Designs at various international locations. Visit www.designshare.com.

Most people reading this book will not have the resources to make significant changes in their existing school architecture, but we all can walk through an existing structure and rethink its use. Possibilities might include pairing certain classrooms or using a space that sits empty because it is assigned a label such as "auditorium" or "band room." With some imagination, these spaces can be used for other types of classroom learning. Could your auditorium be used by the English department for poetry slams, or for screenings of documentaries in science or social studies followed by discussion groups? Could an office adjacent to a library be devoted to a video podcasting station for book talks? Might there be an LCD projector showing PowerPoint slides from field trips or interesting class unit studies projected on a wall in the cafeteria during lunch? Is there a spot in the schoolyard that might be set up with a bench for quiet reflection?

An obvious way to find new space is to leave the classroom for field experiences, both nearby and far away from the school. Local visits to museums and conservation areas with fieldwork observations have been a staple of the school experience for decades, but often they have been special events, such as the annual field trip. We would do well to put both Web-based field experiences as well as ongoing internships and field experiences in the forefront of our planning.

Travel-abroad programs expand the perspectives of our learners for a lifetime when they go beyond the simple tour model to promote a genuine connection with the people in a specific culture. Wilmarth's program for "global ambassadors" (see Chapter 5) exemplifies a level of growth that dislodges students from their school comfort zone.

In thinking about space, we should also respect our learners' need for privacy. Award-winning school designs almost always include a quiet place for reflection. The hectic nature of school life is often amplified by the actual space available to students, with cramped quarters and shared narrow corridors. Even if it is only a small corner of a school, a place for solitude would be welcome.

Four Structures in Search of a Common Platform

I believe that a core reason for the self-imposed limitations we find in schools is the separation of the four program structures—schedules, grouping patterns for learners, groupings of professionals, and space. These four structures are totally intertwined, mutually dependent, and systemic. New school designs, and even the reformation of existing school programs, need to do more than stay out of the box—they need to dump the box entirely.

Long-term new versions of school need to have the capacity to be elastic and responsive. So here is the essential question that drives the provocations in this chapter: *Could your Curriculum 21 review team generate a version of school that had both flexibility and regulation in long-term and daily schedules, supported multiple professional affiliations, offered a wide range of student groupings, and used physical and virtual space in direct response to the actual students you have been charged to educate?* Think like architects.

Sketching Program Blueprints for New School Versions

Frequently, when I have taught curriculum design classes at Columbia University, Teachers College, I have invited an architect to teach with me. What I have learned is that educators would do well to follow many of an architect's design habits. The architect first asks the client (1) whom the building is to serve and (2) what the building's function will be. Then the forms emerge. In a similar way, our Curriculum 21 teams should always begin thinking about new versions of school by asking whom are we serving ultimately, and how can we best meet the needs of our specific learners?

As architects begin with sketches, we, too, should begin by drafting possible solutions. Our versions will *always* need to bring the four structures together. The main contention of this chapter is that a key reason reform efforts often have limited effectiveness is that they are not made in concert with corresponding adjustments in the other structures. The reforms themselves are often tepid and stay within the existing conception of an organization. Most important, the motivation for the specific reform is too often detached from the curricular and instructional needs of the specific learners. Changes in one structure affect the others.

I advocate that Curriculum 21 teams research a range of possibilities in program structures before coming to the table to create a unified programmatic blueprint. Ultimately, form should follow function, and as we expand the possible functions of curriculum and instruction, we should expand the menu of forms available for both formal and informal learning experiences. A worthwhile exercise is to create a flowchart that reflects the reality of a school or educative program. Using visual-thinking software, a school beginning to draft its possible new version should consider the direct flow of decisions for the various components discussed in this chapter. Starting with the supposition that form should follow function, the school group should start with who the students are in order to establish a mission statement based on their needs.

The curriculum should then be established based on their needs, followed by the consideration of each of the major structures in concert. The ultimate goal is an effective environment for learning: students grouped to work with the personnel organized to match their needs in time frames that support their work in both real and virtual spaces.

When I work with planning teams, one of the most eye-opening tasks I ask them to do is to create a flowchart showing the flow of decisions regarding the basic school structures that directly affect the curriculum that reaches the student. It is clear that this flow affects instructional method and whom teachers ultimately work with in terms of both learners and colleagues.

I agree with David Hyerle's conclusions from his masterful work on the power of visual representations to make meaningful changes in both how individuals process information and how groups can make more meaningful decisions. Hyerle (2008, p. 2) writes that change "offer[s] a way through the great dichotomies and supposed polar opposites on which we so endlessly query."

Often, frustration occurs because structures are dated and lead the learning. Rather than being victimized by our program structures, we should be creating new types of learning environments for a new time and for various types of teaching and learning. Not to do so is a declaration not to learn. It is precisely in the area of developing new versions of school that we need risk-taking educators to create bold ideas to transform the whole notion of school. Some might argue that we should hold onto the old notions because it more sensible to do so. I would argue that it is lacking in good sense to hold onto structures that do not match their time and the purpose of education for our century. *Form should follow function. The whole is the sum of the parts.* These two timeless premises support new solutions for a new time.

5

FIVE SOCIO-TECHNOLOGY TRENDS
That Change Everything
in Learning and Teaching

··

Stephen Wilmarth

This chapter is about technology. But it's not only about integrating technology into the curriculum. It's also about social trends and how technology is influencing these trends, and what the implications are for culture, society, learning, and teaching in the 21st century. We live in an age of transformational communications technology. Our world, and all of its many cultures and ways of thinking, is smaller and more connected than ever before in human history. This chapter seeks to define and contextualize how technology and the social adaptations to new technologies change learning and teaching going forward.

In times of great change, it's not unusual to miss the obvious. So I write here about technology trends and the social adaptations that will have profound effects on education in the 21st century. New technologies combined with social and cultural adaptations fundamentally change our understanding of knowledge, its creation and authority. As educators, we have a duty to examine the effect of these trends and respond to the question, "What does it mean to be educated in the 21st century?"

Today's student, nearly everywhere in the world, lives in a technological era in which the Internet and Google and text messaging never *didn't* exist. New technologies result in ubiquitous connectivity and the pervasive proximity of unstructured relationships. As a result, the experience of today's student is the opposite of our own literate-grounded experiences of linearity and hierarchical structures of knowledge commonly accepted and institutionalized in the educational systems that were developed generations ago and that serve as the framework for today's system of education.

All learning is social. It was technology—the development and adoption of a symbolic alphabet—that ended an era of "orality" and began an era we call "literacy." It was technology—the development of moveable type and printing presses—that ended an era of scholastic authority by a selected priesthood and created mass literacy in the vernacular of every culture. And it is dramatic new technology that once again is altering the landscape and redefining our notions of literacy.

Be assured, I am not advocating that children do not need to learn to read. They do. Or that writing will not be necessary. It is. Or that the process of arriving at sums no longer matters. It does. But all of these things are the outcomes of social adaptation to prior technological change and invention. It is the nature and relevance of reading, writing, and sums that change as we enter the postliterate era. Significantly, it is the way in which we make meaning out of information to create new knowledge that is changing.

Social Production

In July 2008, Google engineers announced that they believed there were 1 trillion unique URLs—the unique address of a Web page (Perez, 2008). In the same announcement, Google engineers estimated that the Web is growing by several billion individual Web pages per day. There is only one explanation for the incredible rate of creating, copying, mixing, and remixing of information available to anyone with an Internet

connection, and that is the raw power of *social production* to create information and knowledge artifacts.

Within an incredibly short time—less than five years—the real cost
of publishing and reaching a mass audience has dropped to nearly
zero. This frictionless world of Web 2.0 self-publishing has created a
profound change in how we view the role of producers and creators
(O'Reilly, 2005). The proliferation of types of social media, through
which an entire participatory culture has sprung up, confounds our traditional notion of literary authority.

Are students improving their ability to think critically, to express
themselves, and to develop usable literacies by participating through
blogs, wikis, podcasts, video productions on sites such as YouTube,
e-mail, text messaging, and shared online photostreams (Jenkins,
2006b)? While this question of improved literacy is hotly debated, there
can no longer be a debate over the fact that amateurs, not professional
writers, developers, artists, or programmers, produce the vast majority of
Web content. Our students are no longer primarily consumers of content. They participate as content creators at rates never before seen. And
the trend is accelerating.

Because the World Wide Web is designed to link together digital
knowledge artifacts in any fashion imaginable, old systems of creating
order out of chaos no longer apply. Where once we depended upon
domain experts to categorize and organize knowledge, this task is now
handed over to everyone. And the results are stunning! The power of
the digital disorder (Weinberger, 2007) that arises out of all knowledge
being everywhere at once makes the human capacity for pattern recognition, for critical thinking, for nuanced perceptions, and for dealing
with ambiguity far more important than the search for certain outcomes
(Edelman, 2006). We're forced to replace the metaphor of a tree of
knowledge, organized in a Dewey decimal–like fashion, with a cloud
metaphor as participants in the information bazaar reconstruct the relevance and relationships of knowledge artifacts in ever-changing shapes
and patterns.

The tools and technologies of social production tip the long-held,
customary balance between creators and consumers of information and

culture. Participatory culture means learning takes on a more active role rather than the traditional passive mode. Producers and consumers converge and interact in new ways. The proliferation of devices that merge media types—news feeds delivered over cell phones, video downloadable from YouTube to iPods, global positioning devices that search for restaurants and display menus—don't strengthen mass culture; they destroy it. Everyone participates, and each stands on the shoulders of others to create their own unique version of culture and reality.

New art forms emerge from the proliferation of social media on the Internet—the mashup. Mashups are information formats of a different ilk brought together to create new perspectives and new ways of comparing, contrasting, and recognizing patterns. Mashups have no artificial limits. The participatory culture spawns new ways of putting together information at an ever-increasing rate.

For example, Google Earth takes highly detailed satellite images and three-dimensional landscapes to give us a useful and elegant way to surf an atlas of our home and neighborhood, ocean depths, even the moon and Mars. As impressive as that is, it's not the ultimate power of this tool to teach and inform. The real power of Google Earth isn't in its imagery. It's in its participatory nature. By providing APIs (application program interface codes) to anyone who requests them, amateurs and professionals alike can combine photos and video and blogs and wikis with stunning Google Earth imagery. Participants create their own representations of geophysical-informational knowledge. The wonder of Google Earth is not that so much rich information about people, places, and culture is available to anyone with a computer; it's that all this information is the result of a global, collaborative, work-sharing effort. And the product is free to the ultimate beneficiaries.

Collective intelligence, and the means to tap into it, fundamentally shifts knowledge paradigms through concepts such as mass collaboration, prediction markets (Surowiecki, 2004), and crowdsourcing (Tapscott & Williams, 2008). What are some examples of the power of mass collaboration, the use of prediction markets, and applications of crowdsourcing? Arguably, with more than 2.5 million articles in English and millions more articles in dozens of other languages, Wikipedia is a modern miracle of mass collaboration. The *Wall Street Journal* has reported that General Electric uses prediction market software from Consensus Point to generate new business ideas (Totty, 2006). Dell gives over its computer product research and design functions to its customers, an example of crowdsourcing. The Democratic National Committee launched FlipperTV in November 2007 and McCainpedia in May 2008 (Link, 2008) to crowdsource video gathered by Democratic trackers and research compiled by DNC staff and put it in the hands of the public for any purpose they chose, for example, for a blog post or to create a YouTube video.

Especially as it has evolved since the mid-1990s, the open-source software movement has been the most visible evidence of a shift to collective intelligence through a radical redistribution of social production technologies. Today, thousands of software products are developed by groups of people over distributed networks that make the World Wide Web a cornucopia of productive applications, most of them free under a Creative Commons license, or available at a nominal cost. The more open and distributed the network, the more productive it becomes. Corporations are changing their strategies and redefining missions based on the recognition that social production is an enormously competitive force.

And the phenomenon is no longer reserved for open-source software. Like a highly contagious virus, open sourcing has become the most dominant strategy in globally competitive markets, from product and service design to high-touch customer services. The project team of nearly every corporation in every market is likely to consist of representatives of suppliers, customers, and, yes, competitors! There's even a new word to describe when normally competitive companies work together: *co-opetition* (Bowser, n.d.). The power of open-source social production is routinely applied to designing, organizing, producing, marketing, and supporting products and services, even without the need for formal organizations (Shirky, 2008).

So what does all this have to do with learning and teaching in the networked global knowledge economy of the 21st century? Each of us, from the moment we create a blog post, contribute to a wiki, set up a

MySpace or Facebook page, participate in a chat room, upload pictures to Flickr from a cell phone, make a podcast and post it on iTunes, Twitter with friends, or create a video clip for distribution on YouTube, is a producer of content and knowledge in our connected universe. Social production is a "back to the future" phenomenon applied to learning. This is the apprenticeship model of learning. It is *learning by doing*. It occurs without the need for base knowledge. It is just-in-time learning as you go. It occurs beyond the formal rules and classrooms of traditional education.

Social Networks

Social production has exploded exponentially since 2000 and the mass production of Web 2.0 applications such as blogs, wikis, and other collaborative, interactive tools. Social production is enabled by the incredible power of networks to connect people.

As the Internet has evolved and multimedia forms of person-to-person and group-to-group communications—e-mail, online chat, text messaging, RSS feeds, photo sharing, video streaming, podcasting—proliferate, the implications for mediated connectivity within society have changed. What was thought of as strong and weak ties between members of a social network began to shift as new media for communication became popular. The importance of weak ties to generate heterogeneity in relationships has steadily grown (Haythornthwaite, 2005). As weak ties tend to connect affinity groups within homogeneous interest areas to new ideas, to different ways of thinking, and to innovations in previously disconnected groups, the Internet has generated a profound change in the complexity and value of social networks.

The new power of social media and networking technologies to teach is perhaps the least leveraged technology in formal education systems today. Social networking technologies are powerful tools for enhancing the process of *learning to be*, of defining our identities. Digital social networks are now an essential part of the experience of everyone under the age of 20. Digital social networks may be the biggest game changer in learning and what it means to be educated. And yet the power of social networks to influence the nature of learning and teaching is barely understood by our institutional leaders.

All learners create an identity that determines their place in the social and economic order. Joining communities of interest and shared values (personal, family, cultural, political, economic) has always been essential to a learner's identity. In this case, identity equates to where an individual is on the learning curve. And where traditional community relationships once defined a learner's identity, emerging social networking technologies allow wholly new community associations to spring up organically and globally. These community ties, both strong and weak, exert a powerful influence on learning.

First, keep in mind that social networking technologies are changing rapidly. Second, remember that the technologies are not the point. In social networking, it's important to concentrate on relationships, not technologies. The way people connect with each other—the community that's created—determines how the power of learning shifts. If a technology makes connections more interesting, more varied, or more frequent, it is likely to be more widely adopted and have a disproportionate effect on the creation of dynamic learning communities. Social learning communities spread virally as existing participants recruit new learners to join them. Since its launch in 2003, the popular online social networking community Facebook has grown to 200 million users worldwide. But even more impressive statistics reveal that this community has more than 24 million photos uploaded daily, and more than 6 million active user groups interact on the site. Many of these user groups are related to educational activities and formal learning institutions. YouTube.com is another application of social networking with impressive viral growth statistics. Twitter.com is a service that permits people to broadcast and subscribe to a constant stream of content through mobile phones. Each of these social media applications presents new challenges and opportunities to traditional learning communities.

Do social media applications shift power and responsibility for learning from institutions to individual learners? Writer Clay Shirky (2008) eloquently describes the power of social media to organize without the need for organizations. Social networking and the rapid adoption of social media do indeed demonstrate a trend toward sustainable community-generated content with the power to greatly expand self-determined learning opportunities. The World Wide Web is becoming increasingly social. This sociability is, in turn, making the Web more open and connected, allowing applications to be more socially aware.

The identities created by self-determined learners using all of the available social media are scattered across the Web. An interesting exercise for anyone, student or teacher, is simply to Google (at what point in the evolution of language did the word *Google* become a verb?) your own name. Want to know where you are on the learning curve? This is one indicator—and an increasingly important one for potential employers, university admissions offices, and just plain curious neighbors. In effect, everyone has an electronic portfolio today. Many are empty or sparse, but an increasing number of people, particularly those who are writing, doing, thinking, or acting in public and not-so-public ways, are building extensive electronic portfolios.

So let's think about this for a minute. Our national and state policies are focusing increasingly on high-stakes testing (as in determining the competency of students to go on to the next level, of teachers to teach effectively, and of administrations to manage acceptable outcomes), and yet learners are posting work and reflections and assessments to various Web locations that are, in many cases, easily discoverable through a simple Google search. How do we explain those students who seem disengaged and distracted and are underperforming in the classroom, but who may be producing highly creative, literate, and impressively intellectual content that can be easily viewed on the Web? What is the difference between the test we give students in formal learning settings, versus the work portfolios that we discover in the informal learning spaces on the Web?

Social networks can tell a lot about a person. There is justifiable concern over what risks social networks may pose. The friends people select, the groups where an individual is most welcomed and participates—each interaction can provide insight into a personal profile. Indeed, investigations in the wake of campus or school rampages will often focus on the online affinity groups of the perpetrators. Sophisticated data collection goes on around most individuals' participation in online communities. While we may be losing or voluntarily surrendering aspects of our privacy for the convenience of participating in digital communities, there is also ample evidence that the informal learning gained from social interactions and peer-mediated learning is substantial. And the more diverse, global, and heterogeneous a set of networks that one participates in, the more learning that occurs (Boyd & Ellison, 2007).

A Semantic Web

One problem with today's increasingly short cycles of technological convergence is the lack of time we have to make the necessary intellectual and legal adjustments to the introduction of transforming technologies. The socio-technological trends of social production and social networking are viewed in the context of the World Wide Web as we've watched it evolve over its first 5,000 days. And yet, just as we seem to be accepting the transformational effect of a "read/write" Web, we are about to see a complete transformation of the World Wide Web itself.

If social production can be summarized as radically redistributing the powers of production and knowledge creation and generating a model for learning *to do*, and social networking is a model for learning *to be*, then a semantic Web will become the model for learning *to know* in the next innovation phase of the Internet. A semantic Web, the protocols of which are just emerging, will fundamentally change our understanding of the potential of the Internet to create and deliver new knowledge. A semantic Web will dramatically transform our relationship to new knowledge, our ability to use new knowledge for purposes of creativity, and our definition of what it means to be educated.

A semantic Web will quantitatively and qualitatively improve search, collaboration, and publishing. Don't think of this next generation of information and knowledge management as a linear progression of change. Indeed, a semantic Web will be unlike anything we have experienced before. It will be comparable to the difference between our experience before the emergence of the Web and e-mail and cell phones with text messaging capabilities and our experience after all of these things became intricately woven into our daily lives—so much so that we are often highly stressed when we can't access the Internet, can't get to our e-mail, or lose our cell phone.

How will a semantic Web differ from the Web we've come to depend on? To create a semantic Web, information itself will be tagged, described, and defined so that each bit of information coursing the Web will carry its own DNA. So we now come upon a dawning era of information bits that will be organized, interpreted, and distributed in ways that give implicit and explicit meaning to discourses from humans to humans, and, yes, for those who wonder about brave new worlds, from machines to machines, and from machines to humans in ubiquitous digital domains.

Instead of pages sharing information through hyperlinking, each bit of content itself will share information and stretch our capacity to make meaning out of the mountains of data that otherwise cause us to experience information overload. Search tools that mimic natural language patterns, offering more reliable and specific contextual modes, will replace today's search engines. We are all familiar with the limitations of current-generation search engines. Type some keyword phrases in Google and you're lucky if you don't have thousands of returns to browse through. Of course, Google's search technology has generally been good enough to give us what we want within the first 20 or so returns. But search will take on a whole new dynamic if our queries have context and semantic references added to them. Beyond the semantic Web we can foresee the vague outlines of an intelligent Web.

There are some pretty interesting examples of what it will mean to give information units a digital DNA. Photosynth is a software program that captures and reconstructs spaces in the social environment of the Web and registers collective memories created by hundreds or thousands of contributing photostreams to give us a highly contextualized view of what our world looks like. This technology was put on display by CNN during the Obama inauguration ceremony, gathering in thousands of digital pictures from cell phones and single-lens reflex, or SLR, cameras to re-create a panoramic view from one end of the Washington Mall to the other, from thousands of feet away to close enough to "touch" without any loss of resolution. Using principles of tagging and spatial registration, a model emerges that is greater than the sum of its parts. Photosynth is a potent mixture of two independent breakthroughs: the ability to reconstruct a scene or an object from a bunch of two-dimensional photographs, and the technology to bring that experience to virtually anyone over the Internet.

Using techniques from the field of computer vision, Photosynth examines images for similarities to one another and uses that information to estimate the shape of the subject and the vantage point each photo was taken from. With this information, we re-create the space and use it as a canvas to display and navigate through the photos.

The Photosynth project is a prime example of the potential of the next generation of semantic Web technologies to transform our understanding and creation of knowledge. All of this amazing, jaw-dropping imagery is an example of the Web we will take for granted in three to five years. When each photo pixel or bit (a single unit of data) has been tagged and coded with information about the information, a truly intelligent Web, with powers of reasoning emerging from its DNA-like features, will make it seem as if we've gone from the Stone Age to the Industrial Age in a single leap.

The infrastructure to power a semantic Web is already here. Not only are the bits of infrastructure now in place, but we are also seeing start-ups, research organizations, and enterprises working hard to deliver valuable new applications on top of this sophisticated set of technologies. A semantic Web means many things to different people, because it has lots of pieces. To some, a semantic Web is the web of data, where information is represented in specific technical ways. Others think that a semantic Web is about Web services—applications that bring new services, such as events automatically matched up to a calendar, or connections to people (friends of a friend) even though we use different platforms or applications. For many others, it is about artificial intelligence—computer programs solving complex optimization problems that are beyond the reach of the human mind.

Educators will redefine this potential in terms of student value— whatever the semantic Web is, it needs to have simple and tangible applications for learning and teaching. Much is possible and much can be imagined. If having "Google in your pocket" allows everyone instant access to all knowledge, anytime, anywhere, what is possible when the Web itself possesses a contextual instinct, a natural language interface, and a power of reasoning that is the broad outline of a semantic Web? One thing is certain. Learning *to know* will never be the same.

Media Grids

Think of media grids as three-dimensional representations of space using computing power and the Internet. One of the first applications to be introduced to early computer adopters was a simple video game called Pong, an electronic version of air hockey. Pong's success spawned the video game industry (Miller, 2005). Today's generation of video games simulates highly complex and realistic experiences. The technology is evolving rapidly for creating multidimensional models of digital simulations of reality.

We see it in the popular online role-playing game World of Warcraft, which is revolutionizing online games through complex team strategies and sophisticated graphics. Virtual worlds such as Second Life, Google Lively, There, and Entropia Universe let you create avatars, buildings, and even virtual classrooms and business settings. With Google Earth and Microsoft's Virtual Earth 3-D, you can transcend the map layout and zoom into satellite-mapped locations around the world. All these developments have something in common and point in one direction. Within a very short period, the Internet and the vast wealth of information and services on it will look different, slicker, more realistic, and more interactive and social than anything we experience today through the Web browser.

What do media grids mean for learning? By now the debate about the effect of video immersion on the minds and lives of our students has formed its hard and fast battle lines. There are those who are convinced that video games are the ruination of young minds. Certainly, the social benefits derived from the popular video game Grand Theft Auto are hard to imagine. And so many other video games present themselves simply as opportunities for gratuitous violence and mayhem, even if only of the virtual sort. What could be the benefit of anything in the gaming genre for learning?

Beneath the pop culture veneer of today's shoot-'em-up video games, some trends are emerging that have the potential to revolutionize learning and virtual experience in the near future. Gaming embeds all of the attributes of Howard Gardner's (2007) five minds for the future: the disciplined mind, the synthesizing mind, the creative mind, the respectful mind, and the ethical mind. Games can do something else, as well. Game scenarios can branch, so content is no longer confined to linear structures, as so many learning experiences are in our traditional formal educational settings. If, as evidence shows, experiential learning engages the mind and teaches learners *to do* and *to be* more effectively than the linear application of content so frequently used today, games with an educational orientation can become powerful tools in and out of the formal classroom. We're starting to see real development in this area.

Although games have become popular among the young netizens, many educators are less aware of the emergence of virtual worlds that replicate our social landscapes through 3-D experiences. Second Life is such a 3-D social landscape, with all of the elements found in the real world, including an active economy based on a real, exchangeable currency called Linden dollars. This thriving economy is made up of hucksters and craftspeople who buy and sell virtual real estate, rent out retail outlets or trade show booths, create and sell items of clothing or furniture or floor plans—virtually any item of value, all referred to as "sims."

This virtual world of the future will work differently from our current Web experiences in flat, two-dimensional spaces. In a sense, virtual worlds will become not just a portal into various media, entertainment, and communications services but also a window into a potentially richer real life. Virtual worlds will become the place where we can conveniently engage in familiar real-world activities such as family reunions and shopping trips with friends or in thrilling, only-in-cyberspace adventures.

Above all, virtual worlds hold the potential to transform social interaction online. In contrast to the Web, where there's almost no assumption of a human heartbeat behind the Web page, virtual worlds are inherently social settings. Social activity dominates what people do online today. When you approach an avatar in Second Life, you know there's a real person on the other end. Eventually, virtual worlds may prove to be much more than the fad some folks think they are. World of Warcraft and Second Life may be all the rage now, but they still touch relatively few people's lives, in no small part because they're primitive and awkward to use. But that situation is about to change. And when the virtual world achieves a level of sophistication that makes virtual social interactions nearly indistinguishable from real social interactions, our world and our system of education will be transformed. This will happen in a matter of a few years.

The New Zoo of Nonlinear Learning

Physics proved to be the mother science of the 20th century. All the modern conveniences we take for granted can be traced back, in large measure, to breakthroughs in the general science of physics. Biology may prove to be the mother science of the 21st century. Biology has been making rapid advances in helping us understand the world of the metaphysical so long ago contemplated by Plato, Aristotle, and their descendant philosophers. And out of this understanding comes a new code that we are just learning to work with: the four letters representing the base elements of deoxyribonucleic acid (DNA)—A, C, T, and G. The combination of these base elements in pairs has a singular purpose in nature—to carry information within each cell and to instruct all of the processes arising out of the interaction of cells in complex living organisms. What we couldn't know at the dawn of the 20th century we had to account for through a Cartesian duality of mind and body; today we stand much nearer to a not-so-distant horizon of limitless possibilities through the language derived from the code of A, C, T, and G.

This new science will change everything about our understanding of knowledge creation. As physicist and author Freeman Dyson (2005) states, the Darwinian interlude is over—3 billion years of a process of intense competitive natural selection that gave rise to micro-organisms that replicated their unique gene sets so that they formed the first species, and over the millennia, added and subtracted to the tree of life through species births and extinctions. In the beginning, the soup that made up a microbial sea used a process of horizontal gene transfer (Woese, 2004). This process allowed evolution to be a communal affair. But it was an inefficient process, and the rise of species that no longer shared all genes allowed far more complex organisms to rise and fall throughout the Darwinian epoch.

With the code of life in hand, Dyson speculates that the post-Darwinian era represents a return to a communal form of gene sharing. Humans will achieve the power to create new species at will and transfer genes horizontally as in the pre-Darwinian period. In Dyson's mind, cultural evolution is better than natural selection. "Designing genomes will be a new art form, as creative as painting or sculpture" (2005).

And what role will learning and knowledge play in this revolutionary new world of biotechnology? Our questions will only get more complicated and our answers less certain if we are to survive. But it is too late to wish the progress of science and knowledge would not put such a burden on our systems of education and curriculum design. We can rail against the challenge to God and nature that such science suggests, but technology once introduced into the world never completely disappears. In her 1997 book, author Janine M. Benyus introduces the concept of biomimicry. She writes, "Our planet-mates (plants, animals and microbes) have been patiently perfecting their wares for more than 3.8 billion years ... turning rock and sea into a life-friendly home. What better models could there be?" (p. 8). Her book describes examples of people who are studying nature's achievements, including photosynthesis, natural selection, and self-sustaining ecosystems, among others. Benyus then explains how those researchers use the inspirations found in nature to emulate "life's genius" for the purpose of improving manufacturing processes, creating new medicines, changing the way people grow food, or harnessing energy.

Although all of this may sound strangely futuristic, the seeds of these technologies are here today. Researchers and practitioners are performing experiments that send shivers down the spines of Luddites and futurists alike.

What is the role of education in the 21st century? Can we afford to continue with a system that remains grounded in the linear learning structures and content of bygone eras? Should we still be looking at disciplines as separate, distinct, and unassailable by anyone outside the walled gardens of the academy? The new zoo enabled by biology, a new mother science for a new era of nonlinear learning, should give all those concerned with the direction of learning and teaching pause for thought. Deep thought, and even deeper questions.

From Cathedrals to Bazaars

As educators, we have always placed confidence in the order and scope of the learning process, and striven for certainty of outcomes. We seek a proverbial walled garden of learning in which we can teach and guide and instruct. But our walled gardens are becoming less and less effective at stimulating the messy, nonlinear, highly organic process of learning— at least the kind of learning that seems to be at the core of what it takes to be a successful citizen of the 21st century. The assault on our traditional notions of learning is not some evil force, some cultural decay that has infected the minds and bodies of students of the 21st century. We can raise a cry of angst for the downside view and what it does to our more compact traditional notions of teaching, but we miss a great opportunity if we don't dig deeper into the nature of our own understandings and begin our own shift toward a more practical view of this march of technological progress and the social adaptations it ignites.

As educators, we have a responsibility and a role to play in determining how we respond to the technology trends and social adaptations underway. At the very least, we will have to address not just what we teach our students, but how they (and we) learn. We will have to let the social adaptations of technology inform us on revising best practices to meet the challenges of a less-than-certain outcome of our formal educational institutions and processes.

What we thought we knew about learning and teaching, and the cathedral-like, elegant, top-down, complex systems we designed to support formal processes of learning and teaching, just may not be the relevant model. We may have to reimagine a model that will behave more organically; we may have to develop into a world-class system at a far more rapid pace. The model may not be that which conjures up a cathedral, carefully crafted by wizards and experts working in quiet isolation, but that of a great babbling bazaar that, as if by magic, presents a coherent and stable system that meets the challenges of a transformational time in our understanding of learning and teaching.

6

A CLASSROOM
as Wide as the World

Vivien Stewart

The world in which today's students will graduate is fundamentally different from the world in which we grew up. The quickening pace of globalization over the past 20 years—driven by profound technological changes, the rise of China and India, and the accelerating pace of scientific discovery—has produced a whole new world. Companies manufacture goods around the clock and around the world; ideas and events traverse the Internet in seconds; a financial crisis in the United States affects farmers in Africa; and pollution in China influences the air in Los Angeles.

As never before, education in the United States must prepare students for a world where the opportunities for success require the ability to compete and cooperate on a global scale. But we have not emphasized global knowledge and skills in our schools. Indeed, compared to their peers in other countries, U.S. students are woefully ignorant of other world cultures, international issues, and foreign languages. A 2007 report from the National Academy of Sciences warns, "The pervasive lack of knowledge of foreign cultures and languages threatens the security of the United States as well its ability to compete in the global marketplace and produce an informed citizenry" (Committee to Review the Title VI and Fulbright-Hays International Education Programs, 2007, p. 1).

Moreover, although the United States led the world in high school and college attendance for much of the 20th century, other countries are now catching up and even surpassing us in high school attendance and graduation rates, and in math and science achievement. So we have a gap in both global knowledge and global achievement.

We can no longer afford to be lagging behind other countries in high school graduation rates and in math and science standards, while producing graduates who lack the world knowledge, skills, and perspectives to be successful in this global era. All of our students will be left behind if we don't transform their education with this new global context in mind.

What are the key global trends that we need to pay attention to? What does a well-educated person in the 21st century need to know and be able to do? How can we get all of our students globally ready? This chapter analyzes major global trends that will affect education, describes what innovative schools are doing to produce students who are college-ready and globally competent, and suggests what steps policymakers need to take to make such education available to all our students.

Global Trends

Five global trends are transforming the context for future generations. These trends are related to economics, science and technology, demographics, security and citizenship, and education.

Economic Trends

The globalization of economies and the rise of Asia are central facts of the early 21st century. The economies of China, India, and Japan, which represented 18 percent of the world's gross domestic product (GDP) in 2004, are expected to represent 50 percent of the world's GDP within 30 years (Wilson, 2005). And other parts of the world, such as Russia and Brazil, are also projected to grow in importance, as part of "the rise of the rest" (Zakaria, 2008). Already, one in five U.S. jobs is tied to international trade, a proportion that will continue to increase (U.S. Census Bureau, 2004a). Moreover, the majority of future growth for most U.S. companies, whether small, medium, or large, will be in overseas markets, which means that they will increasingly require a workforce with international competence. According to the Committee for Economic Development (2006), a nonprofit organization of more than 200 business leaders and university presidents,

> to compete successfully in the global marketplace, both U.S.-based multinational corporations as well as small businesses increasingly need employees with knowledge of foreign languages and cultures to market products to customers around the globe and to work effectively with foreign employees and partners. (pp. 1–2)

Trends in Science and Technology

In his famous work *The World Is Flat*, Thomas Friedman (2005) describes how the "wiring of the world" and the digitization of production since 1998 are making it possible for people to do increasing amounts of work anywhere and anytime. As a result, more and more things are going to be made in global supply chains. In addition, scientific research, a key driver of innovation, is increasingly being conducted by international teams as other countries increase their scientific capacity. So the ability to collaborate with people in different time zones, across languages and across cultures, at a professional level, becomes ever more important.

Demographic Trends

If there were just 100 people in the world, only 5 would be American. Although this proportion was not consequential when economies were largely national, since 1990, more than 3 billion people in China, India, and the former Soviet Union have moved from closed economies into the global economy. Another effect of globalization is also readily apparent in our own backyards. New immigrants from regions such as Asia and Central and South America are generating a diversity in U.S. communities that mirrors the diversity of the world, and they are transforming the cultures of local communities, workplaces, and even the local mall. The Hispanic population is 15 percent of the estimated total U.S. population—and will continue to grow. The Asian population is projected to grow 213 percent from 2000 to 2050 compared to a 49 percent increase in the population as a whole over the same period (U.S. Census Bureau, 2004b). Life in the United States increasingly involves interacting and working with individuals from vastly different backgrounds and cultures—a challenge and an opportunity that requires new skills and perspectives.

Trends in Security and Citizenship

The most pressing issues of our time know no boundaries. Challenges facing the United States are both more complex and more global than in the past—from environmental degradation and global warming, to pandemic diseases, to energy and water shortages, to terrorism and weapons proliferation. The effects of poverty, injustice, and lack of education elsewhere spill across borders. What we do affects others, and the actions of others affect us. The only way to solve today's challenges will be through international cooperation among governments and organizations of all kinds. More than ever, our security is intertwined with our understanding of other cultures. And as the line between domestic and international issues increasingly blurs, U.S. citizens will increasingly be called upon to vote and to act on issues—such as alternative energy sources or security measures linked to terrorism—that require greater understanding of the 95 percent of the world's population who live outside our borders.

Trends in Education

In this interconnected world, there is also a growing global talent pool. In the second half of the 20th century, the United States set the world standard of excellence. It was the first country to pursue and achieve mass secondary education and mass higher education. This stock of human capital helped the United States become the dominant economy in the world and take advantage of the globalization and expansion of markets. However, over the past 20 years, other countries have caught up with, and in some cases have passed, the United States. International comparisons from the Organisation for Economic Co-operation and

Development (OECD) show the United States is now 18th in the world in high school graduation rates and 13th in college completion (OECD, 2008). In 2006, U.S. 15-year-olds ranked 25th in math performance and 21st in science (Schleicher & Stewart, 2008). Surveys from the Asia Society and the National Geographic Society have also shown that compared with their peers in other industrialized countries, U.S. high school students lag behind in knowledge of other countries and cultures. And while learning a second language is standard in other industrial countries, only 50 percent of U.S. high school students study a foreign language (Pufahl, Rhodes, & Christian, 2001).

Implications of Global Trends

What are the implications of these global trends for our students? Certainly education as usual won't do. Just as our schools made the transition from teaching skills needed in an agrarian society to those needed in an industrial and scientific society, so too we need to transform our learning systems to equip students with the knowledge and skills they will need to succeed in this new global era.

International knowledge and skills are no longer just a luxury for a few would-be specialists but are a new basic for all students. Preparation for a competitive global job market and for citizenship in the interconnected world of the 21st century is critical for all young people. Our national goal should be that all students must graduate from high school college-ready and globally competent, prepared to *compete, connect, and cooperate* with their peers around the world.

Clearly, many students are at risk of being unprepared for the demands and opportunities of this global age, especially disadvantaged youth for whom U.S. schools have historically fallen short. While agreeing with the need to introduce global content, many educators fear that doing so would divert attention from accountability demands to close the achievement gap in basic skills. Even if that gap is successfully closed, standardized tests of basic skills do not measure the thinking and complex communication skills that spell success in college (Conley, 2005) or the global skills needed for the knowledge-driven global economy. For low-income and minority students, closing the basic-skills gap is only a first step toward real equality of opportunity (Jackson, 2008). Indeed, the Asia Society's International Studies Schools Network, a national network of design-driven secondary schools in low-income and minority areas, has shown that by providing relevant and engaging global content and connections, schools can both improve scores on required standardized tests and give students the global knowledge, skills, and perspectives that will be important in the 21st century.

Global Learning

Over the past few years, schools and districts across the United States have begun to respond to this new reality and are seeking to redesign education to produce students who are both college-ready and globally competent. What is global competence?

We do not yet have an established nomenclature for the dimensions of the newly emerging field of "global competence" or "global literacy," but it is generally agreed to include these elements:

• Knowledge of other world regions, cultures, economies, and global issues

• Skills to communicate in languages other than English, to work in cross-cultural teams, and to assess information from different sources around the world

• Values of respect for other cultures and the disposition to engage responsibly as an actor in the global context

How can schools produce global competence? Consider these examples.

The Walter Payton College Preparatory High School in Chicago, an inner-city magnet school that is one of Chicago's most ethnically diverse schools, has shown how integrating global content enhances academic excellence. Founded in 2000 and now one of the top schools in Illinois, the school's mission is to prepare students for "leadership in their community, the nation and the world." Every student studies a world language for four years and experiences a home-stay exchange with a sister school in China, France, North Africa, Japan, Switzerland, Chile, Italy, or South Africa. Use of technology, including videoconferencing, connects Payton classrooms to their sister schools and to subject matter experts around the world. An array of international visitors, students, and seminars further develops the international spirit of the school. The school is also the flagship of Chicago's Chinese language program, the largest Chinese program in the country.

The John Stanford International School (JSIS) in Seattle is a public elementary immersion school that was started after a survey of the needs of families and the business community. Students spend half the day studying math, science, and literature in either Japanese or Spanish. They spend the other half of the day learning reading, writing, and social studies in English. The school also offers ESL classes for parents. The school is connected to an impoverished school in Mexico, for which the JSIS students raise funds for school supplies. Videoconferencing with students in Japan takes place in an after-school program. The program bridges the time difference because the participants in Seattle can stay late in their after-school program and the Japanese participants can come in early. As a result of the school's success in developing students' fluency in second languages combined with high academic standards in English, Seattle is planning to open several more internationally oriented schools.

These schools, winners of the Goldman Sachs Prizes for Excellence in Education, are clearly outstanding schools. But data collected on hundreds of schools that have applied for the prize—from more than 40 states and from rural and inner-city areas, as well as suburban and private schools—show that many schools are embarking on similar journeys. Our research on these schools and on the Asia Society's own network of internationally themed secondary schools serving low-income and minority communities around the United States shows that schools typically start in a small way, with one or two courses or a single international element such as an exchange, and gradually broaden their approaches. Over time, globally oriented schools develop key common elements (Asia Society, 2008). Typically, they do the following:

- Create a global vision and culture by revising their mission statements and graduate profiles and creating a school culture that supports internationally focused teaching and learning. Although many schools start by creating a single international element or perhaps an international strand, bringing together a school-community group to develop an internationally focused vision and mission statement, such as that of Walter Payton's, can serve as the foundation for creating an inclusive, globally focused school culture. Schools often begin the development of their international culture and focus with external symbols such as maps and flags. But day-to-day practices that go beyond this, such as regular assemblies at which speakers present different perspectives on important world issues, help to develop a school climate that is an intellectually rigorous and emotionally safe place to engage students in serious discussions from multiple vantage points.

A powerful way to gain clarity about an international vision for a school is to develop a profile of the graduate who will emerge from it. A good example of this is the Asia Society's International Studies Schools Network Graduate Profile, which describes the knowledge, skills, and dispositions that define a student's global competency as well as college readiness. Once created, the graduate profile becomes the compass for all school work. Curricular alignment, development of courses of study, and enrichment experiences enable students to meet the learning outcomes that the profile defines. The profile can also provide the yardstick of achievement for student portfolios that demonstrate the dual goals of college readiness and global competence.

- Develop an internationally oriented faculty by recruiting teachers with international interests and encouraging teachers to take advantage of the many professional development and study/travel opportunities offered through universities and international organizations. Although shockingly few teacher preparation institutions as yet prepare teachers to teach about the world (Longview Foundation, 2008), schools can actively recruit teachers who have the dispositions that are essential to effective teaching and have acquired deep international knowledge and interests through study abroad, service in the Peace Corps, or their own linguistic or cultural heritage.

However, recognizing that many teachers have not had exposure to the world outside the United States in their own training, successful schools put in place an array of opportunities for adult learning. Most universities and colleges in the United States have increasing international expertise on their faculties, and developing partnerships with local universities can be a great source of professional development for teachers, enabling them to deepen their own knowledge of world regions and issues. Many travel and study opportunities are available through Fulbright, Rotary, and other programs that can energize and inform teaching through authentic exposure to other cultures. Schools can also create a global learning culture within the school; international book clubs and collaborative curriculum development can encourage thoughtful reflection and extend practice. In a nutshell, successful schools expand opportunities for teachers to increase their own international knowledge and to kindle their excitement about other cultures so that they can foster the same curiosity in their students.

• Integrate international content into all curriculum areas, bringing a global dimension to science and language arts, as well as social studies and languages. Although many people associate international content solely with social studies and world languages, in the 21st century, every discipline can be given a global perspective. Thus, international education is not a separate subject but an analytical framework that can transform curriculum and instruction in every discipline and provide rich content for interdisciplinary work.

Teaching and learning about the world can take place in many ways. Consider these examples:

— Social Studies—Schools can offer world geography, international economics, world history, and world religions, as well as teach U.S. history in a global context.

— English/Language Arts—Classes can be given an international dimension by expanding the traditional canon to include novels and poetry in translation from around the world and by using literary analysis to illuminate both universal themes and differences across cultures. Students can write articles for their peers in other countries, getting real-world practice in cross-cultural communication.

— Science—Schools can use the methods of scientific inquiry to engage with world problems, and students can work collaboratively with students abroad as real scientists do.

— Mathematics—Using the world to understand mathematics and using mathematics to understand the world are key components of global competence.

— Arts—Creativity transcends borders, and the arts are a great way to connect to other cultures. Schools can use international films, cultural performances, and art exhibits, many of which are available free on the Web.

— Career and Technical Education—Courses can offer numerous opportunities to learn about the world as careers and professions of all kinds become global.

Schools use many approaches to "going global." Some use the courses and professional development of the Advanced Placement and International Baccalaureate programs as a framework. Others develop their own approach, building on the universities, businesses, and cultural organizations in their community and the vast international resources available on the Web to create programs that link to state and local standards and circumstances. Whatever approach is taken to improving student learning, this broadened curriculum must be married to the best practices in instruction. These include motivating students through engaging relevant content; combining a focus on deep content knowledge with reasoning skills and analysis of multiple perspectives; using purposeful interdisciplinary inquiry and simulations to answer large questions; using primary sources from around the world; and emphasizing interaction with people in other parts of the world as part and parcel of the learning process.

• Emphasize the learning of world languages, including less commonly taught languages such as Chinese and Arabic. In a globally oriented school, the study of world languages and cultures has to have a prominent place. In fact, opinion polls suggest that the public increasingly understands the importance of languages. A 2007 Phi Delta Kappa/ Gallup poll showed that 85 percent of respondents believe that learning world languages is important, and 70 percent believe it should begin in elementary school (Rose & Gallup, 2007). But language instruction in most schools has simply been too little, too late.

Instead, successful schools are creating new models of effective language learning. Building on the large research base on effective language learning, they start earlier; focus on proficiency rather than seat time; and engage students by giving them meaningful, motivating tasks that allow them to use world language as a tool for communicating with others. Many schools are developing content-based learning, delivering lessons in another subject in a second language, as in the example of the John Stanford International School. And from podcasts to Skype to movies to online language courses, technology is allowing students to immerse themselves in language as never before. Although most world language offerings in schools have remained essentially unchanged for 50 years, a College Board survey reports a more than 200 percent increase from 2005 to 2008 in the number of schools teaching Chinese—a sure sign that parents, students, and schools think language can open doors (Asia Society & College Board, 2008).

Global Connections

Thanks to technology and to the Internet, all children now are children of the globe, not just children of the neighborhood where they live. Today's tech-savvy kids already have the tools for global learning at their fingertips. Gone is the day when education was synonymous with a building housing a teacher and a blackboard. Today, the opportunities for learning beyond the school walls and beyond the school day abound, enabling students to connect the local to the global and back again. Globally oriented schools can do the following:

• Harness technology to tap global information sources, create international collaborations, and offer international courses and languages online, especially to underserved communities. Information and communication technology is our greatest asset in internationalizing education. It allows students to access information from every corner of the world, to overcome geographic barriers, to communicate and collaborate with their peers in other countries, to publish findings, and to share words, images, and videos with a worldwide audience—even to talk to one another in real time.

Lack of timely educational resources about other parts of the world was once a major constraint on teaching about the world. Today's students can tap into free, relevant information and networks from around the world; but at the same time they need to learn critical-thinking skills to assess the wealth of global information that can be found online. Online courses can allow students access to languages or other internationally focused courses that are not available in their local school district. And Internet-based, classroom-to-classroom projects, which allow students to learn *with*, not just *about*, their peers in other countries, are a forerunner of what one day will become truly global classrooms. These learning opportunities made possible through technology are powerful for all students but are especially valuable in rural areas, where global connections or local diversity may be limited.

• Expand learning time to give students more time and support to achieve global skills. Although we live in an interconnected world, many of America's disadvantaged young people are disconnected. Studies show that many young people from low-income communities never travel more than a few miles outside their neighborhood. We now realize that some young people need more learning time and support to reach the goals of schooling and that we need to look at the school day and school year very differently.

According to the Afterschool Alliance (www.afterschoolalliance.org), informal learning programs, such as after-school, before-school, and summer programs that take place in a wide range of settings—including schools, community-based and faith-based organizations, cultural institutions, and museums—now serve more than 6.5 million children. The after-school environment offers many ways to promote global skills. Its traditions of project-based learning can engage young people in learning about world issues; field trips can turn local communities into living museums of local-global connections; and involving families can expose young people to the diverse cultures in their communities and around the world through exploring identity, heritage, and universal cultural pursuits. For older students, programs can provide a voice and an opportunity to develop leadership skills by allowing them to take action on issues of local or global relevance or learn about international options for college or future careers.

Most important, after-school and summer programs can help to extend global literacy opportunities to young people who might be unable to access them otherwise. They can expand horizons—from the neighborhood to the world (Asia Society, 2009a).

• Expand student experiences through internationally oriented travel, service learning, internships, and partnerships and exchanges with schools in other countries. Whether the experience consists of a week of living in a home and attending school classes, or a summer, semester-, or year-long foreign exchange program, living abroad can be life altering, bringing new perspectives, increased intercultural awareness, tolerance, and confidence in dealing with other people (AFS Intercultural Programs, 2008). School partnerships or exchanges, in which a school develops a long-term relationship with a school or schools in another part of the world, are increasing in number and bring added benefits as they enable both U.S. and international students and teachers to participate in regular exchanges, real or virtual, and deepen understanding on both sides.

Many schools value the academic and social benefits of service learning. When it is integrated into courses in a globally oriented school, service learning can also help students see the connections between their local actions and global issues. Finally, internships in local companies or nonprofit organizations can both allow students to apply academic skills to the workplace context and give students insight into growing global interconnectedness.

Going Global: Preparing Our Students for an Interconnected World, a report of the Asia Society (2008), provides further concepts and examples for each of these elements, drawn from more than 70 schools in places as different as Vermont, West Virginia, North Carolina, Texas, Florida, Kansas, Wisconsin, and Oklahoma. The ways in which individual schools harness community resources to link the local to the global demonstrate that teaching and learning about the world is within reach of every type of school. Other approaches and best practices are being collected and shared through the Partnership for Global Learning, a national network of educators dedicated to ensuring that our students are prepared for work and citizenship in an interconnected world (see www.asiasociety.org).

Going to Scale: The Role of States

Across the United States, hundreds of innovative efforts are under way in schools and local districts to add global content and connections. But as encouraging as these efforts are, they are islands of excellence. How can we get all of our students globally ready? For this we will need state and national action to take these approaches to scale.

States are critical to creating internationally oriented school systems. State governments increasingly understand the need for an internationally competitive workforce, recognizing that they are no longer competing with the state next door but with countries around the world. More than 25 states have participated in the States Network on International Education in the Schools, in partnership with the Asia Society and the Longview Foundation. They are beginning to put in place a series of steps to raise awareness about the importance of global knowledge and skills; build leadership among education, business, and political leaders; and create policies and programs that will introduce these new skills. A report by the Council of Chief State School Officers (2008), *Putting the World into World-Class Education*, reviews these developments and proposes a set of recommendations to give *all* students access to a world-class, globally oriented education. The report recommends that each state take stock of its existing efforts and create a framework for systemic change beginning in the elementary grades and extending through high school. The framework should include the following elements:

• Redefining high school graduation requirements to include global knowledge and skills. Every state should include global competence in its overall recasting and modernizing of high school graduation requirements. Requirements should include world languages and assessment of international knowledge and skills across the curriculum. As they redesign middle and high schools to ensure that all students graduate with the skills needed for success in the 21st century, states should consider creating internationally themed schools to act as models and professional development centers.

• International benchmarking of state standards. Across the globe, countries are increasing their high school and college graduation rates, increasing their achievement in math and science, and expanding students' global knowledge and skills. States need to learn about education practices in other high-performing and rapidly improving countries and use the best of what has been observed to help us continue to grow and improve. States should review their curriculum standards and statewide assessments to ensure that they include global knowledge as well as the analytical, higher-order thinking, and cross-cultural communication skills that students will need to face the challenges of a changing world.

• Making world languages a core part of the curriculum from grades 3 through 12. States need to create a long-term plan to expand their capacity in world languages and build on effective approaches to language learning, including starting early and creating longer sequences of study; using more immersion-like experiences; focusing on proficiency rather than seat time; and harnessing technology (such as online language courses). High-quality alternative certification routes should be created to speed up the production of language teachers from heritage communities and enable the development of programs in less commonly taught languages, such as Chinese and Arabic.

• Increasing the capacity of educators to teach the world. Teachers who are being prepared for the learning environments of tomorrow need greater knowledge of the world. States need to work through their teacher certification mechanisms and, with their institutions of higher education (which are themselves becoming more global), to internationalize teacher preparation programs (Longview Foundation, 2008). States should reexamine professional development for teachers in light of the new global context and encourage international experiences for both prospective and practicing educators.

• Using technology to expand global opportunities. The 21st century is both global and digital, and technology is perhaps our biggest asset in internationalizing education. State technology offices should encourage the use of information sources from around the world, help teachers engage in classroom-to-classroom collaborations to connect students with international peers, expand opportunities for students to take internationally oriented courses and world languages online, and promote student-created international projects on the Web.

The National Challenge

The speed of change around the world creates urgency for action at every level. Graduating the next generation of students prepared for the challenges of a diverse, globally interconnected world is a national imperative, not just a state or local one. For 50 years, the federal government has played an important role in fostering foreign language and area studies expertise at the postsecondary level; however, in the 21st century, knowledge of the world is no longer a luxury for a small group of experts but a requirement for any educated person. As the Obama administration and Congress consider the reauthorization of federal funding for elementary and secondary education, a new federal-state-local partnership could make access to an internationally competitive, world-class education and graduating globally competent citizens a national priority. Five areas of investment should help to create 21st century learning environments (Asia Society, 2009b):

• Providing states with incentives to benchmark their educational systems and standards against other countries so that school leaders can understand the changing global skill set and share best practices from around the world.

• Supporting initiatives to redesign middle and high schools to raise high school graduation rates and transform secondary schools for the 21st century in order to create college-ready and globally competent graduates.

• Investing in our education leaders' and teachers' knowledge of the international dimensions of their subjects to modernize our education workforce.

• Building national capacity in world languages from kindergarten through college by offering incentives to begin learning languages in elementary school, promote online language learning, and recruit and train language teachers from our diverse linguistic communities.

• Expanding federal programs that support the engagement of U.S. students with the rest of the world in order to better prepare our students and strengthen America's image abroad.

Concluding Thoughts

What would a truly modern 21st century learning system look like? What would I hope for my grandchildren? I would like to see a day when our students' education is not bound by the four walls of a school but can be as wide as the world:

• When learning languages and cultures begins in the elementary years and can continue anywhere, anytime, through online learning.

• When all our secondary students have access to courses on global issues, whether in science, economics, or the arts.

• When every school in the United States has ongoing partnerships with schools in other parts of the world, enabling students to learn through real or virtual exchanges with their international peers.

• When prospective teachers have the opportunity to study abroad—to kindle their own excitement about other cultures so that they can foster the same curiosity in their students.

• When school leaders, like business leaders, share best practices from around the world, continuously benchmarking their own schools against international standards.

In short, every school would open every student's eyes to the complexity, opportunity, and challenges of a globalized world and equip students with the competence to succeed and to lead in this new era.

Given political will and some focused resources, I believe that educators can rise to these challenges. Doing so not only will make us more successful and innovative in the global economy, but also will lay an important foundation for peace and a shared global future.

7

MAKING LEARNING IRRESISTIBLE:

Extending the Journey of Mabry Middle School

Tim Tyson

The day began like any other: dealing with an unexpected crisis. The school district had just announced a slash in the budget for custodial supplies. How were we going to keep the building clean? I was meeting in my office with the bookkeeper, the head custodian, and teacher leaders to figure out how we could trim budgets. During this meeting, I thought I recognized the voice of an 8th grade student speaking to the secretary out in the main office.

"Mrs. Rosengren, I would like to schedule a meeting with Dr. Tyson. How do I do that?" When an 8th grader wants to schedule a meeting with his principal, I am consumed with curiosity. I yelled out from my office, "Mrs. Rosengren, is that Will I hear? I can meet with him right now."

As Will, in many ways a typical 8th grade boy, walked through my office door, he appeared to bump into an invisible force field when he saw my office was filled with people. "Good morning, son. Come on in. What can I do for you?"

Regaining his composure, Will walked into the office and said with practiced confidence, "Dr. Tyson, all of the students at Mabry are learning how to make podcasts and movies. But, as you know, I can already do this. You probably don't know that I am making a lot of them at home, too. But I don't know how to put them on the Internet so everyone can see them. Dr. Tyson, I want to be the first student at Mabry Middle School to learn how to put my podcasts online so everyone in the world can see them. Will you teach me how to do that?"

I was ecstatic. Many of the key teachers in the building, sitting in my office, got to hear Will's request firsthand. This would be the talk of the teacher lunch table! I nodded thoughtfully and paused as if to reflect on what I already knew would be my positive response. This had to be a dramatic moment worthy of the significance of the request: a student asking his principal to teach him something he thought was relevant, because it wasn't offered in our last-century curriculum.

At Mabry, we were striving to attain an irresistible shared vision. Like Will, we all wanted to be at the top of our game. We wanted to use a new set of tools, the tools of the 21st century, tools that we really were not very familiar with, to move beyond "good." I suspect that when people are already doing a good job, as Mabry certainly was, they have greatness prewired into their DNA.

Welcome to Class

Mabry Middle School, in Marietta, Georgia, has a rich tradition of excellence in academics and in the performing arts. In fact, the band program at the high school to which Mabry students matriculate is considered one of the best in the nation. Walking into a Mabry band or orchestra class, as teachers prepare students for a lifelong love of music, is indeed an exciting experience.

One immediately notices the energy level. Students' class involvement often goes beyond mere participation. Each student is striving to reach a new standard of personal best. They are continuously displaying their work in front of their peers. And a student's work may be singled out at any moment for detailed scrutiny—not to embarrass, but to model best practices or to improve personal practice, thereby helping the other student performers improve. Everyone is a participant in a true community of learners. The teachers are continuously evaluating student work while that work is actually in progress.

At all times, every student contribution in the classroom rehearsal is being measured against the highest standard of all: perfection as a work of art. Teacher talk is frequently laden with metaphors designed to connect the student performers with the higher levels of emotive human experience captured in this abstract artistic expression of meaning through music. Or as one teacher said to his students, "French horns, your job beginning at measure 114 is to make the clarinet part weep!" The ultimate goal of every rehearsal, of each hour spent in personal practice, is to craft a performance that represents the best contribution of the group, a performance that welcomes a public audience to an emotional encounter with beauty.

Absent from Class

That which is absent from class time is equally enlightening. The teachers seldom spend class time defining what a quarter note is. Repetitive practice is rarely outside the context of applying skills to scaffold for improved performance. Worksheets are so seldom used as to be nonexistent. Students are expected to develop their individual musical skills outside class through teacher-structured practice. (On occasion, group practice time, the sectional, is held during class so the teachers can actively teach students how to better practice independently.)

Individual student progress is often assessed outside the classroom in before- or after-school "pass-offs" in which students compete for higher ranking in the class. If given the option, grading would probably seldom exist for reporting purposes, as these teachers continuously monitor and assess skill development to design immediate improvement strategies for each student. Ad hoc groups of student performers often form spontaneously before and after school to enjoy and refine their developing skills. Amazingly, students are not required to take these performing arts courses; yet, at Mabry, the overwhelming majority of elementary students look forward to the day when they can finally go to middle school and sign up for all of this extra work.

But such performance-based instructional practice is not limited to the performing arts. Coaches do a very similar thing: they build teams through a culture of personal contribution, and the team is the product of relentless hard work in skill building for a singular goal—the emotional charge of publicly demonstrating personal-best performance in concert with teammates.

A Typical Classroom

What we see in a typical classroom in a typical American school is sometimes very different from this performance-based focus on holistic learning. Too often, the focus in an academic class is on the individual facts that will most likely be tested on the end-of-year, high-stakes tests. Isolated facts are easy to test, are easy to cover, are easy to drill and practice. Student contributions may well be marginalized, perhaps limited to being on time and prepared for class, paying attention, following a teacher's directions, taking good notes, and filling out worksheets, quizzes, and tests with correct answers—getting good grades in academics and in citizenship. And certainly, with the very real need for efficient, wise use of limited school resources, these rules, routines, rituals, and right answers have a place.

However, music is not about the notes. Language arts is not about the letters and the words. Math is not about the numbers and the symbols. And school is not about grades. The whole is substantially more relevant, more meaningful, and more significant than the sum of the individual parts. Make no mistake, the parts are important. They are just not the goal.

Yet when asking Mabry students in casual conversation what they are supposed to do in school, most of them reply, "Make good grades." And make good grades they do. A significant percentage of Mabry students earns recognition for making the Principal's Honor Roll (straight As) or the Honor Roll (*As* and *Bs*). But when these same students are asked, "Is that the very best you can do?" the answer is inevitably a hesitant "Well, no … not really."

Hard Questions

How do educators move students from this low-level mind-set of just making good grades—or, worse yet, from not even valuing their academic "graded" experiences at all—to personally experiencing the excitement that is the very essence of learning? How do we bring the culture of personal best into the academic experiences of those same children? How do we move from an emphasis on remembering facts for a test on Friday to thinking critically about the larger issues that those disconnected facts can only dimly reflect as stand-alone pieces of information? The educators at Mabry Middle School all participated in a professional journey to explore these questions and many more.

Adequate thinking time is essential to the change process. For more than a year and a half, the administrative team and the subject area coordinators (department heads) at Mabry set aside several hours every week to have honest, open, and always thought-provoking explorations of our school practice. This group did a detailed analysis of student achievement data in each subject area. These school leaders studied horizontal and vertical curriculum alignment. The group had in-depth discussions on books and research about the role of school, the nature of leadership, instructional best practices, research-based literacy strategies, curriculum mapping, grading and assessment, and learning communities, to name only a few topics. The group discussed what was working effectively at our school and what was not.

Frankly, these meetings had a rigorous nature about them as everyone sincerely wanted to improve the professional practice of an already high-performing school—a difficult task at best. One of the subject area coordinators described these meetings as "getting a master's degree on just this school." The subject area coordinators then shared the most important outcomes from these meetings with the teachers in their curriculum area.

Spending this time together had some significant outcomes. Perhaps one of the most important was fashioning a vision, a school mission, built on a common vocabulary about school and achievement. The school moved from a long and somewhat lofty mission statement that could not be easily evaluated to one that would serve as the yardstick against which every action at the school would be measured: "Maximize student achievement in a culture of caring." Does this worksheet, this classroom instructional activity, this administrative action accomplish the school's mission, or is there a better way?

One of the most significant standards that emerged for measuring classroom practice was this: To what extent were students authentically engaged in their own learning? Only two books were given to every teacher on the staff, and Phil Schlechty's *Working on the Work* (2002) was one of the two. Many students at Mabry Middle School are adorable, well-behaved children who are raised by their parents to do what the adults at school tell them to do. Within the framework of *Working on the Work*, these sweet little children were merely passively compliant. The staff wanted to change that.

From Passive Compliance to Global Contribution

The teachers at Mabry were too often the owners of learning, the ones doing most, if not all, of the thinking work in their classrooms. They were the ones who were working really hard every period. The students were typically doing only what was required of them: making grades that were considered "good enough."

At some point since these children had entered kindergarten, learning had become a very passive process. Knowledge, schooling, was being done *for* them, was being given *to* them. They simply had to sit and receive it. Their only responsibility was to remember enough to get the required grade on the test—a grade that was the product of some invisible dance of expectations and excuses between the student, the parents, and the teachers.

Tragically, school had become all about grades. Critical thinking, problem solving, and creative production had given way to memorizing often loosely connected facts that might be tested and therefore "had to be learned." This view of school seemed to have become even more deeply entrenched as the accountability agenda placed increased emphasis on every child's knowing a minimal level of curricular content.

The vision that the staff at Mabry had spent many precious hours crafting seemed to be the exact opposite: maximized achievement for every single child, not minimal performance based on a set of minimum standards for all children. We wanted our students to go above and beyond expectation, to strive for their personal best.

If students were to become more authentically engaged in the art of learning, the classroom would have to be more participatory, as students had to get up out of their mental seats and produce something at least as important as a grade—a product that demonstrated not just content knowledge, but understanding that ultimately makes a contribution. The teachers came to believe that students would take greater ownership of their learning if they were expected to produce a finished product that would be completely public, not just a graded paper that the teacher and the student (and sometimes mom and dad) would see. Peer pressure, after all, is a powerful motivator in middle grades.

As students would take more ownership of their learning, their interest in learning would create an inevitable desire to learn more. (Conversely, those students who have learning "done to them" seem to be the ones who report being bored in school.) Ultimately, the students would want to create something they thought was important, was meaningful, something in which they would take pride and want everyone, including their peers and even mom and dad, to see. The ultimate outcome would be to make learning irresistible—which was to become Mabry's tagline on the school's Web site, MabryOnline.org. People the world over, regardless of age, seem to have an innate desire to make a contribution that is seen as valuable.

Academic Night

Near the end of a year of emphasis on project-based learning, of students creating products they had worked very hard on and took pride in, Mabry held its first Academic Night—the academic concert, as it were.

Enormous displays of hundreds of student projects, with their student creators standing nearby, were placed in the covered play area (a carpeted gym) for the crowd of hundreds to ask questions about and admire. The students were excited to show off their hard work, to explain what they had learned, as parents beamed.

The band and orchestra took turns performing in one corner. The German, French, Spanish, and Latin classes performed dances and served multicultural foods in another area. A computer showed larger-than-life examples of students' digital work on a large screen. Tables laden with exemplary student projects were everywhere. This was a sensory-based display experience: varied items of visual interest, smells and tastes of unusual foods, the sounds of live student musical performances. The attendees could walk up and touch the projects, could sense the excitement of the student presenters. The event was, by all accounts, a huge success.

Interestingly, this event had some unanticipated consequences. Parents, seeing other children's work, were able to place the quality of their own child's work in perspective. Often expectations for their own student's work went up—better helping the school to achieve the school's mission of maximized student achievement. Parents also could see in one place, at one time, an overwhelming amount of exemplary student work created as a direct result of the academic experiences students enjoyed on a daily basis at Mabry. They saw firsthand that the work going on in this public school was impressive.

This event was a positive experience for children, providing them with a powerful emotional connection to the curriculum. As the pride in their work grew, students naturally wanted to share their work with more people. Parents wanted grandparents and other relatives to celebrate their child's achievement. They wanted to brag about the incredible school their child attended. Without doubt, authentic engagement begets an excitement in learning, but the whole story has still not been told. Showcasing this effort was limited to a specific geographical place at a specified time. This limitation became a frustration.

Improving Best Practice with Technology

Every coach is searching for ways to tweak the best plays, and the teachers at Mabry, all focused on becoming even better academic coaches, are no exception. How could we leverage the students' interest in sharing their work? How could we get exemplary student work to a larger audience? How could we increase students' positive emotional connection to curriculum? How could we improve the quality of the students' finished products? How could we entice them to think more deeply, to take even greater ownership of their school work, and to work at even higher levels on Bloom's taxonomy? And, while we're at it, why don't we just have them make the whole world a better place, too?

After some excited discussions with the subject area coordinators about authentically engaging students in a learning process that focused on producing high-quality, digital-knowledge products that everyone—the students, their peers, their parents, the community at large—found of great value, the Mabry PTSA purchased 10 Apple iBooks, and the school purchased one digital video camera. Mabry students, with the help of their teachers, were going to push the boundaries of the classroom and learning in the school setting and attempt to augment the very language of education. We were going to build on the Academic Night in an unprecedented way. We were going to have a film festival, and all of the movies were going to be produced by the students themselves! Could we even do such a thing?

The Film Festival Training

Clearly we needed to begin by learning what would be involved; and so, from that year to this, students, teachers, and parents all sit together for a day-long training in how to make an award-winning movie. The theme for the festival is announced during the training session. All of the criteria by which the quality of each movie will be evaluated are carefully reviewed. All movies must relate to the broad theme for the festival and focus on the curriculum the students studied in one of their courses that year. Two- to three-second movie segments (yes, seconds, as the study was *that* granular) are shown from previous years' winners. Those participating in the training critically analyze these short examples to determine what made them so powerful and how they would make them even more compelling.

Very little of the training time is spent learning how to use a computer program, because the greatest challenge each of these teams faces every year is determining what single point their two-minute movie project is going to make. The overwhelming percentage of time spent on this five-month, schoolwide project does not involve technology (the digital video camera or the movie-making software) at all. Learning the technology was never the purpose of the project. The time is consumed delving deeper into curriculum, doing more research, pitching movie ideas to the team, coming to consensus on the project's thesis (the point of the movie), outlining how best to convey that point in a way that arrests attention and is emotionally compelling, making connections with experts in the field in which their project focuses, writing, editing, revising (over and over again) a script that delivers this curriculum-based storyboard in a way that is engaging to the audience, and determining exactly what digital assets will be needed to accomplish this shared vision. In other words, this is a concert. This is a football game. This is a very public execution of collaborative design and personal best to achieve a shared goal. This is art. This is learning.

Deep Exploration

Teachers increasingly began to realize their critically important role of requiring that projects remain focused on the learning objectives and not on the technology, on guiding the unraveling and exploration of complex issues that were much larger than just the facts themselves. They were able to take students much deeper into content as they guided their search for the single point of the movie project—the thesis statement. The students seemed to be more willing, sometimes even eager, to do more research, to edit, and to revise yet again in their effort, as one 7th grader put it, "to get it just right. It has to be perfect." The fact that the teacher serves as the gatekeeper to actually touching the coveted digital video camera and computer also seemed to motivate high-quality production design.

Only the last few weeks of the project are actually spent filming, importing the footage, and assembling the project on the computer. At this point, the movie-making teams often face a new challenge. As with most creative projects, the movie begins to take on a life all its own. Indeed, the richness of the experience lies in the way the parts combine to create something more important, more compelling, and more powerful than anyone had anticipated. How, then, is each team going to deal with the shots that did not work, or the shots that were so compelling as to illuminate a completely different story line, heretofore invisible, that wants to lead the project in a very new direction? Now, problem solving must come into play. Collaborative effort takes on new meaning. Deep analysis, synthesis, and critical thinking must be the guiding forces of the project.

And although nothing about this learning experience is simple, everything about it is irresistible. In fact, because students always feel compelled to "fix just one more thing," a new mantra has to be emphasized: Your project is never really finished; everyone just agrees to stop working on it until after the film festival. In contrast, students frequently can't wait to get a typical school assignment over with. But the movie projects seem to be very different. These projects are often difficult for the students to "release for global distribution."

Every year, when students submit their "completed" projects, they say they spend an average of 50 hours outside the school day working on their project—a project for which no grade is ever assigned. Why? Isn't school about grades? Don't the red numbers at the top of the graded test paper motivate students to do their work?

Every year student teams ask parents to review their project as it unfolds. Why? Don't most middle school children want to disengage adults from their school work? And every year students take ownership of their projects. As one girl who has significant learning disabilities said to me, "Dr. Tyson, at first this was just an idea in my head. Nobody can see what's in my head. But now everyone can see it. And you know what?

It's really, really good!" She and her team had worked incredibly hard and had accomplished something significant, had created a project that was deeply moving, and she knew it! She was proud of what she had done. And though it was the product of team effort, in her mind, this was hers. She owned it.

This Is Literacy?

Our society appears to be moving away from passive consumption, away from models in which the few broadcast to the many. People want a greater sense of participation and involvement, of community, of network. People innately want to interact. How are schools supporting this desire to contribute, to produce, to create and share? Using digital tools, students can now produce media-rich digital objects that teach them media literacy as well as effective communication strategy.

These are the words of a 6th grade student: Movie making is "so much better than making a poster board for a project at school. A poster board is flat, boring, and doesn't move you. It can't touch you the way our movie can." The fact remains that making a poster board for a school project is much easier than making a movie, but this child sees the value of the extra effort and hard work needed to produce a movie. A mere poster board would hold her and her audience back, would get in the way of her using the language of her generation to make meaning.

A 6th grade boy commented, "When you write a report, people can't see it, can't understand it as well." Another student said that making a documentary "really is social studies." And a 7th grader said, "Making a movie? That's like learning on steroids." The act of creation through this medium is authentic, is real, and is meaningful to these students.

Education in the Technology Ecosystem

If, indeed, our media-rich culture is shaping the way students think and express themselves, how are we as educators to use these new, expressive, creative forms to empower learning? For the first time in history, our students have the capacity to produce high-quality products that rival those of professional production companies. However, more often than not, the instinct of a child is to use these powerful tools in very simple, childlike ways. We found that the students at Mabry frequently wanted to explore the fun and amusing technical possibilities that the movie-making process affords.

The role of the teachers is not really to teach students what buttons to push to make the software and hardware do this or that. Perhaps the most important role of the educator is to keep students focused on the point of the movie, to keep them centered in meaningful curriculum content and message, to guide and facilitate the creation process. Just like the coach and the performing arts teachers, the academic teachers are helping children take the pieces, the facts, the building blocks of understanding and create something more impressive than the individual pieces, assembling them in meaningful and compelling ways that are worthy of attention. Helping students evaluate the progress of their work toward their shared goals in real time is of much greater value than assigning any grade to the work.

Some teachers began reaching out into the community to establish working relationships with medical professionals, research scientists, community organizations, Holocaust survivors, and others who, when they saw the quality of work these middle school students and their teachers were producing, were willing to share their expertise, their personal story, were eager to contribute to the movie projects and to participate in other special school projects. The learning community was growing—and the growth was born of respect. Students saw the authenticity and value of their work in the eyes of adult leaders who were eager to be part of their learning, their projects, not because they were fun or cute, but because those projects had substance and quality.

As the school principal, I could now issue an unprecedented challenge: "Students, if you do exemplary work, the very best of the best, I will consider placing your work into global distribution." This is a challenge that every educator should offer students. Never before has such a possibility existed for schools. Indeed, every person on the planet with Internet access has the capacity to see the work of Mabry students. Students can have a global voice, can connect in meaningful ways on a planetary scale.

Online Content Distribution

The Mabry Web site at the time, a collection of nearly 100 blogs, served as a means of communicating with our school community, of connecting parents and others with what was going on in the classroom. We began placing the work of our students, teachers, and administrators on the site to make it a rich repository showing who we are, what we value, and what we do every day to make learning irresistible for children. Little did we know that people around the world would soon be looking at it. The site quickly began serving up more than 1.5 million files a month, and e-mails began to pour in. I will never forget the first e-mail I received from outside the United States. It came from Tasmania.

People everywhere were watching the academic work of the Mabry community of learners. We began to have visitors come to the school from around the nation and around the world. They would meet with the Mabry teachers and students to learn how they were doing the exemplary work they did.

As the school principal, I wanted to find ways to leverage this newfound capacity to help us take the school's mission, maximizing student achievement, to new levels heretofore impossible. This, then, became the Mabry challenge that made learning too irresistible to ignore—looking the children in the eyes and saying to them, "Students, what do you have to say that is so important, so vital, that everyone in the world needs to hear it? What do you, as a 6th, 7th, or 8th grader, have to say that will cause others on our planet to do something that matters, something that will make our world a better place, because they saw your schoolwork, the movie that you made at Mabry this year?"

These were not meaningless words, for the students who heard them knew of their friends who had sat down with educators from the United Kingdom, from Perth, Australia, from the Republic of Georgia in the former Soviet Union to talk about their schoolwork, how they did it so well, and why the project was important to them. They knew their friends had sat down with the state superintendent of schools, with members of the Chamber of Commerce, had sat in front of a crowd of thousands at the National Educational Computing Conference in 2007 to talk about their schoolwork—work that really mattered to them, work in which they took genuine personal pride.

World Debut

Each year, once the student movie projects are turned in, each is placed in at least one category—Best Picture, Best Cinematography, Best Teaching and Learning, Best Documentary, and so on—and presented to a panel of judges who are completely unrelated to the school: members of the Georgia Film Commission, professionals in the broadcast industry, university professors, technology integration specialists from other schools in the metropolitan area, educators from the state department of education, and business professionals. The astounding quality of the student work requires that difficult decisions be made and the results placed in sealed envelopes. The programming director for Georgia Public Broadcasting said of one movie one year, "This is better than anything I've put on television."

The topics of the movies produced year after year represent complex, demanding, even highly controversial issues worthy of a global audience. Indeed, students want and need to learn how to grapple with difficult, real-world issues that matter to everyone. They want to make a contribution. They actually want to make our world a better place! What better way than through a synthesis of curriculum focused on larger issues and presented on the big screen for everyone to see and then shared with the world through the Web and through iTunes.

Beyond Create, Connect, and Contribute

Mabry's first efforts to find real ways to infuse authentic student engagement into classroom learning experiences through technology proved to be transformative. The schoolwide use of frequent blogging and the sharing of hundreds of student-, teacher-, and administration-created digital media objects through the blogs and through iTunes welcomed parents into a more participatory role in their children's education at Mabry. This new level of transparency showed everyone the impressive work of the students and teachers. Unexpectedly, teachers from around the nation and the world, including from China, began inquiring about working at Mabry.

But the technology served the instructional setting well only when it was invisible to the learning experience and was used in new ways, which required infrastructure and continuous training. If digital technology is used in low-level ways—to do the same things we have always been doing in schools, just doing them now with computers—then we have failed to grasp the metamorphosis this technological ecosystem offers. In so doing, we perpetuate an emphasis on student passivity, on students' "receiving" school as if learning were given to them by teachers and as if computers served only for such low-level tasks as grading, reporting, and word processing.

Extending the Vision

Mabry's explorations in engaging students to produce meaningful contributions were just first, tentative steps in moving school practice in a completely new direction. Imagine extending these first awkward steps, infusing them more deeply into instructional practice. What would that look like in your class, in your school, with your students?

If access to information is indeed at the foundation of teaching and learning, what about pervasive access? Would schools proffer a better learning experience if they empowered students themselves, under the professional and informed coaching of their teachers, to actively create high-quality, media-rich, digital curricular contributions that are aggregated and shared with learners of all ages, the world over? These learning materials would not only represent students' personal academic achievement at high levels but also could be used to teach other students—and adults. The aggregated media could be made available for any time/ any place learning via the Internet and through highly portable media devices, such as the pervasive iPod, at little expense to schools.

We now have the capacity to change what we do and, just as important, what we do not do in the instructional period—class time. When instructional content is delivered through digital media, it no longer must be taught in the physical classroom space at a specified time of the day. Schools can leverage digital content delivery systems to add enhanced value to the interactions between teachers and students in class. Teachers then have more class time to do those things that we all value that too often get pushed aside because class time is limited. We can begin to affect the very structure of school.

Today, teachers can, at no cost, actually broadcast their classroom instruction live while also recording it for later viewing. In other words, you can broadcast and record the audio and video of your teaching of a math lesson on the distributive property, including everything you write on your interactive whiteboard, in class this year, so next year's students can watch that lesson on their home computers for homework, thus allowing you to use class time in new ways that enhance learning. Students who are absent can watch the class in real time. Students who did not completely understand the content can review it at home that night. Parents can better assist their struggling student. Students can now have shared learning experiences around this content delivered to their computers in their homes, even on their iPods. Now, just as in life itself, learning can happen any time, in any place. Academic learning can be pervasive.

In this vision, students are taking greater ownership of their own learning. They come to class with the fact-based content already presented to them through the digital-media product assigned as homework. Now class time can be spent reinforcing that learning, building on that content, focusing on the larger issues, on contextual significance, on application and problem solving, digitally engaging students in intellectual collaborations with professionals in the field through desktop video conferencing, wikis, and blogs. Class time can be used in differentiated instructional activities based on students' prior learning and interests in exploring curriculum at deeper levels, and on engaging students in creating media objects to teach more clearly those areas of content in which students may have struggled. Indeed, class time can now be a richer personal encounter between the student and the teacher because of technological affordances.

Imagine aggregating exemplary student and teacher products on a school-, system-, or statewide level that would be shared with everyone the world over. A small yet growing number of state departments of education are beginning to take initial steps to implement this vision. Instructional practice that focuses on the generative, creative potential of our students and teachers, that empowers them to produce high-quality knowledge products that are shared globally for worldwide review, would have profound, long-term, positive implications for our world and would leverage a cognitive capacity that has heretofore been largely underestimated, even ignored. Now we have the affordable tools to accomplish such a vision.

8

MEDIA LITERACY:
21st Century Literacy Skills

Frank W. Baker

In 1960, communications scholar and theorist Marshall McLuhan wrote the following: "Without an understanding of media grammars, we cannot hope to achieve a contemporary awareness of the world in which we live" (Carpenter & McLuhan, 1960, p. xii). His point remains relevant today, even though the context has changed to a remarkable extent.

Educators in the 21st century are slowly starting to appreciate that we no longer live solely in a print-centric world; we are surrounded by a culture filled with visual images and messages, many of which work on a subconscious level. In the 21st century, "texts" and "literacy" are not limited to words on the page: they also apply to still and moving images, such as photographs, television, and film. Today, being literate also means understanding wikis, blogs, nings, digital media, and other new and emerging technologies. Unfortunately, many K–12 educators have yet to realize the benefits of teaching students with and about non-print media, what is today recognized as an important part of "media literacy."

Proficient teachers know how to meet teaching standards, including those that today make more references than ever to media and media literacy. The problem is that many teachers are not proficient in teaching media literacy. Few educators have been trained in the effective use of media in instruction. Fewer still know how to embrace youth media and culture to engage students in learning. A recent national survey by Cable in the Classroom found that 60 percent of the educators polled believe their schools are not giving media literacy the attention it deserves (Grunwald Associates, 2006). The 5th Annual Speak Up survey of teachers and students revealed what many in K–12 education already knew: students come to school media savvy, but their teachers are ill prepared to put new media tools and technology to use, thus creating what the survey called a growing "digital disconnect" (PRWeb, 2008).

In the 21st century, these "digital natives"—a term attributed to education consultant Marc Prensky—already know how to do the following:

- Upload, download, and remix music, photos, videos, and movies
- Text and instant message using mobile phones and other handheld devices
- Connect and communicate via social networking Web sites
- Operate digital still and video cameras
- Edit and post online videos
- Create blogs, podcasts, video games, digital productions, and graphic novels
- Participate in virtual reality games and forums

And where are students learning how to use these new media and technology tools? Certainly not in schools.

Young people are also exposed to television programs and commercial messages in an increasingly hypermedia world. Television and advertising are now available to them via their mobile phones and computers. Researchers worry about the effect of their exposure levels and the implications of their multitasking behaviors. Media educator Renee Hobbs observes, "Our students are growing up in a world saturated with media messages.... Yet [they] receive little to no training in the skills of analyzing or evaluating these messages, many of which make use of language, moving images, music, sound effects, special visual effects and other techniques" (Hobbs, 1998).

Many educators agree that what we teach young people, and the way we teach them, must change. We can no longer afford to ignore the Internet, television, music, or the movies. These media are the domain of today's students, just as their mobile phones have become the convergent media tools of tomorrow. Filmmaker George Lucas equates media literacy, particularly as it relates to films, with more traditional forms of literacy:

> When people talk to me about the digital divide, I think of it not being so much about who has access to what technology as who knows how to create and express themselves in this new language of the screen. If students aren't taught the language of sound and images, shouldn't they be considered as illiterate as if they left college without being able to read and write? (Daly, 2004)

In a report to schools about this new media world, the MacArthur Foundation echoes the need for educators to do more than just teach the basics: "The ability to negotiate and evaluate information online, to recognize manipulation and propaganda, and to assimilate ethical values is becoming as basic to education as reading and writing." (Fanton, 2007).

Schools in the United States, for the most part, have failed to recognize not only young people's fascination with new media and technology, but also how teachers could use these new media tools to connect with their students and teach a myriad of subjects. Many schools have not yet accepted blogs, iPods, or digital cameras as teaching tools, because they don't understand their application or worthiness. Most textbooks make no references to "media literacy," and training teachers in this area is certainly not on most schools' radar screens. School libraries, for the most part, have also failed to respond: scanning the shelves of these 21st century media centers, I find little in the way of resources for students or teachers about popular media, media issues, or media literacy.

The No Child Left Behind legislation is also seen as a detriment to teaching media literacy, as teachers admit to concentrating their lessons on only those subjects being tested. But education consultant Jim Burke (2003), writing in *The English Teacher's Companion*, sees incorporating media in the classroom as vital for teaching's future: "Movies, advertisements, and all other visual media are tools teachers need to use and media we must master if we are to maintain our credibility in the coming years" (p. 341). The National Council of Teachers of English (NCTE) agrees. Commenting on the organization's resolution on visual literacy adopted in 1997, Michael Day, then chair of NCTE's Assembly for Computers in English, urged educators not to ignore

> the rhetorical power of visual displays. Visual forms of media, by themselves, and in combination with text and sound, come at our students from all directions, including television and the World Wide Web. The critical media literacy we need to teach must include evaluation of these media, lest our students fail to see, understand, and learn to harness the persuasive power of visual media. (NCTE, 1997)

NCTE is not alone. Sue Swaim (2002), past executive director of the National Middle School Association, says media literacy should not be relegated to just the English classroom: "Media literacy is an important topic to be integrated throughout the curriculum so that every student has an opportunity to become actively engaged in learning about it multiple times and in multiple ways throughout each school year."

As educators, we have the opportunity and the responsibility to use media literacy as one of our key strategies for helping students develop critical thinking skills. A large number of organizations and institutions have already recognized, recommended, or endorsed media literacy education. Among them are the American Association of School Librarians, the American Academy of Pediatrics, the International Reading Association, the National Board for Professional Teaching Standards, and the National Middle School Association.

The Partnership for 21st Century Skills (www.21stcenturyskills.org) recognized the startling gap between what young people need to learn and what schools need to teach in order to prepare them for careers in a competitive global economy. The partnership, which started as a collaboration among technology companies, quickly attracted the attention of many education-related organizations, including NCTE. Among the skills the partnership urges schools to teach are collaboration and teamwork, making global connections, critical thinking, and media literacy.

Media and Media Literacy: A Brief History

After *The Wizard of Oz* was first broadcast on nationwide television in 1956, libraries reported a tremendous demand for the L. Frank Baum books. Television, it seemed, could be a catalyst for student literacy and learning. For years, the media were portrayed as the enemy of learning. The introduction of television in the classroom in the 1960s was widely criticized; today, television is a staple of learning. The rise of the Public Broadcasting Service (PBS) and the creation of the cable industry's Cable in the Classroom initiative are just two examples of how instructional and educational media continue to prosper. With the advent of streaming technologies, K–12 teachers now have more access to resources and can better use snippets, rather than whole programs, in instruction.

In 1970, NCTE recognized the growing influence of both television and film. It issued a position statement to study their effects and urged its members to consider teaching with these "non-print texts." At the same time, the National Telemedia Council, based in Madison, Wisconsin, continued to publish *Telemedium* (now called *The Journal of Media Literacy*), a regular periodical designed to report on the new but expanding media literacy movement.

In 1978, U.S. Senator William Proxmire of Wisconsin helped throw cold water on the growing movement to teach "critical television viewing skills" when he awarded one of his "Golden Fleece Awards" (given to projects that wasted taxpayer funds) to the development of several national curricula designed to help students better understand the power and influence of television. Despite this setback, the Center for Media Literacy developed media literacy curriculum kits in the 1970s and 1980s for schools and community groups. The kits addressed diverse topics such as "Living in the Image Culture," "Images of Conflict," and "Break the Lies That Bind: Sexism in the Media," to name a few.

In the 1990s, the Partnership for Media Education morphed into the Alliance for a Media Literate America, a national membership organization designed to raise awareness of media literacy education in U.S. schools. The alliance sponsors and organizes a biannual national media education conference. In 2008, the group became known as the National Association for Media Literacy Education.

In 1993, the New Mexico Media Literacy Project was the first statewide initiative to take media literacy education to schools and to provide regular teacher training. (The project has created a popular series of media literacy DVDs for classroom use.) In 1999, Robert Kubey, a media professor at Rutgers University, and I reported that almost every state had developed teaching standards that included "elements of media literacy"; those elements could be found predominantly in the standards for English/language arts, social studies, and health (Kubey & Baker, 1999). Shortly after the Columbine school shootings, and partially in response to school violence, Discovery Communications, based in Bethesda, Maryland, created Assignment Media Literacy, a comprehensive K–12 media literacy curriculum. Teachers in every school in the state were trained to incorporate standards-based media literacy lesson plans into the classroom. For more information, see www.marylandpublic schools.org/MSDE/programs/medialit. With growing concerns about commercialism, obesity, violence and sex in the media, bias, representation, body image, and other stereotypes, classroom educators are not lacking in topics and issues involving media literacy.

Critical Thinking:
An Important Element in Media Literacy

Media educator David Considine (2002) highlights an important rationale for including media literacy in the curriculum:

> While more young people have access to the Internet and other media than any generation in history, they do not necessarily possess the ethics, the intellectual skills, or the predisposition to critically analyze and

evaluate their relationship with these technologies or the information they encounter. Good hand/eye co-ordination and the ability to multi-task are not substitutes for critical thinking. (p. 5)

In my travels around the United States as a professional development teacher trainer, I hear the same refrain from teachers: "My students believe *everything* they see, read, and hear." These same teachers admit that they haven't had sufficient training in how to incorporate critical thinking about the media in their classrooms. So it's no wonder students are persuaded and influenced by the media. In my visits to schools, I instantly see evidence of student loyalty to brands through the prominent labels on their clothes. They don't have a clue that they are walking billboards. These corporations depend on media-illiterate young people to advertise their clothes to their peers. Despite the best efforts to limit advertising in schools, it is the students who are the worst offenders.

For media literacy to flourish, schools must offer professional development opportunities, and teachers must be willing to invest more time in teaching critical-thinking skills—and these skills can be taught. The Center for Media Literacy's Elizabeth Thoman says, "At the heart of media literacy is the principle of inquiry" (Thoman, n.d.).

Following the lead of media educators in Australia, Great Britain, and Canada, the Center for Media Literacy (www.medialit.org) helped create a U.S. version of five core concepts of media literacy: (1) all media messages are constructed, (2) media messages are constructed using a creative language with its own rules, (3) different people experience the same media message differently, (4) media have embedded values and points of view, and (5) most media messages are organized to gain profit and/or power.

Using these core concepts, Thoman and other media educators have created a list of corresponding critical-thinking questions designed for students to consider and apply to each media message they encounter. Among the questions are these:

- Who created or paid for the message? (authorship, producer)
- Why was it created? (purpose)

- Who is the message designed to reach? (target audience)

- How does the message get my attention; in what ways is the message credible? (techniques, methods)

- How might different people from me understand this message differently? (audiences negotiating meaning)

- What values, lifestyles, points of view are included or excluded and why? Where can I get more information, different perspectives, or verify the information? (research, critical thinking)

- What can I do with this information? (decision making)

A media-literate person, according to Thoman, has

> the ability to create personal meaning from verbal and visual symbols
> we take in every day through television, radio, computers, newspapers
> and magazines, and, of course, advertising. It's the ability to choose
> and select, the ability to challenge and question, the ability to be con-
> scious about what's going on around us—and not be passive and vul-
> nerable. (Thoman, quoted in Schwarz, 2001, p. 112)

Media Literacy: What Does It Mean?

Today, the phrase "media literacy" has been co-opted by different groups to mean different things. Due to fears about Internet predators and cyberbullying, schools are currently interested in what they call "media literacy" as a way to teach young people the rules regarding proper behavior on the Internet. The phrase has also been used by those who really mean "information literacy," that is, searching for and locating accurate, reliable information on the Internet. The Google generation believes that the popular search engine is both the official library and their answer to conducting research. Media specialists in school libraries have been fighting this battle for years and will continue to do so.

The problem with the phrase "media literacy" is that it does mean different things to different people. So what *does* it mean? Media literacy encompasses both analysis of media messages as well as creation of media productions. Students need to know how to read media messages and to understand the process of making media.

In 1989, a group of Canadian media educators formulated this definition, one of my personal favorites:

> Media literacy is concerned with helping students develop an informed and critical understanding of the nature of mass media, the techniques used by them, and the impact of these techniques. More specifically, it is education that aims to increase the students' understanding and enjoyment of how the media work, how they produce meaning, how they are organized, and how they construct reality. Media literacy also aims to provide students with the ability to create media products. (Ontario Ministry of Education, 1989, pp. 6–7)

In 2000, the Alliance for a Media Literate America proposed its own definition:

> Media literacy empowers people to be both critical thinkers and creative producers of an increasingly wide range of messages using image, language, and sound. It is the skillful application of literacy skills to media and technology messages. As communication technologies transform society, they impact our understanding of ourselves, our communities, and our diverse cultures, making media literacy an essential life-skill for the 21st century. (National Association for Media Literacy Education at namle.net/media-literacy/definitions)

In 2007, the Partnership for 21st Century Skills offered its own version, stating that media literacy involves the following:

Analyze Media
- Understand both how and why media messages are constructed, and for what purposes
- Examine how individuals interpret messages differently, how values and points of view are included or excluded, and how media can influence beliefs and behaviors
- Apply a fundamental understanding of the ethical/legal issues surrounding the access and use of media

Create Media Products
- Understand and utilize the most appropriate media creation tools, characteristics and conventions
- Understand and effectively utilize the most appropriate expressions and interpretations in diverse, multi-cultural environments (www.21stcenturyskills.org/index.php?option+com_content&task+view&id+349&Itemid=120)

Media Literacy in the Classroom

Most K–12 textbooks used in the United States lack any references to the elements that make up media literacy. That situation is slowly beginning to change. (Holt, Rinehart, and Winston's *Elements of Language* was one of the first widely adopted textbooks to incorporate elements of media literacy. More recently, McDougal Littell created a series of DVDs entitled *Media Smart: Strategies for Analyzing Media.*) Teachers looking at most state-adopted textbooks are not likely to find up-to-date information on how to incorporate the media, media issues, or media literacy into instruction.

Some state teaching standards refer to elements of media literacy. Here are examples of typical references for various subject areas:

- English/Language Arts
  - Recognize bias
  - Recognize parody
  - Recognize persuasive and propaganda techniques

- Social Studies
  - Analyze campaign and political marketing and advertising
  - Examine the role of mass media in American history
  - Identify the types of media that comprise mass communication

- Health
  - Analyze health ads
  - Evaluate health information

— Evaluate how media affect body image

— Evaluate alcohol, tobacco, and other drug media message and marketing techniques

In 1998, I created the Media Literacy Clearinghouse Web site (www.frankwbaker.com) in part as a response to the lack of information about media literacy in textbooks. The site is a compendium of lesson plans, readings, activities, and other resources designed to help teachers (and their students) better understand media literacy and its place in the curriculum.

What does the research say about media literacy? Some of the earliest approaches to teaching media literacy in the United States used an approach called "inoculation." As the word suggests, it was thought that effective media education would protect students from the potentially "bad" effects of media exposure. But over time, this approach was abandoned. It is not consistent with the stated goals of media literacy education: to create critical thinkers and viewers who have the skills, knowledge, and abilities necessary to understand, analyze, and create media messages, as well as to comprehend their purpose and audiences. Later studies sought to address student learning outcomes.

In 2005, two educators writing in *Access Learning* magazine reported that "a growing body of research suggests that media literacy instruction improves student reading, viewing, and listening comprehension of print, audio, and video texts; message analysis and interpretation; and writing skills" (Johnson-Towles & Shessler, 2005, p. 10). A three-year research project (2003–2006) involving two middle schools in the San Francisco area showed that students' critical and creative thinking skills measurably increased following their participation in a media literacy curriculum. Educational researcher Michael Cohen reported that "the results of the evaluation clearly indicate that those students exposed to the Media Education, Arts and Literacy (MEAL) curriculum showed significant increases in their acquisition of knowledge in core curriculum areas—and even shifts in attitudes toward learning" (Just Think Foundation, 2007).

In 2003, the Kaiser Family Foundation published *Media Literacy: Key Facts* to inform policymakers and others about the state of media literacy education. The report's conclusions are paraphrased here.

Media Violence, Aggression, and Antisocial Behavior. Several studies have shown that incorporating lessons on media literacy into the curriculum can help reduce potentially harmful effects, such as verbal and physical aggression, on young viewers of TV violence and can lead to children watching less TV. Other studies have shown that media literacy efforts can help at-risk youth become more responsible in their decision making, think critically about the consequences of risky behaviors, and resist impulses to engage in such behaviors.

Body Image, Nutrition, and Fitness. An evaluation of a media education program created by the National Eating Disorders Association found that media literacy skills can help enhance high school girls' self-acceptance, and other studies suggest that even brief peer-guided workshops can counteract messages that perpetuate unrealistic body images and promote unhealthy eating. A study of a team-centered media literacy intervention for high school male athletes found that the program helped develop skepticism about steroids and supplements while increasing knowledge about strength training. After one year, the athletes reported less intention to use steroids and a reduction in their use of illicit drugs. Other long-term effects included less use of supplements, improved nutrition, and fewer reports of drinking and driving.

Alcohol, Tobacco, and Drugs. An evaluation found that media literacy education increased children's understanding of the persuasive intent of ads for alcoholic beverages and influenced their decision making about drinking alcohol. Participants were less likely to believe that drinking had positive consequences, to choose alcohol-related products, and to want to be like characters who drank. A comprehensive high school curriculum on media literacy, developed and taught by teen leaders with the guidance of adult coaches, influenced tobacco use at different stages of the decision-making process, leading teens who had never tried tobacco to develop skills to resist it and teens who had tried tobacco to feel less susceptible to peer pressure to smoke. Various studies suggest that media literacy programs can help children and adolescents understand the persuasive intent of tobacco advertising messages.

Benefits of Education in Media Literacy

One of the primary benefits of education in media literacy is that it helps educators meet state teaching standards. Increasingly, those standards refer to understanding, analyzing, and producing media. After a workshop with high school students on the techniques used by television commercial producers, I overheard a student leaving the classroom proclaim, "I will *never* look at television the same way again." This is exactly the response all educators should hope for: students who not only are critical viewers, but also are skeptical and willing to reexamine media messages. Students whose teachers include media literacy in the curriculum are presented with familiar media texts but are challenged to look at them through a new, different lens.

Another major benefit of media literacy is that it allows teachers to bring familiar youth-media culture into the classroom. Teachers who are comfortable with and trained in media literacy will find students who are more engaged. Additionally, students who are media literate are better able to resist messages deemed biased, harmful, or inappropriate.

Other benefits noted by researcher David Considine (quoted in Schwarz, 2001) include the following:

- Media literacy is interdisciplinary and easy to integrate into key elements of the existing/emerging curriculum.
- Media literacy is inquiry based and consistent with reflective teaching and critical thinking.
- Media literacy includes hands-on experiential learning and is consistent with learning styles research.
- Media literacy works well in teams and groups, fostering cooperative learning.
- Media literacy has been successful in appealing to at-risk students and in improving retention rates.
- Media literacy is compatible with SCANS (Secretary's Commission on Achieving Necessary Skills) and fosters employment opportunities.
- Media literacy connects the curriculum of the classroom to the curriculum of the living room.

Classroom Applications

What might media literacy look like in various subject area classrooms? Here are ideas for teaching media literacy in English/language arts, social studies, health, and math and science.

English/Language Arts

Ideally, students should be both analyzing and creating texts in all forms—print and nonprint. Teachers should be familiar not only with new media, but also with the popular culture of the students they teach: social network sites, blogs, music videos, and more. Television content (news, game shows, sitcoms, talk shows, sports, reality shows) offer teachers a wide array of possibilities for study.

Writing is a logical starting place for an exploration of media's role. All media messages start out as writing—whether it is news, editorials, motion pictures, commercials, blogs, music, or a TV situation comedy. Each medium and genre has its own codes and conventions, and it is critical for students to both understand and use them. Students should learn scriptwriting and the visual representation process of storyboarding, both essential elements in the media production process.

Because young people consume so many media products, they are already familiar with many programs, genres, plots, and characters. One of the most popular genres with young people is parody. From *The Simpsons* to *MAD* magazine to *Shrek*, media are ripe with examples. The Read-Write-Think Web site, developed by NCTE and the International Reading Association (www.readwritethink.org/), offers teachers a number of parody-related lesson plans and activities.

Advertising is another rich area for students to both study and produce. Advertising exists in so many forms and in so many places that it is convenient for classroom teachers to use magazine or newspaper ads, TV commercials, or product placement in films as topics for student research and exploration. (The holiday toy season and the annual Super Bowl football game are good times of year to explore this topic.)

The language of film is another rich source of media literacy in the English/language arts classroom. Students love film, and studying how films are created is another way for teachers to teach media literacy. If your students have watched either the Academy Awards or the Emmy Awards, they are already familiar with the award categories. Each award honors those people who are the experts in lighting, camera work, editing, sound, acting, and set design, to name just a few categories. The language of film involves understanding how each of these is used to create meaning. Today, a number of excellent film-study curricula are available to help students (and teachers) better understand the power and influence of film. For example, students might watch a documentary to study the way the filmmaker uses bias, camera angles, and music to convey a particular message.

Those same students might decide to collaborate to shoot their own short film about a topic of interest. Today's young people are becoming civically engaged by using new media and technology to express their points of view. Numerous Web sites allow students to upload their school-created productions and share their work with their peers.

To further encourage media literacy in the English/language arts classroom, NCTE published *Lesson Plans for Creating Media-Rich Classrooms* (Christel & Sullivan, 2007), a book with contributions from secondary English teachers. Topics addressed include photography, video games, graphic novels, and popular music.

Social Studies

Many states' social studies teaching standards include having students consider the role and rise of mass media in U.S. history. The invention and use of photography is a prominent example of an appropriate focus for this topic. Using photographic images in a history classroom is a great way to teach visual literacy skills. (Most arts educators and students already know how to read a painting, and many of the same analytical skills can be applied to photographs.) Because of the rich resources on the Library of Congress Web site (www.loc.gov/index.html) and other sites, students can easily locate and research the background and history of photography in U.S. and world history. Topics to consider include the Civil War, Dorothea Lange's Depression-era photos, and images from contemporary world conflicts, among many others. The more recent topic of digital manipulation of images should also be introduced so that students understand and recognize when images have been altered.

Political campaigns and political advertising are other rich sources of media literacy lessons for social studies teachers. Thirty-second campaign commercials alone can be a focus of study in techniques of persuasion as well as production. A campaign's use of new media and technology (such as MySpace, Facebook, YouTube, and blogs) is also a topic that students can relate to.

In 2007, documentary producer Ken Burns presented *The War,* a multipart series for PBS about World War II. The series encouraged classroom teachers to have their students identify veterans and document their stories. The series' Web site (www.pbs.org/thewar) offers teachers and students guidelines on how to conduct interviews, position the video camera and microphone, and incorporate photographs, video clips, and other mementos from that era for use in student productions. Creating these original video war stories is a perfect example of hands-on, engaging media literacy work. Students not only learn the production aspects of conducting the interview, but also how to research and retell the story using images and sounds. Students begin to take ownership of their productions in new and powerful ways. Today the result is called "digital storytelling."

News magazines, editorial cartoons, newspapers, and online news sources also offer social studies educators a wealth of teaching material. With the advent of the Internet, teachers and students no longer need to have the print edition of a source in hand—many of these sources are available freely online. For example, comparing the U.S. news coverage of President Obama's Middle East trip with news coverage from Egypt and Israel would serve as powerful examples of point of view, bias, and perspective.

Health Education

Most of us rely on the media for all of our information, including health information. The health education classroom offers another opportunity to both use the media and teach media literacy as it relates to nutrition, body image, alcohol, tobacco, drugs, sex, and other topics. It has already been documented that young people are influenced by what they see on television. Those who watch large amounts of television are exposed to many junk food ads. As a result of that exposure, many health-related problems have been recognized, including diabetes, high blood pressure, attention deficit disorder, and more. The junk food and health problem relationship was confirmed in December 2008, when the National Institutes of Health and Common Sense Media, reported on their analysis of 173 previous studies. The study's authors concluded that screen time exposure impacts both the physical and mental health of young people (www.commonsensemedia.org/sites/default/files/ CSM_media+health_v2c%20110708.pdf).

As noted in the earlier mention of the Kaiser Family Foundation report, media literacy curricula have been included in many health education curricula as an effective strategy to shape student attitudes and behaviors, including those related to smoking and alcohol. One curriculum, *Media Sharp: Analyzing Tobacco and Alcohol Messages*, was created and distributed by the Centers for Disease Control and Prevention (CDC). The CDC later produced a curriculum entitled *Scene Smoking* that addressed the increasing use of tobacco in film. Other CDC resources can be found at this Web site: www.cdc.gov/tobacco/youth/ educational_materials/videos_dvds/index.htm. Georgetown University's Center on Alcohol Marketing and Youth studies alcohol advertising and provides educators and policymakers with a wealth of information and resources, including those available on its Web site: www.camy.org.

Pick up any women's magazine and you will find a cover photo of a 100-pound model whose appearance has been digitally manipulated to perfection. Researchers have called attention to the powerful influence these and other images have on women. Body image is a growing topic of discussion in many health education classrooms. One of the leading researchers in the field, Jean Kilbourne, has advocated for media literacy education: "It's important that parents and citizens really lobby for media literacy to be taught in schools, starting with kindergarten. We're doing our students a real disservice if we don't teach them to become critical consumers of the media" (*Christian Science Monitor*, 1999).

Like it or not, young people learn a lot about sex from the media. What they understand is often skewed by Hollywood and other media producers. Advertisers have known for years that "sex sells." Some well-known advertisers such as Calvin Klein, Dolce & Gabanna, and Abercrombie & Fitch have made news with their often provocative ad campaigns aimed at teens. Teachers should consider how sexual content messages in magazines, music lyrics, television shows, and popular movies can be used as ways to address this topic.

Mathematics and Science[1]

Pick up a math or science textbook and you won't find the phrase "media literacy" in the index. But it should be. Consider all of the ways the media use numbers—in everything from the monthly Consumer Price Index to the weekend box office reports and TV program ratings.

Numbers abound in news. Math teachers should be encouraged to consider incorporating these news reports in their instruction. Teachers can engage their students by helping them understand how these numbers are generated and how they are used.

I created the Math in the Media Web site (www.frankwbaker.com/math_in_the_media.htm) to help math educators incorporate "numbers in the news" into their classrooms. One of the major lesson plans and activities centers around ratings for TV programs. The ratings and shares of audience numbers, reported weekly, are simply percentages. Students could research how TV and radio stations and their advertisers use these numbers. They could also research the differing costs of ad time from one television market to another.

Science is another popular topic both on television and in the movies. In the 1998 movie *Contact*, actress Jody Foster portrayed a scientist responsible for deciphering the first extraterrestrial message sent to Earth. The movie was generally applauded by scientists for its authenticity. But it is rare for Hollywood to accurately portray a female scientist.

---

[1]Much of this section is adapted from the author's previous essay: "Media Literacy: Yes, It Fits in Math and Science Classrooms," *Becoming Literate in Mathematics and Science*, ENC FOCUS, Vol. 8, No. 3 (Summer 2001).

Stereotypes and misconceptions are frequently generated by television and movie producers.

Classroom teachers can take advantage of students' interest in popular movies to help them analyze the misconceptions. For example, the motion pictures *Deep Impact* and *Armageddon* both posed the question: What would happen if the planet Earth was in danger of being hit by an asteroid or a large comet? Even though scientists tell us the chances of such a collision are small, these movies offer teachers an opportunity to explore how science is portrayed. Every teacher who uses a video, a CD-ROM, or the Internet as part of instruction should ask questions such as this: How does the selection of images by the producer shape our understanding of science concepts?

Even the wealth of science programming by well-known documentary producers such as the Discovery Channel should not be exempt from some inquiry by teachers and students. The same questions that apply to commercial movies should also be asked of documentaries: Who is the producer? What are the producer's motives? What techniques does the filmmaker use to convey the desired message?

Final Thoughts and Recommendations

For media literacy to become widespread, several things need to happen:

• Teachers should demand media literacy education as a vital component of teaching and learning.

• Media literacy should not be a separate class but should be incorporated into all subject areas.

• Schools and districts should offer professional development training to meet media literacy requirements related to state standards.

• Courses in media and technology must incorporate analysis along with production and creation.

• School library media specialists should consider media and media literacy resources both for student and professional collections.

• Colleges of education must include media literacy training in their teacher preparation courses.

- More textbook publishers must embrace and include media literacy in their publications.

- Schools should consider programs for parents on media literacy awareness.

9

DIGITAL PORTFOLIOS AND CURRICULUM MAPS:

Linking Teacher and Student Work

David Niguidula

What makes a successful year of teaching? When the final bell rings on the last day of school, what should the students know and be able to do? How will those students be different from how they were on the first day of school?

Teachers know that the answers to these questions can be complex. Sure, there are lists of standards that neatly outline what 6th graders should know about math or what biology students should gain from their course. But the process of teaching is about far more than checking standards off a list or "getting through" the curriculum. It's about getting to know students as individuals and as groups; it's about recognizing that Olivia's interest in science fiction lights up her interest in writing or that Mario's skill at assembling (and disassembling) indicates that he prefers hands-on experiments.

Ultimately, the measure of a successful year stems from looking at the student work. It's one thing for a teacher to cover everything that a student should know and be able to do; it's quite another to see whether students can *demonstrate* their skills and knowledge. It's wonderful when a teacher reaches out to a student and makes a connection; it's even better when that connection translates into improved understanding and performance.

Digital portfolios represent a powerful way to collect student work. When done well, a digital portfolio outlines a student's learning journey in much the same way that a curriculum map describes a teacher's teaching journey. The collection of work in a portfolio can do two things: it can show that a student has met standards and show who the student is as an individual learner.

In this chapter, we explore the links between curriculum maps and digital portfolios—and how these explorations of teacher work and student work can provide feedback to each other.

What Is a Digital Portfolio?

A digital portfolio is a multimedia collection of student work that provides evidence of a student's skills and knowledge. In the early 1990s, when the Coalition of Essential Schools (CES) conducted the first study of digital portfolios (Niguidula, 1993, 1997), technology in schools was just emerging; the concept of putting video into a computer was a novelty, and the Internet was largely the domain of universities. The first digital portfolios ran on individual computers; now, they can live on the Web and provide a link between home and school.

The results of the initial CES study yielded a set of essential questions that schools need to address for portfolios to be more than glorified file cabinets. As we reported (Niguidula, 2005), these essential questions include the following:

- Vision: What should a student know and be able to do?
- Purpose: Why do we collect student work?
- Audience: What audiences are important to us?
- Assessment: How can students demonstrate the school vision? How do we know what's good?

- Technology: What hardware, software, and networking will we need? Who will support the system?

  - Logistics: When will information be digitized? Who will do it?

  - Culture: Is the school used to discussing student work?

The first three questions—vision, purpose, and audience—are critical to a school's success. A portfolio should not contain *everything* that a student does in school, and determining the purpose and audience for the portfolio will help students and teachers focus on what they want to collect and select.

A typical portfolio for a high school student might begin with a table of contents organized around a set of expectations—the school's vision of what a graduate should know and be able to do. The expectations can be organized by subject areas (representing state standards in English, math, and so on) or categorized under interdisciplinary headings, with headings such as communication, problem solving, and research.

Different portfolio tools allow readers to see the student work in different ways. In the Richer Picture portfolio tool, the contents page lists the student's specific entries that illustrated each of these expectations. For example, the expectation "creates a persuasive argument based on evidence" could link to several student entries, including an essay on *Romeo and Juliet*, a biology lab report, and a presentation on the effects of Reconstruction.

The contents page provides links to the student entries. Students can upload multiple artifacts—word-processed documents, images, presentations, audioclips or videoclips—that contain their actual work. For example, students in one class were given the assignment of taking pictures of geometric concepts (parallel lines, concentric circles) within their hometown. These pictures are the artifacts—the samples of student work—that are uploaded to the portfolio.

When students add entries to the portfolio, it's important that their work be placed in some context. It's helpful, for example, to see the original assignment as offered by the teacher, and to see the links between this work and the list of school expectations. Some kind of reflection or self-evaluation—preferably including an action plan describing how the student can improve on the next performance—helps the readers to see that the student understands what the work represents. In the case of the geometry scavenger hunt, the students connected their work to specific expectations, such as "The student can communicate mathematically," and "The student uses 21st century tools to create information within the context of the core subjects."

Elementary digital portfolios can capture work in similar ways. For example, in one 4th grade class, students kept a paper folder of open-ended math problems. At key points during the year, the teacher asked each student to select a problem from the folder for inclusion in the digital portfolio. Students scanned their work and put it into the portfolio to demonstrate their skills. After selecting their samples, students also had to explain the problem-solving process to the teacher, and the explanation was videotaped. The video clips were also included in the students' portfolios.

The teacher's focus here was on problem-solving skills. It did not matter, for this example, whether the problem dealt with fractions or with multiplication; much more important was the fact that the student could go through the problem-solving process. By capturing this work, the teacher was better able to understand a student's thinking process and what areas of mathematical problem solving—from reading the problem to working through a strategy—might be causing the student difficulty. Students selected and reflected on their work several times during the year. Through this process, the teacher could see the progress of the student's problem-solving ability, even as the topics in the math curriculum changed.

How Are Digital Portfolios Used?

On a bright afternoon in May, Neale, a junior at Mt. Hope High School in the Bristol-Warren (Rhode Island) school district, arrived for his digital portfolio review. Neale went to the library; joining him was a group of three faculty members, including one of his own teachers, the assistant superintendent, and a teacher from another school in the district.

For the next 20 minutes, something happened that is all too uncommon in most U.S. high schools: They had a conversation. At first, the adults listened closely as Neale displayed his best work from the year—and they continued to listen as he reflected on his overall growth as a learner. After that, the faculty asked questions and talked to Neale about his goals (he wants be a dentist) and his passion (playing music). Based on the work Neale showed and his own reflection, the adults gently pushed Neale to make specific plans for his senior year that were connected to his long-term goals.

At Mt. Hope, portfolios meet multiple needs. The first purpose that the portfolios serve is to fulfill Rhode Island's innovative Graduation by Proficiency policy. To receive a diploma from a Rhode Island high school, students must demonstrate proficiency in a variety of subject areas (English, math, science, social studies, technology, and the arts), and that demonstration must come from a variety of assessments. Most districts in the state have implemented portfolios as one of these demonstrations.

Although the policy pushes schools to begin creating portfolios, the mark of success comes when the schools take the process seriously. The end-of-year reviews serve as a public demonstration of the school's work. Both teachers and students are demonstrating what they have accomplished in the past year, and by presenting the work to an audience, students want to put their best work on display. This student desire is very much in line with what researchers (such as Darling-Hammond, Ancess, & Falk, 1995; Stiggins, 2005; Wiggins, 1998) have long been saying about authentic or performance assessment; in a nutshell, when a student has a stake in the process of assessment, and when teachers and others provide useful and meaningful feedback, student performance improves. Using the portfolio process in place at Mt. Hope, Neale was much more likely to show high-quality work to his assessment committee than if he was simply asked to turn in a paper folder to a teacher at the end of the term.

More subtly, the process of presenting work also encourages teachers to improve their assignments. Most work in the portfolio comes from assignments that teachers give in class. When the portfolios are reviewed, the quality of the student work is at least partially dependent on the quality of the assignment and the usefulness of the teacher's feedback. Teachers in these situations identify "portfolio-worthy" assignments: tasks that provide evidence linked to expectations and that provide opportunities for students to demonstrate their skills.

Increasingly, schools are allowing students to include work from outside school, and this is a welcome development. Schools need to acknowledge that a student's best piece of writing may not have come from class, but from an impassioned essay written for a blog, or that a best demonstration of leadership may be from engagement with a church group.

In the original CES research (Niguidula, 1993), our team observed that the most important feature in a successful portfolio system is the feedback from the teachers. Students need to know that the work they put into compiling a portfolio will get more than a "Nice job!" or a check-plus. Teachers need to know that they aren't just helping students work on projects that will never be seen again.

Portfolios can be used to create an ongoing dialogue between students and teachers. With a digital portfolio, teachers can use online rubrics to assess student work. For example, the elementary school described in the last section uses a common rubric when students are demonstrating problem solving. The rubric focuses on key areas, such as "identifying the problem" and "creating a strategy," which can be used no matter what type of problem the student is solving. Figure 9.1 shows part of the rubric completed for one student's response. (The Exemplars Problem Solving Rubric [Exemplars, 2008] was adapted from the NCTM Standards rubric and used with the Exemplars performance assessment materials.)

Because the portfolio is digital, the data in the rubric can be used to improve the process of teaching. The district uses software that allows the teacher to look at a single table showing all students' performances on a particular task. In this way, the teacher can identify areas of strengths or weakness for the class as a whole, or note which specific students might benefit from a minilesson on one component of the problem-solving process.

Figure 9.1 | Problem-Solving Rubric

	5—Expert	4—Practitioner	3—Advanced Apprentice	2—Apprentice	1—Novice	Comments
Problem Solving	Correct answer. Finds more than one way to solve. Efficient strategy is chosen.	Correct answer. Correct strategy.	Correct strategy is chosen, but minor computational errors may lead to an incorrect answer.	A partially correct strategy is chosen and incorrect answer is given, or strategy would lead to solving only part of the problem.	No strategy is chosen, or strategy can only lead to an incorrect answer.	
Reasoning and Proof	Goes beyond what problem asks. Shows correct reasoning, verifies solution, and justifies formulas or rules (extends, generalizes, hypothesizes, predicts).	Shows correct reasoning through a systematic approach.	Shows correct thinking but not enough reasoning to support answer.	Little evidence of reasoning or the reasoning is flawed.	No correct reasoning is evident.	
Communication	Clear explanation of solution, with precise mathematical language and notation.	Clear explanation using all mathematical language and notations accurately.	Uses some mathematical language and/or notations appropriately.	Attempts to use mathematical language but not always appropriate.	Incorrect or no use of mathematical language.	

Teachers have long given responses to students in a variety of ways—from red marks on an essay to individual conferences. By recording at least some of these responses in an online portfolio, teachers can more closely track student progress over time and, as we shall see, look for improvements in their own teaching.

The Feedback Loop

In this brief discussion, we've seen how digital portfolios can document a student's work. Similarly, curriculum maps are an organizing tool that document a teacher's work. Put together, mapping and portfolios can provide a feedback loop for continuous improvement.

The use of a feedback loop for improving organizations was popularized by MIT professor Peter Senge in his book *The Fifth Discipline* (1990). A true "learning organization" is able to adjust to new situations by reacting to data as it occurs. A classroom, by all rights, *should* be a learning organization—but all too often, a teacher's daily work is dictated by external forces ("We have to get to Chapter 23 by next Friday!") rather than the reality of what is happening in the classroom.

Figure 9.2 illustrates the feedback loop between portfolios and maps. The loop can begin at any point, but let's start at the left. A teacher begins by creating her curriculum map, outlining the content, skills, and assessments that will be in her course in the coming year.

At certain points in the year, the teacher gives the assessments to the student. (The number of times this happens can vary; typically, teachers have found two to four assessments for any elementary subject area or middle/high school course to be sufficient.)

The student responds to the assessment, and the student's work is entered into the portfolio. The teacher can also use the portfolio (including the online rubrics) to assess the student work.

At the bottom of the cycle is the critical event: by analyzing the results of the student assessment, the teacher can then make revisions to the map. In the analysis, we can ask questions such as these: Did students do as well as expected? What areas need improvement? Do the students need additional instruction on the concepts, or just some more time to practice?

Figure 9.2 | Feedback Loop

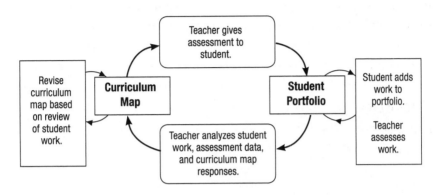

As Kallick and Colosimo (2009) put it, the data in the curriculum maps, "when taken into account with assessment data, can be the basis for informed decisions to improve student learning" (p. 5). The data need not be purely quantitative; the comments from students and the observations by a teacher during class can also provide critical evidence for making changes in instruction. Still, the portfolio provides the opportunity for gathering evidence so it can be analyzed at all.

The key to the feedback loop is that each step is an *action*. The revision to the curriculum map represents a change in what the teacher will do in the classroom. If the assessments are saying that the students are not at the expected level, then an appropriate action must be taken to reverse that trend. By pairing the curriculum map with the detailed results of an online rubric, the teacher can pinpoint the areas that need more attention—or target specific students who could benefit from additional instruction.

A Story in Revision

Let's consider an example. Beth Beckwith teaches computer technology at a suburban Minnesota middle school. In this district, middle school technology, art, music, and certain other courses are taught in "wheels." Rather than having a group of students every Monday all year, the school divides the school year into fifths; thus a teacher has a set of students every day for seven or eight weeks. This schedule means that Beth has the opportunity to revise her course five times during the same year.

One element of Beckwith's course is the teaching of online safety. In the first two wheels of the year, Beckwith took a relatively traditional approach to the topic. She identified some of the primary areas of concern about online activities and led a class discussion on how students should not reveal private information. In her curriculum map, the skills section included the following:

- G1. Determine orally ways the cyber community is like a physical community.
- G2. State ways to handle inappropriate Web sites.
- G3. Determine ways the cyber community is accessed by peers.

These topics were then covered in an end-of-unit assessment: a fill-in-the-blank and short-answer paper-and-pencil test. Students dutifully filled in the responses—but when it came time to give feedback to the students, Beckwith noted that the student responses weren't very reflective. From this assessment data, it wasn't clear that the students were "getting it."

In the third wheel, then, Beckwith altered her map and used a different kind of assessment. She set up a simulated online chat area; that is, the chat area was accessible only by the students in the class and the teacher, and was available only inside Beckwith's computer lab. In the simulation, each student was given a state to use as a screen name (student 1 was Alabama, student 2 was Alaska, and so on). Students were told not to reveal their screen names to their classmates.

Then, in the online chat, students were given different tasks to find out information about other online users. One student might be asked, "Is Illinois a boy or a girl?" or "What part of town does Colorado live in?" Amazingly, even though students had all agreed that they should not give out personal information, the students had little difficulty discovering this information about their classmates. The simulation showed them, clearly, that it was easy to let down their guard and reveal information that they hadn't intended.

This change in the curriculum was a direct result of observing the student work. By placing work into the portfolio, students and teachers have to connect their work to the overall set of standards; in reviewing the work, the teacher can determine if the students are achieving the appropriate skills and knowledge, and make the appropriate revision. In this case, the revision was an actual change in the assessment itself; in other cases, it might be a further change in instruction or a decision to alter the number of skills addressed in a unit. What makes the revision work, however, is that it is based on actual student work rather than gut feelings about what students are doing.

Student Maps and Tours

We have seen how teachers can use student portfolios to inform their day-to-day activities in the classroom. Conversely, it is also possible for students to use teachers' curriculum maps to get a better sense of their own journey.

Beth Beckwith used her maps directly in her middle school instruction. Her curriculum mapping software allowed her to output a portion of the map to a word processing document, which she then distributed to her students. Students then added their comments to the map. At the beginning of the term, students can look over the list of skills and electronically highlight them according to this scheme:

- Green: I can do this skill.
- Yellow: I know what this skill is, but I'm not confident that I can do it.
- Red: I don't know what this skill is.

Gathering this information at the beginning of the term allows the teacher to understand the knowledge that the students are bringing to the class. This exercise also allows the student to understand what is going to happen in the coming term; a list of familiar skills means that this term should enhance existing knowledge, whereas a list of unfamiliar skills shows where the student is going to have to get up to speed.

The curriculum maps can also be used at the end of the term, when they provide an opportunity for teachers and students to discuss their learning journeys. In Beckwith's case, she organized the "content" column into a set of essential questions and supporting questions, some of which are shown in Figure 9.3. Students were given an electronic copy of the document and responded to these questions directly on the map. Similarly, students were given the list of assessments in the third column and asked to describe if those assessments provided a reasonable demonstration of the skills.

When students were presented with this project, some of the initial reaction was confusion: We're just about finished with the term; what's the point of reflecting on it? Many students dread reflection, considering it to be a waste of time. Many see it as a trap; teachers ask a seemingly open-ended question, but the students believe that the teacher is only looking for certain buzzwords or validation about the "value" of the lesson—a kind of mandatory reflective response.

When Beckwith made clear, however, that their responses to the map were going to be valuable pieces of information for the next class, students perked up. When Beckwith gave examples of how the responses from the previous class actually changed the experience of the current class, they paid more attention. When Beckwith added another component, asking them to provide "advice to teachers," the students typed more than they ever had previously. The opportunity to shape the classroom—and the sense of trust that their opinions would actually be read and used—became an irresistible chance for students to provide useful feedback.

Although it can be powerful for students to respond to teacher maps, it can be even more energizing for them to create and document their own learning journeys. Students using the portfolio software can create "tours" of their work; in the example described earlier, Neale had about 16 entries for each year of his high school career; when he sat down with his committee, Neale selected just 6 entries to use as evidence of his progress.

Figure 9.3 | Student Response to a Curriculum Map

Content	Skills	Assessment
Essential Question: How can tools be used to accomplish tasks? *Student response:* I can use digital cameras to take photos and then, for example, you could use fireworks to put words in the photo for a Christmas card or if you wanted to send a picture to a friend then you could use the cropping tool to make the picture look more clear or if you have wrinkles on your face that you don't want any one to see then you could blur it just a little so that you wouldn't be able to see the wrinkles. **E. Digital Imaging** *Supporting Question:* When should I use what type of image file? *Student response:* Well if you know what file does what then it makes things a lot easier. For example .jpg can be used for photographs and gradients, .pdf can be used for making the document look exactly like the original, and .png can be used for photos.	*Skills:* *Please indicate your comfort level with the skills listed below. Solid lines = most comfortable; dashed lines = not quite comfortable; dotted lines = least comfortable.* E1. Scanned a drawing or photo at the correct resolution with the correct file type (jpg, tiff, or pdf) for the intended output. E2. Took a digital image with a digital camera using appropriate handling techniques. E3. Downloaded photos from camera to computer. E4. Modified image content (e.g., added layers, special effects, text, cropped, feathered). E5. Identified and modified image size and resolution. E6. Explored image editing options within digital image editing software.	*Assessments this term:* E1. Scanned Image (Evaluation: teacher observation) E2. Digital Photo and Download Project (Evaluation: teacher observation) E3–E4. Digital Image Modification E5. Photo Play Project (Evaluation: teacher observation) *Question to student: Do these assessments fairly demonstrate your skills?* Yes, because for me physically doing things really helps me to learn how to do it and also you can tell if we were listening in class or if we were just clicking buttons when you told us to.

Source: Curriculum map created by Beth Beckwith, Kenwood Trail Middle School, Lakeville, MN. Used by permission.

In Beckwith's school, the middle schoolers created tours of their work from their English, math, science, social studies, and technology classes. The selection of the work needs to be purposeful; the tour can show evidence that a student is ready to move to the next grade (or to graduate), can show strength in a particular area, or can show growth over time. The essential questions of purpose and audience will help dictate what pieces the student will select.

However, selecting the pieces is not enough; if readers are going to look at the portfolio, they need a narrative to describe what the work represents. This experience is analogous to an exhibit of artwork in a gallery or a coffeehouse; the artist selects items for display but also includes a narrative guide to help the viewers put the work in context. In a student-led conference, a portfolio tour might begin with a personal statement, in which the student talks about his goals for this year and for the future. The tour then can contain the specific pieces of evidence that show the progress toward those goals, and a final action plan, outlining what the student has done well and what next steps need to be taken.

The specific prompts for the tours have varied from school to school. In New Hampshire, where middle school students create tours to demonstrate Information and Communication Technologies (ICT) standards, the students need to show that they are meeting technology skills—but the entries need to show how technology applies to all subject areas. In elementary schools, students might select specific entries for a student-parent-teacher conference; in areas of writing, for example, the student can focus on the use of the "6 traits" rubric and identify which traits come easily in her writing and which need more work. At the high school level, the student could be asked to write a letter to a college admissions office or to an employer and present evidence that the student is ready for that particular postsecondary activity. Elements of the tour can correspond to elements in the common application for college or elements required for certification in a vocational area.

In short, the process of collecting, selecting, and reflecting on the work in a portfolio is what makes it powerful. The portfolio is a representation of what students know and are able to do, and the opportunity to present that work to an audience of peers, parents, and teachers shows that the world can take the students' work seriously.

At the heart of the classroom activity is the interaction between teacher and student. Curriculum maps and digital portfolios are, in and of themselves, just tools. Used in a thoughtful way, though, maps and portfolios can provide the background to make those interactions more informative and more meaningful.

10

EDUCATING
for a Sustainable Future

....

Jaimie P. Cloud

What does education have to do with making the shift toward a sustainable future?

A practice (or set of practices) is unsustainable when it undermines the health of the very systems upon which it depends and therefore cannot be continued or sustained over time. The practice of spending more money than you earn cannot be sustained over time without adverse consequences. Eating too much without exercising enough undermines the health of the body.

In contrast, a sustainable practice enhances the health of the systems upon which it depends by creating favorable conditions for it to thrive indefinitely. Mutually beneficial relationships, healthy food and exercise, saving for a rainy day—all are natural, healthy ways we have learned to behave in our everyday lives because they make it possible for us to thrive. The same concept can be used at any scale: healthy body system, healthy family system, healthy schools and communities, healthy local and global economic, social, and ecological systems.

What makes our current reality unsustainable is that the interdependent systems within which we live and upon which we depend are, simply put, out of whack. Social and economic indicators of unsustainable practices include the widening gap between rich and poor; the rising rate of obesity and diabetes in our children; and the declining graduation rate of U.S. high school students, estimated at being as low as 54 percent for urban minorities (Greene, 2002). Despite evidence that there is enough food grown on our planet to feed everyone 3,500 calories a day (Lappe, 1977, 1991), more and more people are going hungry, particularly farmers.

Ecological indicators of unsustainable practices include unprecedented and disturbing changes in our global climate due to the release of more carbon into the atmosphere at a rate that is faster than Earth's absorption rate. Similarly, our ecological footprint, an indicator of the human demand on biological capacity, exceeds the Earth's replenishment rate of biological supply by 20 percent (Wackernagel, 2008). All these are interconnected indicators—symptoms, if you will—of unsustainability. They are all the results of practices that are inadvertently causing the decline of the systems upon which we and our loved ones depend.

But the question of sustainability is much deeper than environmentalism or "greening," despite the tendency to examine it in these terms. Central to the essential question, How can we all live well within the means of nature? is a sense of agency, engagement, and hope that inspires us to create a better future for ourselves and our children. Here, too, our systems are in decline. Roper studies and Gallup polls indicate that as many as 70 percent of school-age youth feel hopeless about the future and disempowered in their daily lives (Wheeler & Bijur, 2000).

Now, this is *not* news. We have all been informed. The data have been accumulating and publicized for decades.

What *is* news is that it doesn't have to be that way. We can choose a different destination. We can learn. We can trump the habits that reside in the hardwiring of our brains that got us into this situation in the first place, and we can exercise our free will to move toward a healthy and sustainable future. A midcourse correction is required.

However, most of us have not been *educated* to grapple effectively with our current reality. Nor have we been educated to make the connections between our thinking, our behavior, and the results of that behavior on our current reality. Most people in the United States do not have a shared understanding of the knowledge, skills, and habits of mind required to make the shift toward a sustainable future. If they did, they would have learned them in school, because the foundations of our knowledge, skills, and habits of mind are cultivated in our schools.

We have to *learn* how to live well in our places without undermining their ability to sustain us over time. To ensure healthy and sustainable communities, we need to apply an ever-expanding body of knowledge; to employ an ever-changing set of skills; and to develop the attitudes that are most likely to create favorable conditions for us to thrive. We can, and I believe we must, increase our capacity to make the shift toward a sustainable future.

Educating for Sustainability

Thankfully, "intelligence is learnable" (Johnson, 2008). Therefore, those of us who educate for sustainability spend the bulk of our time preparing people in schools and communities to learn why and how to move toward a healthy and sustainable future for ourselves, for future generations, and for the living systems upon which we and, indeed, all life depend. This is a distinguishing characteristic of education for sustainability. There would be no need to educate for sustainability if there was no such thing as unsustainable. Educators for sustainability work to develop in young people and adults the knowledge, skills, attitudes, and enduring understandings required to individually and collectively contribute to a healthy and sustainable future.

What is education *for*? To address that essential question, educators for sustainability address a series of guiding questions:

Q. What kind of future do we want?

A. A healthy and sustainable future for generations to come.

Q. What do we want to sustain, for whom, and for how long?

A. A quality of life, for all, within the means of nature, indefinitely.

Q. What does our thinking have to do with our current reality and our ability to achieve the kind of future we want?

A. Our mental maps (paradigms, frames, mental models) drive the designs we create, the rules we make, the strategies we use, our behaviors and their consequences.

Q. What does our education have to do with our thinking?

A. Everything.

Education for Sustainability (EfS) was officially born in 1992 in Chapter 36 of Agenda 21, the international agreement to move toward sustainability signed by every country in the world at a UN Summit in Rio de Janeiro. The history of EfS as a field of study, before and after 1992, is well documented. One good rendition of that history is in a chapter (Federico, Cloud, Byrne, & Wheeler, 2002) of a book entitled *Stumbling Toward Sustainability* (Dernbach, 2002). A sequel, *Agenda for a Sustainable America* (Dernbach, 2009), includes updated information on EfS activity in the United States.

The Cloud Institute

At the Cloud Institute for Sustainability Education, we equip preK–12 school systems and their communities with the core content, competencies, and habits of mind that characterize education for a sustainable future. We do this by inspiring educators and engaging students through meaningful content and student-centered instruction.

Our vision is as follows:

IMAGINE   There is a shared understanding that schools have a responsibility to contribute to our individual and collective potential, and to that of the living systems upon which all life depends.

IMAGINE   Schools are learning organizations.

IMAGINE   The potential of having all our children in school with their teachers and mentors during the *most favorable time* in their lives for learning and paradigm shifting (*for creating new functional pathways*) in young people, and that we honor them with transformative learning experiences that prepare them to participate in, and to lead with us, the shift toward a sustainable future.

The Cloud Institute Framework for Education for Sustainability draws upon the original work of educators from around the world as noted in Chapter 36 of Agenda 21; the U.S. Task Force on Education for Sustainability; Harland Cleveland, Paul Hawken, Daniella Tillsbury, David Orr, Keith Wheeler, Jack Byrne, and Stephen Sterling; ministries of education in Germany, Switzerland, the United Kingdom, and Australia; colleagues and counterparts in the United States, Japan, Mexico, Canada, Hungary, the Czech Republic, Slovakia, and Russia, to name a few; and 15 years of experience in purposefully educating for a sustainable future in schools and school systems in New York City, around the United States, and throughout the world.

As outlined in our EfS Framework, the Cloud Institute (www.cloudinstitute.org) advocates that students learn (and act upon) the following:

Cultural Preservation and Transformation—How the preservation of cultural histories and heritages, and the transformation of cultural identities and practices, contribute to sustainable communities. Students will develop the ability to discern with others what to preserve and what to change in order for future generations to thrive.

Responsible Local/Global Citizenship—The rights, responsibilities, and actions associated with leadership and participation toward healthy and sustainable communities. Students will know and understand these rights and responsibilities and assume their roles of leadership and participation.

The Dynamics of Systems and Change—Fundamental patterns of systems including growth, decline, and vacillation. Students will know and understand the dynamic nature of complex living systems and change over time. They will be able to apply the tools and concepts of system dynamics and systems thinking in their present lives, and to inform the choices that will affect our future.

Sustainable Economics—The evolving theories and practices of economics and the shift toward integrating our economic, natural, and social systems, to support and maintain life on the planet. Students will know and understand 21st century economic practices and will produce and consume in ways that contribute to the health of the financial, social, and natural capital.

Healthy Commons—That upon which we all depend and for which we are all responsible (i.e., air, trust, biodiversity, climate regulation, our collective future, water, libraries, public health, heritage sites, top soil, etc.). Students will be able to recognize and value the vital importance of the Commons in our lives and for our future. They will assume the rights, responsibilities, and actions to care for the Commons.

Living Within Ecological/Natural Laws and Principles—The laws of nature and science principles of sustainability. Students will see themselves as interdependent with each other, all living things, and natural systems. They will be able to put their knowledge and understanding to use in the service of their lives, their communities, and the places in which they live.

Inventing and Affecting the Future—The vital role of vision, imagination, and intention in creating the desired future. Students will design, implement, and assess actions in the service of their individual and collective visions.

Multiple Perspectives—The perspectives, life experiences, and cultures of others, as well as our own. Students will know, understand, value, and draw from multiple perspectives to co-create with diverse stakeholders shared and evolving visions and actions in the service of a healthy and sustainable future locally and globally.

A Sense of Place—The strong connection to the place in which one lives. Students will recognize and value the interrelationships between the social, economic, ecological, and architectural history of that place and contribute to its continuous health.

Real-Life Examples

Educating for Sustainability is not just a theoretical construct. Here are some real-life examples of schools and school systems that aspire to educate for sustainability.

Putnam/Northern Westchester BOCES, New York

Supported by the Putnam/Northern Westchester BOCES Curriculum Council, made up of representatives from 27 school districts in Westchester, New York, the P/NW BOCES Curriculum Center is developing and distributing K–12 Education for Sustainability Curriculum Exemplars. The center believes this curriculum project is timely, important, and urgent and will prepare students for a democratic society, a global economy, and a sustainable future. The goal of the project is to create multidisciplinary, Web-based curriculum units that combine engaging and relevant content with the highest-quality pedagogy.

This multiyear undertaking includes building the capacity of administrators to lead in this area and working with teams of teachers to develop cutting-edge sustainability education curriculum exemplars. The first year of curriculum writing focused on creating units for grades 6 through 8. During the summer of 2008, more than 100 talented middle school educators from 17 districts worked together to draft a multidisciplinary curriculum unit for sustainability education that incorporated English/language arts, social studies, math, science, and the arts. The teachers built the sustainability education units around an overarching question: "How are we all going to live well within the means of nature?" The question, in turn, was inspired by the definition of *sustainability*: providing a rich quality of life for all and accomplishing this within the means of nature. Each grade level then chose an essential question to drive inquiry across the disciplines. These essential questions were based on the teachers' work with the Cloud Institute for Sustainability Education and addressed the Education for Sustainability Core Content Standards.

To implement this ambitious project, P/NW BOCES assembled experts on sustainability, curriculum design, and instructional technology to work with the educators involved in the project. Once the curriculum units were created, they were refined by the P/NW BOCES experts and placed on the Web for teacher-writers to pilot during the year. Teacher feedback and examination of student work will continue to enhance the curriculum, and the curriculum development cycle will continue until the K–12 curriculum units are complete. Thereafter, P/NW BOCES will use a continuous improvement model to ensure that the units remain at the cutting edge of content and instruction. Districts anywhere can subscribe to these units from the P/NW BOCES Curriculum Center. Used by permission. © 2009 P/NW BOCES.

The Willow School, Gladstone, New Jersey

The Willow School, a small, independent day school for students in kindergarten through 8th grade, is committed to combining academic excellence and the joy of learning and experiencing the wonder of the natural world. The 34-acre forested site on which the school was built is integral to all aspects of the curriculum. The site has many regenerative design features, such as constructed wetlands for the filtration of wastewater that provide for the return of an abundance of clean water to the groundwater system. Natural meadows, butterfly gardens, water harvesting, and hedgerows are incorporated into the site. The Willow School believes humans are an integral part of the natural world and that the health and sustainability of our natural systems has a profound effect on the quality of our lives. How we relate to each other goes hand-in-hand with how we relate to our natural surroundings.

Since the Willow School began in 2001, students have learned to become aware of their natural surroundings and to take care of those surroundings. The Willow School setting exemplifies a commitment to living healthily and wisely. The buildings and grounds are a laboratory for academic inspiration and sustainability education where students develop a sense of place, become stewards of their environment, and learn to appreciate their role in restoring balance to the natural world.

In 2007 the Cloud Institute was asked to help the faculty develop the new middle school curriculum. The elementary school faculty joined the process to seamlessly embed the attributes of Education for Sustainability across the curriculum, K–8, through professional development, curriculum and assessment development and mapping, analysis of EfS strengths, observations, coaching, analysis of student work, and program planning and assessment. Teachers are motivated and committed to educating for sustainability and believe that they are better teachers as a result. Everyone is committed to the role of schools and young people in contributing to the shift toward sustainability.

Some of the school's specific curriculum exemplars include the following:

- Using the school garden as a laboratory for basic agricultural techniques, 1st graders have the opportunity to plant, weed, and harvest crops.

- Third graders explore the land-use history of the country and begin to understand why different groups of people viewed and treated land the way they did.

- In 4th and 5th grade social studies, students study cultures and consider the reciprocal relationship between humans and their environment.

- In language arts, students explore place and its influence on the mythology and folk writings of a culture.

- Middle school students formally study ecology in their sciences classes. Each subject—from furniture design to language arts—seeks to make connections between the content and the core theme of sustainability. For example, in English, students discuss the concept of "place" in novels and its effect upon characters.

NYC Public Schools: The Empowerment Schools

For 25 years, the Cloud Institute has worked with the New York City Public Schools on various initiatives. The latest work involves the network leaders and superintendents of 500 Empowerment Schools, which are based on the belief that decisions about how to educate students should be made as close as possible to those who work with them—the principals in collaboration with the school community.

The network leaders and administrators of these schools are interested in using systems thinking and learning-organization theory to create excellent schools in healthy communities as an entry point into educating for a sustainable future. Peter Senge, Linda Booth Sweeney (author of *When a Butterfly Sneezes, The Systems Thinking Playbook, Connected Wisdom*), and I have cofacilitated a series of professional development sessions that are preparing network leaders to design learning networks of schools in the service of systemic change and continuous improvement.

In addition, School Food Services, the Empowerment Schools, and the Cloud Institute are working to bring a variety of "farm and garden to cafeteria" programs to interested Empowerment Schools so that students will be exposed more to fresh produce and foods that are regional, seasonal, and organic, when possible. These efforts, aligned with appropriate curriculum content and instructional practices, enhance students' abilities to think well, particularly about the relationship between their health and well-being and sustainable food systems.

Marin Country Day School

In 2008 the Cloud Institute and Marin Country Day School (MCDS) began working together. Two important strands began this process. Having arrived at MCDS in 2004, Head of School Lucinda Katz began her tenure at the beginning of a strategic-planning process by including the many voices representing the various school constituencies. As part of their strategic plan for 2006, they identified three initiatives—technology, environmental sustainability, and community and global education—that were to be integrated into the curriculum and daily teaching.

Simultaneously, MCDS's Sibley Award, typically given to one person at the school who lived the mission of the school, was instead given to a group of faculty and staff to develop EfS curriculum unit exemplars to demonstrate the elegant integration of the three strategic initiatives and the curriculum review in the service of educating for a sustainable future. In 2007, Dianne Maxon and Alice Moore led the team of Sibley awardees through the beginning of the process.

Thus far the Cloud Institute's work with the Sibley team has included professional development, assistance and coaching on EfS curriculum design, a self-assessment of the attributes of a learning organization, and reviews of exemplary curriculum units and student work samples. The entire faculty and the majority of staff members have begun to develop a shared understanding of sustainability and Education for Sustainability through some introductory professional development, and the trustees and parent board also began this process in 2009.

Unity Charter School, Morristown, New Jersey

The mission of Unity Charter School is to teach the importance of protecting and improving the environment by educating students on the principles of sustainability, ecology, and diversity in a way that celebrates and honors this planet and all its inhabitants. Through a generous grant from the Geraldine R. Dodge Foundation, the Cloud Institute has been working with Unity Charter School since 2007 to go to the next level in accomplishing its mission. In the first phase of the work, the school developed an awareness and a shared understanding of sustainability and Education for Sustainability among the faculty and administration; it acquired and applied a shared EfS vocabulary; and it collected baseline data and self-assessed the extent to which Unity is already a learning organization and the extent to which it is already educating for and assessing for sustainability. The school developed K–8 outcomes and indicators for sense of place, one of the core content standards in EfS, and teachers developed pilot units of study that assessed for at least one of the sense of place performances.

The continuing work will address a number of areas. The school plans to differentiate professional development and coaching with the faculty, develop Unity as a learning organization, provide increased and improved communication to the board of directors and the parent community, develop more and improved curriculum unit exemplars, map the curriculum units the teachers have designed and developed, and share exemplary work with interested educators in its learning communities.

Cambridge Montessori School, Cambridge, Massachusetts

Cambridge Montessori School encourages independent, self-directed learning for life in a child-centered, international community valuing peace, respect for others, and pride in individual differences. When this preK–9 school contacted the Cloud Institute, they, like the Willow School, wanted to begin working with the institute to educate for sustainability through the development of their new middle school. In addition, the school plans to move to a new site and to do a green renovation on that site as a demonstration of their commitment to sustainability. The preschool faculty and administration *and* the elementary faculty were also ready to "sustainablize" (our word) their curriculum, which makes for an elegant preK–9 scope and sequence.

In the first phase of our work, we developed a shared understanding of education for sustainability among the faculty and some administrators; we acquired and applied a shared EfS vocabulary; we began to collect baseline data; and many (not all) teachers self-assessed the extent to which they are already educating for sustainability by conducting a "strengths assessment." Teachers began to think about EfS outcomes and indicators for their grade levels and disciplines, and a few teachers began to develop pilot units of study. The Middle School mapped out an interdisciplinary scope and sequence for 7th grade and sketched the 8th and 9th grade curriculum maps. In addition, we increased and improved the shared understanding of EfS by the board of directors and the parent community.

Next on the agenda is to finish documenting the strengths assessment to have baseline data for assessing our work over time; and increasing and improving EfS curriculum units and curriculum documentation. These efforts involve differentiating professional development, deepening understanding and application of the Cloud Institute's core EfS Content and Performance Standards and curriculum design, assessment, mapping, and coaching with the faculty.

St. Paul's Episcopal School, New Orleans

St. Paul's Episcopal School opened its doors in 1961 with 52 students, all boys. Over the decades, St. Paul's grew into an independent coeducational day school educating, on average, 270 students per year from 3 years old through 8th graders. The school is living its mission to instill in its children strength of intellect and strength of character in a Christian environment that is positive, respectful, and familial. St. Paul's students are encouraged to strive to do their best, to be humane, and to appreciate the beauty of life.

Located near the 17th Street Canal breach, St. Paul's was devastated by floodwater after Hurricane Katrina, as were the homes of most of its families. Student enrollment was, in 2009, about half of what it was before the storm, as was the size of the faculty. A combination of faith, determination, hard work, and help from around the country brought the school's campus back to life. Still, there are serious issues threatening both St. Paul's and the surrounding community.

The future of the school, the neighborhood, and the city are intrinsically interwoven. As a result, St. Paul's is looking to the future with a bold vision for the study of the sciences that will incorporate the highest standards of sustainable "green" planning and design, along with a comprehensive curriculum incorporating Education for Sustainability at every grade level. They see this as an opportunity for their students to learn about, and to learn to be responsible for, their community in a different way, and to learn for a sustainable future in a way that will allow them to meet their full potential and to shape their futures and the futures of generations to come.

In 2008, the Cloud Institute began working with St. Paul's faculty, parents, rectory personnel, and community partners to develop a shared understanding of sustainability, and of the attributes of Education for Sustainability. We will follow this introductory work with the use of tools and exemplars from the Cloud Institute's EfS Curriculum Design Studio; the use of tools, concepts, and methodologies of *Schools That Learn* (Senge, 2000) and *Communities That Learn, Lead, and Last* (Martin-Kniep, 2008); strategic planning; and deepening EfS knowledge, skills, and attitudes through professional development and coaching over time. This project is a proactive way for St. Paul's community and students to positively affect and protect their environment and regain if not a sense of safety, at least a sense of competency and responsibility about the future. It is potentially a silver lining to their story in the wake of Katrina.

The UN Decade of Education for Sustainable Development

In December 2002, resolution 57/254 on the United Nations Decade of Education for Sustainable Development (2005–2014) was adopted by the UN General Assembly, and UNESCO was designated as lead agency for the promotion of the decade. The National Association of Independent

Schools officially committed to the goals of the decade shortly thereafter, as have hundreds of organizations, professional associations, consortia, and colleges and universities in the United States. Ministries of education and schools of education at colleges and universities around the world have been taking responsibility for their role as educators for sustainability. In the United States, a small handful of schools of education have begun to develop significant programming in EfS.

Examples of EfS Curriculum and Instruction

What determines the extent to which a curriculum unit is exemplary of EfS attributes? Evidence of a rich combination of EfS Content Standards and Performance Indicators designed, delivered, and assessed through one or more best practices. The more, the richer.

As noted, the Cloud Institute is working with leading independent and public schools and school systems in the United States to design, develop, assess, and map exemplary EfS curriculum units and full courses of study. In addition, many are also teaching or adapting existing units and courses published by EfS organizations.

Publishers of Exemplary Curriculum Materials

To date, only a handful of publishers are producing exemplary curriculum materials specifically designed to educate for sustainability in K–12 schools. Among them are the Cloud Institute for Sustainability Education, the Shelburne Farms Sustainable Schools Project, Facing the Future, Creative Change, the Lawrence Hall of Science at UC Berkeley, the Creative Learning Exchange, Dr. Art Sussman, Teachers College, and the Center for Eco Literacy. (See References and Resources for more information.)

A Case Study of "Inventing the Future: Leadership and Participation for the 21st Century"

The Cloud Institute has published several units of study and two full courses of study. The following is a case study of one exemplar among the Cloud Institute materials, a one-semester course entitled "Inventing the Future: Leadership and Participation for the 21st Century."

Inventing the Future was codesigned with Giselle Martin-Kniep and Joanne Piccone Zoccia of Communities for Learning to meet EfS content standards for responsible local and global citizenship; healthy commons; a sense of place; multiple perspectives; sustainable economics; inventing and affecting the future; and the dynamics of systems and change. In addition, it is exemplary in its expression of the attributes of excellent curriculum and best instructional practices from which EfS draws.

Inventing the Future engages students in inventing a sustainable future as citizens of our democracy and includes a project-based learning component that is student-designed and student-led, and can be linked to service learning requirements where appropriate. Students who take this course do the following:

- DEVELOP a sense of place and value local knowledge, in an effort to begin the process of restoring and improving the beauty, integrity, and health of the places in which we live and work.

- EXPLORE the roles, rights, and responsibilities of citizens in a democratic society, and study the range of ways in which to participate.

- DISCOVER "the commons" in our communities and our society—that which is shared by all, upon which we are all dependent, and for which we are all responsible.

- INVESTIGATE new ways of thinking about the relationship between society, the economy, and the environment.

- ENVISION the future of our communities and develop quality-of-life indicators.

- DOCUMENT and examine the assets (what do we have going for us?) and the liabilities (what are the challenges we are facing?) that exist in our communities.

- RESEARCH the world of public policy and policymaking and how policies influence our lives and our future.

- SCAN the driving forces that are at work in the world and develop projects that contribute to positive change.

In 2006–07, the Academy for Educational Development's Center for Schools and Community Services carried out an 18-month evaluation of Inventing the Future, which was funded by the Ewing Marion Kauffman Foundation and the Carnegie Corporation. The following is a summary of student and teacher outcomes.

Students demonstrated statistically significant increases in the strength of their attitudes about civic engagement in the following areas:

• Their personal obligation to contribute in some way to the community

• Their plans to become actively involved in issues that positively affect the community

• Their feeling that state and local issues are everybody's responsibility

Students increased their familiarity with all of the course content items, including basic science principles, the "commons," community mapping, and sustainability. Here are some representative comments from students:

• "I learned about being a citizen of your community, your city, of [the] USA, and of the world."

• "Because of this class I am 100 percent more interested in government."

• "We did a description of our community and then came up with a plan that would make the community better."

The course seemed to raise student consciousness about elements that impede sustainability and need to be changed. Again, here are representative comments:

• "I think about what I can do now that will make things better 20 years from now."

• "We are the future; if we don't change it we are going to suffer the repercussions."

Students demonstrated a greater awareness of community, a greater appreciation of the democratic process, and an appreciation of how current actions affect the future. Students also demonstrated a keener awareness of the need to solve problems facing communities.

Statistically significant increases between the precourse and postcourse surveys were noted in the number of students who felt that they "had more confidence and intelligence." There were also significant decreases in the number of students who selected "low grades" (from 38.5 percent to 15.8 percent) or "I don't think I can succeed" (from 29.9 percent to 6.0 percent) as barriers to their educational success.

Teachers reported that their professional development activities increased their preparedness to teach the curriculum and further increased their own perceptions of themselves as educators who can teach others about sustainability and as citizens who can work with others toward a sustainable future.

Parting Thoughts

Education for Sustainability is made up of an elegant system of core EfS Content Standards and Performance Indicators, aligned with robust instructional, organizational, and youth leadership attributes and practices. It is most advantageous to educate for sustainability in "green" buildings and in schools that exercise sustainable procurement practices, develop sustainable investment portfolios (specifically appropriate for independent schools), and serve delicious, healthy, and sustainable food—some of which might have come from their garden or local farmers, and have rich authentic relationships with their communities.

As educators and students who want to contribute to a healthy and sustainable future, we will envision, design, and assess with the desired future in mind. We will develop goals in the service of our vision, we will determine our strengths and our challenges, and we will operate from our strengths. We will distinguish problems from symptoms and identify the most "upstream" problems we can address, neither underestimating nor overestimating our sphere of influence. We will strive to solve more than one problem at a time and minimize the creation of new problems.

We will identify the nonnegotiable limits—the parameters within which we are operating. We will learn how to tap the power of limits because healthy systems have them. We will thrive within the natural laws and principles, within our means, and within the means of nature. We will "not incur debts greater than can be paid in our lifetime" (Jefferson, personal communication to James Madison, 1789).

We will become strongly connected to the places in which we live, and identify and create healthy commons because we all depend on them and we are all responsible for them. We will work to reconcile the conflicts that exist between our individual rights and our responsibilities as citizens to tend the commons.

We will have fun, breathe easily, find meaningful and prosperous work, and aspire to a rich quality of life for all, within the means of nature.

11

POWER DOWN
or Power Up?

Alan November

Have you ever been surprised when you have watched a young child pick up a friend's cell phone and intuitively use all of its functions? YouTube is filled with videos of adorable 2-year-olds using many of the features of an iPhone. You can watch the children gleefully zip their little fingers across the touch screen to take pictures, send e-mail, watch videos, and make calls. These images will either generate warm, fuzzy feelings or conjure up scary thoughts. You may even believe that these devices have no place in our classrooms.

The need to maintain control of the traditional classroom has led many school districts to ban a wide range of powerful tools that could be used for learning. It is not unusual to have cell phones, iPods, blogging sites, wikis, and free global communication tools such as Skype forbidden within a school. Either the list of forbidden resources will grow as new, powerful, easy-to-use tools are invented, or it will disappear as we learn to co-opt these devices for learning.

Rethinking Control in Our Classrooms

This is the first time in history when many children are learning to use powerful tools outside the range of adult supervision. What concerns many of us is that our worst fear of students abusing these tools has a much higher chance of happening without teachers and parents providing appropriate role models. Eventually we must realize that it does not make sense to simply ban all of the exciting technologies children want to use from their learning experiences in school. Not realizing this will only expand the disconnect that many students currently feel as they enter our classrooms. Of course, the problem is that these tools can be very disruptive to the traditional management of a classroom. Teachers have told me that they fear losing control of their classes if their students are allowed to bring these devices to school, or if the network allowed access to Facebook and MySpace.

I think these teachers are right. These are disruptive technologies that will not work well in the current culture of industrialized classrooms.

What if we were to transform the culture of teaching and learning to adapt to the power of these tools? After all, our children are growing up at a time when they have instant access to the Web for information and global communication in their back pocket. And it is nearly free.

What many educators find objectionable is the content that students can encounter when using these devices. Reports in the media warn us about online predators, identity theft, cyberbullying, and more. Pornography and hate messages can be found with only a few mouse clicks.

This isn't the first time that these issues have come to the forefront. For years there has been ongoing debate over content delivered through television, books, movies, and magazines. Regulations have been developed over time to help parents and teachers deal with content delivered in these formats. We have become so comfortable with these regulations that we no longer worry about them as much. We put ratings on television shows that tell parents that the content might be inappropriate. We put age restrictions on movies to keep kids out of theaters or on magazines to prevent them from being sold to minors. We have learned how to deal with these media. But what about the Internet? There are no widespread safety regulations. Many students are carrying digital devices right now that have unfettered access to just about anything—both good and bad. It should be no surprise that when children are not taught the social responsibility of using powerful tools, there will be abuse and distraction.

New Roles for Developing Empowered Learners

Shouldn't we be providing role models for our students about how to harness the power of information and global communication? What if we could tap our students' interest in these digital tools to design more rigorous and motivating assignments?

Before the Industrial Revolution and the invention of powerful machines such as the tractor and the combine, children were responsible for performing meaningful jobs that were vital to each family's success. Depending on their age, children would care for animals, repair farm equipment, prepare food to sell at local markets, and more. Children were essential to the very survival of the family and the farm. At the same time, these jobs taught children the value of hard work, leading them to become more productive citizens within their communities as adults.

As mechanized tools and other technologies developed, our communities no longer needed young children to work. Although technology freed children to leave the farm and go to school, there was a loss of real work and contributions to the community by children.

Across the country, pioneering teachers are providing students with new roles that have students making contributions to their learning communities. We have powerful, easy-to-use tools such as screencasting and podcasting that give students opportunities to contribute content to the class. At the same time, we can also provide them with rigorous and more motivating assignments that better prepare them to become more productive in our new global economy. It's an exciting time.

Student as Contributor: The Digital Farm

As I visit schools all over the world, I have met teachers who have pioneered new roles for the learner. It is exciting to watch empowered students tap the tools they want to use to become more engaged and rigorous in their own learning.

The six jobs described in this section outline only a sampling of creative ways that teachers have provided students with opportunities to make valuable contributions to their learning community. Although in many cases these jobs are being successfully implemented individually, by bringing them together in harmony, we can create a more balanced vision of teaching and learning. The real problem is not adding technology to the current organization of the classroom, but changing the culture of teaching and learning.

Tutorial Designers

Students from Lincoln Middle School in Santa Monica, California, have energized their school through the use of screencasted tutorials. With the leadership of their teacher, Eric Marcos, these kids have begun documenting their learning by recording themselves solving problems based on material discussed in class.

Marcos has been using Camtasia (www.techsmith.com) to allow students in his class to record the actions being performed on their computer screens while also recording their explanations about how to solve each problem. When completed, these movies are uploaded and become part of an online database that Marcos's students—or anyone else around the world—can access at any time. Another option from TechSmith that is free and equally powerful is Jing (www.jingproject.com). With this software, and a single click of the mouse, students can begin recording their work easily and at any time.

Marcos has found this task to be so motivating that he has worked to build a new YouTube–like Web site (www.mathtrain.tv) that he and the rest of his school's math department use to share the growing number of screencasts that students are creating. He has found that allowing students to create material for this site increases engagement and provides struggling students with more opportunities for reviewing troubling concepts.

Official Scribes

Do all of your students take excellent notes every day? What if there were online collaboration tools that would give your class the opportunity to collaboratively build one set of perfect notes? Using a shared blog, wiki, or another collaborative writing tool like Google Docs (http://docs. google.com), students can share this responsibility and create a detailed set of notes that can be used by the entire class.

Darren Kuropatwa, a high school calculus teacher, has transformed his classroom from individual students working on "their stuff" to a collaborative learning community. His "scribe of the day" program (http:// tinyurl.com/68djoz) has been a great success. Each day, a new student is responsible for taking notes and collecting diagrams that become part of his class's online calculus textbook.

Kuropatwa has found that students who never took notes in the past are now doing so, knowing that their peers are dependent on what is published in the class blog. At the same time, students who struggle to take good notes are getting better as they see constant high-quality models being posted from others.

Researchers

Many classrooms have one rarely used computer sitting in the back. What if that computer became the official research station, where one student each day was responsible for finding answers to all the questions that came up in class—including the teacher's?

This activity might not sound imaginative, but it can be very effective. Each day, assign a different student to sit at that computer. When questions come up during class, it is that student's responsibility to search out the correct answer. Once sites are found that give details about the questions being asked, you might consider adding them to your own

search engine built using Google's Custom Search Engine creator (www.
google.com/coop/cse/). This search engine can be designed to meet
standards, coordinate with your curriculum, and consist of sites from
reputable resources. Imagine creating a global warming search engine
that cuts through the hype on both sides of the issue and accesses only
factual information from NASA, NOAA, and other scientific research
organizations.

Don't expect this activity to work easily right from the beginning.
Most educators know that there is a great amount of misinformation
online and also acknowledge that students don't always use the most
effective search techniques. Understanding this reality makes this student job that much more important. We should be providing students
with guided opportunities and teachable moments that allow them to
practice and hone their research skills.

Collaboration Coordinators

It wasn't that long ago when it was cost prohibitive to have your class
connect with other classes and subject experts around the world. That
time is gone! In an ever-shrinking world, we now have free access to
make these very connections.

Using Skype (www.skype.com), a collaboration team could be
responsible for establishing and maintaining working relationships via
the Internet with classrooms around the world. How can you leverage
that power? Before a discussion of the American Revolution, charge your
collaboration team with the responsibility of finding a class of British
students who would be willing to discuss the issues that led to the start
of the American Revolution. How many eyes do you think would be
opened by the differing views that occur during the debate?

Connections can also be established with experts who might be
willing to talk to your students regarding other meaningful topics. For
example, middle school students from one Chicago suburb were learning about the effects of globalization. Their teacher, Andrea Trudeau,
could have provided students with a short passage from a textbook or
a few magazine articles. Instead, she facilitated a project that had her
students creating interview questions for an American factory owner

who felt he had to outsource his production to China, as well as a businessman in China who was managing a factory for the U.S. market (see http://dps109.wikispaces.com/Skype). The questions that the students developed became part of a series of interviews that were recorded, providing students with a learning experience that went far beyond any textbook or article. This project attracted a global audience, including a teacher in the United Kingdom who repurposed this material for his class as they were discussing similar issues.

Hundreds of other opportunities like this are waiting for any adventurous group of students looking for opportunities to bring the world into the classroom.

Contributors to Society

It's almost impossible to watch TV or listen to the radio without hearing about issues concerning various countries around the world. Although they seem distant, these issues are important, and we can use them to teach students about social justice and empathy.

Kiva (www.kiva.org) is one of today's most important social responsibility Web sites. This site opens the doors of learning and gives students the opportunity to make a small but meaningful difference in the lives of others. Through this site, your class can join others in making small loans to entrepreneurs in developing countries who are trying to make better lives for themselves and their families. These loans are repaid over time as students are kept informed on the successes and struggles of those in whom they have made investments.

You might consider pulling together a team that seeks investments that the class finds important and that relate to their current studies. They might organize snack sales or penny drives while educating other classes about their mission. This team would then work with the research team to investigate what is happening in these distant places. They might work with the collaboration coordinators to find experts whom they could talk to about how loans work. The learning cycle could go on and on, as loans are repaid and reinvested. Your students could be tracking the results of their micro-investments long after the school year ends.

Curriculum Reviewers

As the resources described here come together, the curriculum review team can jump into action to create material for continuous review. This team can combine visual and audio components into podcasts that can be posted online for individuals to download into their MP3 players.

Bob Sprankle and his class at Wells Elementary School in Wells, Maine, are well known for doing exactly this. Their Room 208 Podcast burst onto the scene several years ago and provided classes with a fantastic model that can be duplicated by others. Weekly, during their snack time, Sprankle's students organized, recorded, and edited their podcasts before publishing them to a global audience (www.bobsprankle.com/podcasts/0506/rm208vodcast.mov).

If you attempt this, you may want to ask your school to purchase a few generic MP3 players that can be used by students who might not have their own. These devices can be loaded at school with podcasts that cover multiple courses, and the material on these players can be accessed anywhere, at any time.

Parting Thoughts

If our children are to grow up to make important contributions to our society, it is essential that we provide them with powerful tools and experiences across the curriculum. This goal will require a new culture of teaching and learning that engages students as contributors. Our students have already chosen tools such as MySpace and Facebook for their own communications and social interaction. Now is the time to take elements of these tools and provide students with the appropriate role models of how to use them to make important and rigorous contributions to their own school and beyond.

The essential question is not "What technology should we buy for our schools?" The much more important question is one of control: "Can we change our traditional culture of teaching and learning so that students are empowered to take more responsibility for making important contributions to their own learning and to their learning community?"

If we can make this change, we have the opportunity to expand the quality of learning in our schools. In fact, we might find that our students' contributions can raise the level of engagement and provide more depth and rigor to the curriculum than was ever possible before.

....

Visit www.novemberlearning.com to learn more about my work and to gain access to a variety of useful resources.

12

CREATING LEARNING CONNECTIONS

with Today's Tech-Savvy Student

Bill Sheskey

In September 2002, I brought a new digital camera into my 9th grade physical science classroom to show it off to the students. I showed them all of the features and told them that I was excited about what great pictures I could take with a 3.2-megapixel camera. This show-and-tell took place at the beginning of class, and then I put the camera away. We proceeded to the lab table to build electric motors with wire, magnets, and a 9-volt battery. The students were engaged in this lab, and the groups progressed smoothly through all the steps. The lab activity was going so smoothly that I decided to get out my new camera and play with it while the students were working. For fun, I decided to take pictures of the electric-motor lab setups being built by each lab group. I was trying out the different features of the camera as I went around, without really thinking about the pictures I was taking.

As the lab time wound down, I went to my classroom computer and uploaded the pictures from my digital camera. Coincidentally, I had a

195

computer projector checked out from the media center that day. Without any premeditation, I asked the students to come back to their seats, and I told them that I wanted to show them the pictures that I had taken during the lab activity. The last 10 minutes of that class were a revelation for my teaching career! As I started showing the pictures of their electric motors on the big screen, they began to critique each other's work without any prompting from me. They started asking each other excellent questions about the lab setups. Why did you do it that way? Did that way work better? They were also complimenting each other on their work. Complimenting each other's work is not a common practice of 9th graders. One student who was usually not motivated by lab activities asked me very quietly if he could go back and rebuild his motor. After the bell rang to end the class period, the student was still there. He asked if I could retake the picture and put it on the big screen at the beginning of the next class period for everyone to see. That was the first time that student had ever shown any interest in a class activity.

The Light Goes On

During the entire lab and camera activity, I never said a word. The simple act of photographing the students' lab work and projecting the images through the computer on a big screen led to a profound change in how I conducted my science classes. The fact that the students' work was going to be displayed digitally in front of peers motivated them to complete higher-quality work. After that day, I started photographing all of their lab work and displaying it. I checked out digital cameras for them and asked them to take their own digital photographs and insert them into their lab write-ups. That easy activity became something the students looked forward to as part of their lab experiences in the class, and it significantly increased their motivation to produce high-quality lab reports.

It was at this moment in my science lab that I realized that integrating technology into the classroom was going to allow me to make authentic connections with the students. From there I began the journey of exploration to make stronger and better connections using technology tools that are relevant to tech-savvy students. Using images, audio and video recording tools, interactive software, and Web-based collaborative tools allows the students to demonstrate what they are learning using modern literacy tools.

Students Demand a Change

Educators in the 21st century realize that students entering the classroom today are much different from those who have come before. Today's students are demanding a change in the classroom because of their ability to gather information faster than any previous generation. In 2006, the Kaiser Family Foundation reported that two-thirds of infants and toddlers watch a screen an average of two hours per day. Children under age 6 watch an average of about two hours of screen media per day, primarily TV and videos or DVDs. Children and teens 8 to 18 years old spend nearly four hours a day in front of a TV screen and almost two additional hours on the computer (outside of schoolwork) and playing video games (Kaiser Family Foundation, 2006).

To make authentic connections with students, we must change our strategies to fit this new age of students. With the resources available today for use in the classroom, such as interactive software, digital imaging, audio and video creation tools, on-demand video libraries, computers and LCD projectors, and Web 2.0 tools, the hardest job may be choosing which tool to use and how to integrate it into the classroom. It is the greatest time in history to be in a classroom because learning technology is changing at an exponential rate, and our students can thrive with it.

Before the time of television and mass-produced multimedia, the teacher brought the curriculum to the students through textbooks, pictures, maps, and the teacher's own methods and strategies for instruction—as many teachers still do today. Effective teachers encouraged students to share experiences with each other and connected with students using instructional tools that were available at the time. In the 1960s, reel-to-reel, 16mm film projectors brought educational media to the classroom. The filmstrip projector and overhead projector displayed images that would have been impossible to display on a chalkboard or bulletin board. The television did not become commonplace in the classroom until the invention of the video cassette recorder (VCR) in 1972 and the video home system (VHS) format for cassette tapes in 1977. At the high school where I had my first teaching job in 1979, teachers had to sign up weeks in advance to use the VCR and participate in an extensive training session to learn how to insert the tape and push the "play" button. In the 1980s, televisions were installed in classrooms when the cost of the VCR decreased and cable TV channels with educational content became available through the public broadcasting system.

In the late 1980s, the mass production of computers made it possible to bring them into the public school classroom. The early introduction of computers into classrooms failed because most teachers did not understand how to use them as a teaching tool. In a 1986 book, *Teachers and Machines: The Classroom Use of Technology Since 1920*, Larry Cuban, former Stanford professor and school superintendent, wrote the following:

> The cycle always began with big promises, backed by the technology developers' research. In the classroom, teachers never really embraced the new tools, and no significant academic improvement occurred. This provoked a consistent response from technology promoters: The problem was money, or teacher resistance, or the paralyzing school bureaucracy. Meanwhile, few people questioned the technology advocates' claims. As results continued to lag, the blame was finally laid on the machines. Soon schools were sold on the next generation of technology, and the lucrative cycle started all over again. (Oppenheimer, 2003, p. 6)

The technology that broke the cycle of failure with computers for classroom teachers was the development of easier-to-use operating systems such as the Windows and Apple desktop operating systems. Software and Web-based applications have now been programmed to reduce the learning curve to use the software as an instructional tool. Since the beginning of the 21st century, the decrease in the cost of computer-projection systems has enabled large screens to visually display the computer screen for all students in the classroom to see and interact with. One-to-one computing in classrooms is growing throughout the United States, but we are still a few years away from this happening in the majority of school systems because of the cost and the logistics of wireless connection. It is a crucial time to begin looking at what is truly driving change in the 21st century classroom: the students.

The Digital Child Arrives at School

Anyone over 45 years old remembers the time before cable television and computers. Anyone over 35 years old remembers the time before digital video games and the Internet. Anyone younger than 25 years old has lived in the world of digital electronic images her entire life. Let's examine the students in our public schools today at age 18 and younger. They have experienced the time when video gaming, television, and the Internet have reached new heights of popularity.

In his 1995 book *Being Digital*, Nicholas Negroponte of the MIT Media Lab claims that

> the growth of video gaming is just another indication of the way computers are increasingly transforming so many aspects of human communication. We are not waiting on any invention. It is here. It is now. It is almost genetic in its nature, in that each generation will become more digital than the preceding one. (p. 231)

Negroponte's profound writing in 1995 was the platform for his now famous "One Laptop per Child" project, which is bringing inexpensive laptops to disadvantaged students around the globe.

Today's students have the frontal lobe of their brains stimulated by video games, television, cellular devices, and instantaneous Web-based communication for many hours each day. One of the common causes of boredom in the classroom is students' perception that the methods of how the curriculum is delivered to them are irrelevant to how they learn. "There is a perception that class assignments or tasks are irrelevant. Why work hard when what you're working on doesn't seem to matter?" (Jensen, 2005, p. 103). The teachers in today's classrooms face the challenge of making standardized curriculum rich and relevant to students who have instant access to anything that they want to learn on their own.

It is time, right now, for us to develop strategies that connect with students in the 21st century classroom. Understanding the concept of the digital native and the digital immigrant as developed by Marc Prensky (2005/2006) will help us understand the modern student's engagement with technology:

> I've coined the term *digital native* to refer to today's students.... They are native speakers of technology, fluent in the digital language of computers, video games, and the Internet. I refer to those of us who were not born into the digital world as *digital immigrants*. We have adopted many aspects of the technology, but just like those who learn another language later in life, we retain an "accent" because we still have one foot in the past. We will read a manual, for example, to understand a program before we think to let the program teach itself. Our accent from the predigital world often makes it difficult for us to effectively communicate with our students. (p. 9)

Engaging students with tools that they use outside of the classroom every day will help teachers make strong connections.

Tools for the Interactive Classroom

Teachers do not have time to adapt to hardware and software that require high learning curves. The hardware tools discussed in this section are designed for ease of use by the teacher. Most Web 2.0 software applications are free, Web-based, and easy to use.

Bringing the Computer to the Big Screen

The visual backbone of the 21st century classroom is the computer projector, also referred to as a data projector or LCD projector. This tool connects to a central computer in the classroom and displays the image on the computer screen to a large screen or interactive whiteboard. The traditional overhead projector screen was 4 feet by 4 feet. The computer projector can produce an image up to 8 feet by 8 feet. The larger image is much more stimulating to the eye and benefits all students, especially those with visual impairments, because it makes the screen more visible. The projector makes a classroom with only one computer much more interactive.

The cost of LCD projectors is decreasing, much like the cost of high-definition televisions. Mounting the projector opens up additional space at the center of the classroom. As a replacement for the television and VCR combination, many states are using on-demand educational video services. These services give teachers and students access to thousands of media clips and images that are correlated to state standards. The streamed video makes the VHS tape obsolete because teachers add the electronically digitized media clips to presentation delivery systems such as PowerPoint.

An instructional tool that complements the computer and LCD projector is the wireless mouse and keyboard, which give teachers mobility in their classrooms. Being stuck behind the computer can make it difficult to manage a classroom full of students. The presentation mouse allows teachers to move around the classroom and interact with students while controlling the computer simultaneously. The wireless mouse and keyboard also enable the teacher to give a student or a group of students control of the computer to present to the class.

Interactive Software

Another popular wireless presentation tool is the wireless tablet. Students are more responsive to the digital writing software than to the traditional marker pen used with an overhead projector.

Interactive whiteboards, which are large electronic touch screens, are increasing in popularity and make the computer directly interactive for the students. Primary-grade students who are still developing their writing skills benefit from being able to touch the whiteboard to operate the functions of the computer. A drawback to the interactive whiteboard in secondary classrooms is its limited screen size, making it difficult for students in a large class to view the screen.

A relatively new hardware tool for the 21st century classroom is the student-response system, in which each student has a remote control device that can be used to respond to questions that the teacher programs into the system. The screen displays the students' individual answers and gives the teacher immediate feedback on the class's response to the question. The software grades each student automatically, and the results can be quickly transferred to the teacher's grade book. Teachers and students enjoy the power of the remote response system because they know that everyone must participate and no one can meekly hide during the activity. The use of this type of tool creates connections with students and raises the level of engagement in the classroom.

Using Images to Stimulate Creative Writing

Since 2004, I have trained teachers at all grade levels and in various content areas in the power of digital photography in the classroom. A picture really can say a thousand words and stimulate the writing of more than a thousand words. The synthesis of traditional storytelling activities and digital image production stimulates students to be more creative in the telling of their stories. Susan Kraft stated that

> Digital storytelling has become one of my students' favorite technological activities. Not only does it allow me to integrate the curriculum in a nurturing environment where students' unique learning styles are recognized and validated, it also allows students to think and express themselves in an environment free of fear and negative consequences because there are no wrong answers. (Kraft, 2006, p. 45)

Combining images into slide shows or simple movies that can be presented using Microsoft PowerPoint, Photo Story 3, and Movie Maker, or Apple's iPhoto and iMovie, gives students the opportunity to link their writing skills and technology skills. This process makes the assignment more of a project and takes away the stigma of its being just another boring writing task. Jason Ohler reports

> As digital storytelling enters the academic mainstream, the technique shows great promise. Creating a digital story taps skills and talents in art, media production, storytelling, and project development that might otherwise lie dormant within many students but that will serve them well in school, at work, and expressing themselves personally. (Ohler, 2006, p. 47)

The creation of a digital storyboard for a novel that is required reading for middle school students allows them to discover the literary value of the story in a visual context.

Web 2.0 Tools for Collaborative Learning

The concept of the new Internet, or Web 2.0, has changed the Internet from an information source to a platform for collaborative learning and information sharing. Blogs, wikis, document-sharing Web sites, podcasting, and message boards are all forms of Web-based communication tools that students use to socialize and interact outside school. These tools have the potential to organize thematic messages that students use to create journals and to upload pictures and videos.

Teachers can also use a Web-based communication tool to stimulate a strand of thought with an essential question such as this: "How did Rosa Parks's refusal to move to the back of the city bus in Montgomery, Alabama, affect today's society in the United States?" This kind of open-ended, provocative question can stimulate high-quality literary discussion through a Web-based communication tool that students can access 24 hours a day. As the strands of online discussion develop, the teacher can stimulate classroom discussion based on the responses expressed in the Web-based communication tool outside of class. The students will connect with this form of communication in a much more positive way than they would with the traditional homework assignment that would ask them to research Rosa Parks and report back to the class. Using Web-based communication tools also gives teachers the ability to provide feedback at any time on the quality of the writing.

Web-Based Tools to Stimulate Writing

Every school district in the United States has some form of initiative that focuses on literacy. Web-based communication tools provide a modern delivery system that students can easily connect with. Tools such as Blogger, Wikispaces, EduBlog, and Google Docs all offer free platforms with various levels of security for the teacher to facilitate discussions that stay on task and prevent student abuse of the tool. As author and educator Will Richardson (2005/2006) notes:

Tens of millions of bloggers around the world, many of them high school students, regularly add their ideas and perspectives to the massive body of information that is the Web. Although many students treat blogs as simple online diaries, some students and teachers use them as vehicles to draw out critical thinking. Teachers are using Web-based communication tools to build classroom resource portals and to foster online learning communities. Students create online, reflective, interactive portfolios of their work to share with worldwide audiences. (p. 24)

The Web-based communication tool is an excellent platform for connecting students because it uses methods that many students already use for social communication.

Social Network–Style Demonstrations of Learning

The popularity of social communication online venues such as MySpace and Facebook has enticed large numbers of teenagers to build their own social portfolios on the Web as a way to interact with their peers. A MySpace marketing slogan is "A Place for Friends to Meet." Since launching on the Web in 2004, MySpace has attracted more than 100 million users, the majority of whom are teenagers. Without even realizing it, teenagers are creating portfolios about themselves with the opportunity to be quite creative. Just like any other open and free form of communication, there is some inappropriate activity on sites like MySpace and Facebook, but the vast majority of young people who use these sites do so for normal social communication and expression.

If more than 100 million young people are using a personal portfolio platform for social expression, why not ask teachers to bring that portfolio to the classroom and give students the power to use electronic portfolios as a form of assessment? More colleges and universities are asking for an electronic portfolio of student work as part of the admission process. It is an excellent means to evaluate student work and abilities. The task of building the portfolio reaches across the curriculum because it demands the literacy skills required for high-quality writing and the creative artistic skills needed for layout and display of images. The literacy and the artistic abilities must be integrated with the technology skills to organize electronic files and decide how the actual portfolio will be delivered to the Internet.

Commenting on the role of Web-based portfolios, DiMarco (2005) states the following:

> Global networked information systems such as the World Wide Web are changing nearly every aspect of our lives. These technologies should be prominent within our curriculum. Often, they are not. Web-based portfolios offer a meaningful way for technology students to gain a thorough understanding of these critical new technologies beyond mere Web research. Web-based portfolios provide benefits that can never be realized with conventional portfolios. (p. 3)

The Web-based electronic portfolio can also be a valuable alternative assessment tool for teachers and students in the 21st century classroom.

Script Writing and the MP3 Player

One of the most popular technological innovations is the MP3 player. It is a simple audio file storage chip that plays music and audio clips in the MP3 format. The MP3 player has revolutionized the music industry and even started a firestorm of illegal copying and transferring of electronic music files. Apple's development of the iPod MP3 player targets young people and makes the image of a person using an iPod very chic in American culture; iPods and other brands of MP3 players are everywhere in schools, on university campuses, and in airports as a sign of a person's technological status.

The first MP3 players played only music. In 2004, programmers for Apple's iTunes developed a technology called podcasting. This allows any digitally recorded sound file to be formatted into an MP3 file and published to a Web server that makes the file available to anyone who has an Internet connection. The podcast can be streamed live from the Internet, downloaded, or set to be received automatically on a computer via a subscription.

It did not take long for technology-savvy teachers to harness the power of the podcast and the MP3 player that most students already had in their book bags. With a simple, inexpensive microphone connected to the computer and free downloaded digital recording software, teachers and students can publish their own podcasts. Teachers can record lessons, materials to review for tests, class assignment information, and reflections on class activities and post them to a Web site or a commercial podcast delivery location such as iTunes. The students can transfer the teacher's audio files to their personal MP3 player for listening at their convenience. An even more powerful instructional tool is having the students create electronic audio files. "Students across the United States are podcasting audio tours of local museums and points of interest, weekly news programs about their classrooms, oral histories and interviews, and more" (Richardson, 2005/2006, p. 24). Teachers who allow students to create their own podcasts stimulate freedom of expression through a delivery technology that the students are already familiar with.

Another technology using podcasting is the video podcast (vodcast). Students' multimedia video projects can be used as a powerful form of alternative assessment. "New and easier ways to publish multimedia screen captures and digital video on the Web create even more opportunities for sending multimedia creations to a potentially large audience" (Richardson, 2005/2006, p. 24).

Podcasting is still new to many teachers, but the number of MP3 players in students' book bags increases daily. The following are two examples of how audio and video podcasts might be used in the classroom.

Middle school science. Students are asked to visualize ahead to the year 2022. They will be the first Americans to walk on the surface of the moon since Eugene Cernan and Harrison Schmitt in December 1972. NASA has asked the astronaut teams to hold a press conference from the moon. The students form teams and must create a script for a 60-second opening statement for the press conference, which will be broadcast and podcasted to every country on Earth. When the students have prepared the rough draft of the script, they can use any digital recording device (MP3 recorder or computer microphone) to rehearse the script and do a final presentation. The presentation could be in the form of an audio podcast or a more formal presentation using a video recorder to make a vodcast. This authentic assessment stimulates the writing process because the students are scripting a press conference that will be broadcast back to Earth.

Elementary art. Students have learned about French painter Henri Rousseau and used his artistic style to create their own paintings of jungle scenes. Upon completion of their work, students must write a postcard from the scene depicted in their painting and describe what life is like there. The students must read and record their postcard using a microphone and a computer. Then the teacher takes a picture of each student's work. Using a video editor such as Photo Story 3 or Windows Movie Maker, the teacher creates a video that displays the paintings and incorporates the audio recordings for each postcard. This project requires students to learn about a specific topic, paint a picture, write a script, and record their work. Students tend to put more effort into a project or an assignment when they know that their work and script will be displayed on the classroom's big screen in the form of a movie.

From the Printing Press to the Search Engine

I believe the early 21st century is the greatest time in history to be in a classroom because we are still in the infancy of an electronic information revolution. In its January 2000 millennium issue, *Time* magazine published an article rating the most important innovations in the history of mankind. The number one innovation was the portable printing press, invented around 1450. As part of the Renaissance in Europe in the middle 1400s, the printing press allowed for the rapid movement of ideas and gave more people access to information.

When we fast-forward to the present day and look at how fast students can access information, it is evident that we are living in a time of great change in education. The evolution of the search engine has changed how students gather information. Consider the following statement from the CEO of Google, Eric Schmidt:

> Search is so highly personal that searching is empowering for humans like nothing else; it is about self-empowerment; it is antithesis of being told or taught. It is empowering individuals to do what they think best

with the information they want. It is very different from anything else that preceded it. Radio was one-to-many. TV was one-to-many. The telephone was one-to-one. Search is the ultimate expression of the power of the individual; using a computer, looking at the world, and finding exactly what they want, everyone is different when it comes to that. (Friedman, 2005, p. 156)

Before the Internet and mass media, people who earned advanced degrees in the traditional education system were considered scholars. One could become highly knowledgeable in a particular field through years of study from books, lectures, and experimentation. Today, instant access to just about any fact, knowledge base, or piece of information created by any scholar can be accessed with one click of the mouse. Problem-solving methods are changing because we have instant access to information and an unprecedented ability to collaborate to solve problems. All the strategies and tools discussed in this chapter empower this generation of students in unprecedented ways.

It Isn't the Answer Anymore— It's the Question

Students in today's schools can access all the information they need to know, but they must learn how to ask the right questions. Roger C. Schank, a leading researcher in artificial intelligence, offers the following thoughts:

> Is intelligence an absolute? Does mankind get smarter as time goes by? It depends on what you mean by intelligence, of course. Certainly we are getting more knowledgeable. Or at least it seems that way. While the average child has access to a wealth of information, considerably more than was available to children fifty years ago, there are people who claim that our children are not as well educated as they were fifty years ago and that our schools have failed us. (Schank, 2002, p. 206)

At this point in the history of formal education, a change is occurring. Whereas before we gathered knowledge to become intelligent, now intelligence is measured by how well we apply knowledge to ask the right questions about how to solve the world's problems. Schank elaborates on this point:

> Is intelligence simply the ability to be informed of answers to your questions, or is it the ability to know what questions to ask? As answers become devalued, questions become more valued. We have lived for a very long time in an answer-based society. Signs of it are everywhere: in the television shows that people watch, such as *Jeopardy* and *Who Wants to Be a Millionaire?*; in the games that people play, such as Trivial Pursuit; and most of all in school, where answers are king. Increasingly, the chief concern of our schools is testing. School has become a regimen for learning answers rather than learning to inquire. New technologies will change all this. When the pocket calculator was introduced, people asked whether calculators might as well be used in math tests, since from now on such devices would always be available. As a result, math tests began to focus on more substantive issues than long division. (2002, p. 209)

Schank's key point here is that instructional technology tools can engage students and give more opportunity for deeper thinking. Teachers who train themselves to ask deeper-level essential questions will develop better problem-solving skills in their students.

What Now? What Next?

When educational historians study the early 21st century classroom, they will say that it was a time of great change and that change was driven by the technology skills that tech-savvy students brought to the classroom. All teachers want authentic learning connections with their students, and the tools discussed in this chapter give every teacher the opportunity to make those connections. As educators reflect on the various philosophies of education and how they relate to the 21st century student, they will realize that the children entering our schools are different than earlier generations. If veteran educators look at themselves as "digital immigrants" and understand that the young people today are "digital natives," they will be equipped to launch the process of change in the classroom.

13

IT TAKES SOME GETTING USED TO:

Rethinking Curriculum for the 21st Century

··

Arthur L. Costa and Bena Kallick

Bena bought a new car. It has some gadgets that her old one didn't have. To put it in "park," for example, she has to press a button on top of the gear lever. That's not like the procedure she used in the old car, where she advanced the gearshift to the "P" in the farthest forward position. "I can do it, but it takes some getting used to," she sighs.

Marie has an interactive whiteboard in her 4th grade classroom. She always projects her PowerPoint presentations to students with an LCD projector. Now she can get on the Internet as well as make her Power-Point presentations. "But," she says, "it takes some getting used to."

Tom, an experienced high school science teacher, knows that he must break the apathy of his students by providing more hands-on, high-tech kinds of problems to solve. However, he has been successfully teaching his students using the more typical lab experiences for the past 15 years. It is only in the past five years that he has realized that the content of the curriculum is not all that is important. He must also engage his students with processes of thinking and problem solving. "I really have to rethink everything that I have been doing in light of new technologies and a more diverse student population," he says as he maps revisions to his curriculum for the fourth time in four years. "It takes some getting used to."

Jose is sitting in the class drumming his fingers, waiting for the time when he can get on the Internet. His teacher has been talking for a long time, and he is ready for some action. He wants to do some research on the periodic table. He is intrigued by how someone actually identified the elements. He found a really good Web site that provides this history, and he cannot wait to get back to it. Natasha is developing a documentary film that will show how the civil rights movement served as a stepping-stone for the candidacy of Barack Obama. She has been working on her home computer to edit the film and cannot wait for the school day to end so that she can get back to her homework project.

Our students are *in* the 21st century, and they are waiting for the teachers and the curriculum to catch up.

Shifting Our Mental Models

Changing our mental models about what we teach, how we teach it, and how we assess students' learning growth will take some getting used to. Such changes require open-mindedness, flexibility, patience, and courage. Changing curriculum is about changing your mind first and then forming some new habits and routines as you abandon old ones. As educators, we are all really futurists because we are trying to prepare students for the present and, at the same time, for a future that does not yet exist. We need a shared vision of the skills and dispositions that students will need to be successful regardless of the content.

Educators are realizing that the new vision for educating students is more concerned with survival skills needed for our children's future, for the perpetuation of our democratic society, and even for our planetary existence. In its Framework for 21st Century Learning, the Partnership for 21st Century Skills (n.d.) lists the following "Learning and Innovation Skills":

- Creativity and Innovation
- Critical Thinking and Problem Solving
- Communication and Collaboration

Tony Wagner (2008) talks about "rigor redefined" and suggests that such skills as critical thinking, problem solving, collaboration and leadership, agility and adaptability, initiative and entrepreneurialism, effective oral and written communication, accessing and analyzing information, curiosity and imagination are necessary for learning in school, in the workplace, and in life.

This vision reflects a curriculum of *processes* that serve as leverage for learning any content. It is a curriculum that gives students practice engaging with complex problems, dilemmas, and conflicts whose resolutions are not immediately apparent. And what is most significant about these processes is that they are as significant for adults as they are for students. We refer to these processes as Habits of Mind—dispositions or attitudes that reflect the necessary skillful behaviors that students will need to practice as they become more thoughtful in their learning and in their lives.

We have identified 16 vital habits that are necessary for success in school, work, and life (Costa & Kallick, 2000, 2009). The 16 Habits of Mind are as follows:

1. Persisting: *Stick to it!* Persevering in a task through to completion; remaining focused.

2. Managing impulsivity: *Take your time!* Thinking before acting; remaining calm, thoughtful, and deliberative.

3. Listening with understanding and empathy: *Understand others!* Devoting mental energy to another person's thoughts and ideas; holding in abeyance one's own thoughts in order to perceive another's point of view and emotions.

4. Thinking flexibly: *Look at it another way!* Being able to change perspectives, generate alternatives, consider options.

5. **Thinking about your thinking (metacognition):** *Know your knowing!* Being aware of one's own thoughts, strategies, feelings, and actions and their effects on others.

6. **Striving for accuracy and precision:** *Check it again!* A desire for exactness, fidelity, craftsmanship, and truthfulness.

7. **Questioning and problem posing:** *How do you know?* Having a questioning attitude; knowing what data are needed and developing questioning strategies to generate information.

8. **Applying past knowledge to novel situations:** *Use what you learn!* Accessing prior knowledge; transferring knowledge beyond the situation in which it was learned.

9. **Thinking and communicating with clarity and precision:** *Be clear!* Striving for accurate communication in both written and oral form; avoiding overgeneralizations, distortions, and deletions.

10. **Gathering data through all senses:** *Use your natural pathways!* Gathering data through all the sensory pathways—gustatory, olfactory, tactile, kinesthetic, auditory, and visual.

11. **Creating, imagining, and innovating:** *Try a different way!* Generating new and novel ideas, fluency, originality.

12. **Responding with wonderment and awe:** *Have fun figuring it out!* Finding the world awesome and mysterious, and being intrigued with phenomena and beauty.

13. **Taking responsible risks:** *Venture out!* Being adventuresome; living on the edge of one's competence.

14. **Finding humor:** *Laugh a little!* Finding the whimsical, incongruous, and unexpected. Being able to laugh at oneself.

15. **Thinking interdependently:** *Work together!* Being able to work with and learn from others in reciprocal situations.

16. **Remaining open to continuous learning:** *Learn from experiences!* Having humility and pride when admitting we don't know; resisting complacency.

Mapping the Development
of the Habits of Mind

Although many authors and futurists are expressing the broad ideas behind 21st century skills, they do not use sufficient specificity to describe how to integrate them into the curriculum, instruction, and assessment. The Habits of Mind detail those behaviors, and although the habits are never fully mastered, learners must continually practice, modify, and refine them. They become an internal compass to guide one's actions, decisions, and thoughts.

Metacognition serves as a rich example of how to map the development of a habit. Occurring in the neocortex, metacognition, or thinking about thinking, is our ability to know what we know and what we don't know. It is our ability to plan a strategy for producing whatever information is needed, to be conscious of our own steps and strategies during the act of problem solving, and to reflect on and evaluate the productiveness of our own thinking.

When confronted with a problem to solve, we develop a plan of action, we keep that plan in mind over a period of time, and then we reflect on and evaluate the plan upon its implementation. Planning a strategy before embarking on a course of action helps us keep track of the steps in the sequence of planned behavior at the conscious awareness level for the duration of the activity. It facilitates making temporal and comparative judgments; assessing the readiness for more or different activities; and monitoring our interpretations, perceptions, decisions, and behaviors. An example would be what superior teachers do daily: developing a teaching strategy for a lesson, keeping that strategy in mind throughout the instruction, and then reflecting on the strategy to evaluate its effectiveness in producing the desired student outcomes, and modifying plans for future applications.

Effective thinkers plan for, reflect on, and evaluate the quality of their own thinking skills, strategies, and Habits of Mind. Metacognition means becoming increasingly aware of one's actions and the effects of those actions on others and on the environment; forming internal questions in the search for information and meaning; developing mental maps or plans of action; mentally rehearsing before a performance;

monitoring plans as they are employed (being conscious of the need for midcourse correction if the plan is not meeting expectations); reflecting on the completed plan for self-evaluation; and editing mental pictures for improved performance (Costa, 2001).

Students do not progress from "awareness of our thinking" to getting into the habit of effective thinking in one easy step. It takes practice, reflection, evaluation, and persistence. Teachers can help students become more metacognitive by inviting students to be aware of, reflect on, talk about, and evaluate their thinking. Learning to think about their thinking can be a powerful tool in shaping, improving, internalizing, and habituating their thinking.

This progression might be thought of as a reflective staircase. Each step represents progressive levels of metacognition that serve the purposes of facilitating the internalization of habits of mind and their self-directed use by effective thinkers. Although we are never perfect in all situations in which the habits are called for, the staircase serves as a reminder of how to build the capacity for stepping back, reflecting on the situation and the habits of mind that were called for in that context. As a result of that conscious awareness, we learn, improve, and become more facile with the appropriate uses of the Habits of Mind.

Becoming Aware of Habits of Mind

The first step of this staircase involves being aware of the kind of thinking we are doing by recognizing, identifying, and labeling the habits of mind that we have been using to help us become a productive thinker. Classifying a specific thinking disposition requires a conceptual name and language that can be used to describe and define it. It helps to be clear about what the behavior is and what the behavior is *not*. For example, persisting is not giving up; striving for accuracy means not settling for mediocrity; managing impulsivity means not jumping to conclusions or acting too soon without scoping out the situation. As adults, most of us know the names of the thinking dispositions and understand their meanings, though we do not always practice the behaviors. Our students need to learn what the behaviors are by labeling them and identifying them when the student is using the behavior on behalf of more effective thinking ("you really *persisted* with that problem," or "I notice that you are *thinking flexibly* as you work on solving this problem"). By formally introducing the Habits of Mind terminology, using the labels repeatedly and explicitly, and by instructing students in the skills and strategies for using the habit, they will know how to persist, think flexibility, and listen with understanding. When we make the students conscious of these behaviors, we are leading them up the staircase to greater capacity for independence with the habits.

Employing Habits of Mind Strategically

Climbing up on the second step of the staircase involves not only knowing the label of the Habit of Mind we are using, but also understanding the strategy we are using. Students can describe how and why they are or have been using this habit. They can analyze the sequence of steps of the process they are using. Students can link and sequence this habit with others they intend to use. They can give reasons why they are using this Habit of Mind, what clues in the problem prompted them to use it, and what questions they might be trying to answer as a result.

Evaluating Effectiveness

On step three, the thinking shifts from descriptive and analytical thinking to evaluative thinking and critical thinking. Students must monitor the effectiveness of the strategy to determine if it is producing the effects they desire: "Is this a good and effective way to use this habit of mind?" They must apply a set of criteria to judge the effectiveness of our thinking strategy.

Applying Habits in Other Situations

On step four, the thinking becomes predictive. Students are sensitive to situations in which this habit of mind may be used again. Students predict the consequences of such thinking and are aware of times when these habits are not appropriate. They plan how they will apply these strategies in the future, based on everything they have done so far.

Making a Commitment to Improve Use

At the top of the staircase, students take matters into their own hands by committing to a mindful way of thinking, one in which they are aware of when they have used the habits to their advantage and when they have not. In addition, they determine what they must focus on to become more effective in their thinking and communicating. They decide to deliberately follow the steps they think will work best in the future. They gather data as to the effectiveness of their use of Habits of Mind strategies, reflect on and evaluate the data, and modify their thinking accordingly. Students voluntarily set goals for themselves with the intention of using Habits of Mind strategies the next time the habits are called for. When students follow this thinking plan, they are taking charge of their own thinking and become more effective as a result.

Prompting the Climb up the Metacognitive Staircase

Keeping the staircase in mind, teachers can invite students to think at each level by posing invitational questions intended to elicit that level of thinking. Figure 13.1 (pp. 218–219) shows examples of how a teacher might prompt students to ascend the metacognitive staircase before, during, and after the thinking task is completed.

We can think about our own thinking in a variety of ways. The metacognitive staircase is a framework for a series of repeated experiences with metacognition that is aimed at helping students become more reflective and take charge of how they engage with Habits of Mind. Teaching students to think more critically, creatively, and skillfully should also include teaching them to think independently and spontaneously. Helping them to develop the habit of ascending this staircase will help them to achieve this bigger, even more important goal as they make their way through life.

Building a commitment to continuous improvement in the use of the Habits of Mind occurs when learners increasingly become self-directed.

Figure 13.1 | Up the Reflective Staircase:
Questions That Prompt the Climb

Step	Reflective Level	Questions Posed by the Teacher
5	Making a Commitment to Improve the Use of Habits of Mind	• Why is it important to you to _____? • What goals are you setting to become more mindful of your own Habits of Mind? • As you anticipate similar problems in the future, what insights about the habits might you carry forth about how to think through such problems?
4	Applying Habits of Mind in Other Situations	• How might you do this thinking next time? • As you anticipate similar problems in the future, what insights about the Habits of Mind might you carry forth about how to think through such problems? • What makes you think that strategy will work in this situation? • What has worked for you in the past that you might draw upon? • When in [this course/school/life/work] might this Habit of Mind strategy prove useful? • What situation cues will remind you to think this way?
3	Evaluating the Effectiveness of Using Habits of Mind	• How well did your strategy work? • How do you know your strategy is working? • What corrections and alterations in your strategy are you making? • What will you pay attention to while you are solving this problem to determine if your strategy is working? • What alternative strategies might you use if your strategy is not working? • Why do you think this is the best strategy? • What has worked for you in the past? • What makes you think that this strategy will work in this situation? • By what criteria will you judge that this is the best way to approach this problem?

Figure 13.1 | *Continued*

Step	Reflective Level	Questions Posed by the Teacher
2	Employing Habits of Mind More Strategically	*Going to use:* • What approaches will you use? • As you approach this problem, what other Habits of Mind will you use? *Are using:* • As you consider the steps in the skillful problem-solving process, where are you? • What patterns are you noticing in your approach to solving this problem? • What questions are you asking yourself? *Did use:* • As you reflect on your strategy for using the habit, what did it involve? • What led you to the decision to _____? • What questions were you asking yourself?
1	Becoming More Aware of Habits of Mind	• Describe the Habit of Mind you will be/are/were using. • How might that habit serve you as you are working on this problem? • What might it sound like or look like if you are using that habit? • What might you hear yourself saying about how this habit relates to this problem?

Self-improvement is recognized as learners become self-managing by setting goals for themselves, self-monitoring as they "observe themselves" in action, and more self-reflective as they evaluate themselves, modify their behaviors, and set new and increasingly higher standards for their own performance. Self-evaluation moves from being the quantitative recognition of the use of the Habits of Mind in themselves to being increasingly more descriptive and qualitative. For example, students recognize that it is not merely that they demonstrated flexibility in their thinking but also that they knew why use of that habit helped them to produce a better interaction with their peers and, ultimately, better work. They are able to describe the situations in which the habits are most powerfully used and when not. They recognize that thinking interdependently might not always be possible, and they know how to call on their own thinking with clarity and precision when necessary. Rather than merely saying "I used the habit," they are able to describe how and when they are using it to enhance their learning as well as the learning of others. They most likely have replaced some old habits with new ones.

The following are entries that two 10th grade students from Sir Francis Drake High School in Marin County, California, wrote in their journals as they reflected on their meanings, values, and commitment to improve their Habits of Mind.

> At first I was not a good group worker because I felt controlling and perfectionist. I had to step back and examine my thinking and adjust to be cooperative and open. I changed the way I thought about my role in the group process.

> Every time I finished a project, I was able to enter the next one with more knowledge of the group process. Also, with each project I became more technologically advanced, which helped me add value to the group.

And here is what two 4th grade students at Crow Island School in Winnetka, Illinois, wrote:

> *Persisting.* I have used my perseverance. When I was doing long division. It was very long and hard but I did it. I still want to improve for the future when I'm in high school.

> *Thinking and Communicating with Clarity and Precision.* I'm too shy sometimes and then I think all my work is poorly done. But my work is really not that poor like when I write. So I want to improve on my communication skills.

Although school staffs might lament the absence of these attributes in their students, it should be obvious that all of us—parents, teachers, and administrators—can continue on this journey toward internalization. What gives a curriculum "dignity" is that it is as good for the adults in the school as it is for students. Over time, as the vision embodied in the Habits of Mind becomes increasingly shared, the school takes on a culture in which the habits become the norms—"the way we do things around here." One student, one classroom, one school at a time, the world is becoming a more thought-full place.

Getting into the Habit

Our experiences with many schools and school districts both nationally and internationally indicate that the best way to develop these habits is through practice. It is not possible to learn the habits merely through rhetoric. Everyone in the school community—including parents, teachers, administrators, and support staff—needs to believe in the habits as being significant to student learning.

The ultimate goal is for students to become self-directed in their learning. They need to take responsibility for managing, monitoring, and modifying their behavior as they learn. We have organized the habits around those key concepts in our book *Assessment Strategies for Self-Directed Learning* (Costa & Kallick, 2004). To achieve this goal of self-directed learners, teachers need to find the appropriate places in the curriculum—integrating the habits into the curriculum so that the unit designs include not only authentic performances but also the habits that are required to make certain that the students learn how to struggle with the issues of uncertainty and ambiguity embedded in the designs.

For example, we know that students are required to do research in many of their classes. Research serves as the foundation for a high-quality project. When students use the Internet for information, are they striving for truth and accuracy? Are they in the habit of checking the sources to ascertain credibility of information? Are they flexible in their thinking? Do they realize that there is often more than one perspective on a particular issue and that they need to consider all perspectives? When they are choosing the best photos and text as a part of their project, are they making certain that they are communicating with clarity and precision? Given the overwhelming number of possible sources for any given project, students need to be in the habit of persisting. The first draft is not the last draft. They need to question and pose problems, to think interdependently, and to persist when the answers are not immediately apparent. In addition, teachers need to create a classroom that is open to continuous learning, making certain that there are many opportunities for coaching and formative assessment. It needs to be clear that taking responsible risks is valued and that discussions encourage students to think flexibly. Students need to have the opportunity to practice the habits or ... they don't become a habit!

Leading Schools with the Habits of Mind in Mind

For teachers to embrace the Habits of Mind and value them in their classroom instruction, the school administrators must also adopt the habits. This often implies a shift in the schedule of a school so that there is more time for students to work with greater depth. It may also require that teachers and administrators learn how to become better coaches for critical thinking. Administrators will need to demonstrate their willingness to remain open to continuous learning by readily accepting what they know and what they need to know. The teachers will respond with greater belief in the long-term sustainability of the habits when they observe and experience the administrators listening with understanding and empathy.

Furthermore, school board members need to adopt the habits not only for the students but also for themselves. They need to evidence questioning and problem posing, listening with understanding and empathy, thinking and communicating with clarity and precision. The students will behave only as well as the adult models who surround them. As one school board member said to another after a workshop that focused on using the habits as the basis for norms for decision making,

"If we can really adhere to listening to one another with understanding and empathy, we will serve as good models for the community and students, [showing] that we really mean to be open to being influenced."

Curriculum Mind Shifts

As we consider changing our curriculum so that it focuses on process as well as content, we need to attend to three major decisions: (1) what should be taught—*goals and outcomes*; (2) how to organize and teach toward those goals—*instruction*; and (3) how we might know if those goals are being achieved using these instructional strategies—*assessment*. Embracing the Habits of Mind as educational outcomes requires some curriculum mind shifts in thinking as we move from what we are presently doing toward a more 21st century form of education.

Mind shift #1: FROM knowing right answers TO knowing how to behave when answers are not readily apparent. As Abigail Adams noted, "The habits of a vigorous mind are formed in contending with difficulties." Schools tend to teach, assess, and reward convergent thinking and the acquisition of content with a limited range of acceptable answers. Life in the real world, however, demands multiple ways to do something well. A fundamental shift is required from valuing right answers as the purpose for learning, to knowing how to behave when we don't know answers—knowing what to do when confronted with those paradoxical, dichotomous, enigmatic, confusing, ambiguous, discrepant, and sometimes overwhelming situations that plague our lives. A mind shift is essential—from valuing knowledge *acquisition* as an outcome to valuing knowledge *production* as an outcome. We want students to learn how to develop a critical stance with their work: inquiring, thinking flexibly, and learning from another person's perspective. The critical attribute of intelligent human beings is not only having information, but also knowing how to act on it.

By definition, a problem is any stimulus, question, task, phenomenon, or discrepancy, the explanation for which is not immediately known. Thus we are interested in focusing on student performance under those challenging conditions that demand strategic reasoning, insightfulness, perseverance, creativity, and precision to resolve a complex problem.

As our paradigm shifts, we will need to let go of our obsession with acquiring content knowledge as an end in itself and make room for viewing content as a vehicle for developing broader, more pervasive, and complex goals such as those incorporated in the list of the Habits of Mind. These *are* the subject matters of instruction. Content, selectively abandoned and judiciously selected because of its fecund contributions to the practice of these Habits of Mind, becomes the vehicle to carry the processes of learning. The focus is on learning *from* the objectives instead of learning *of* the objectives.

Mind shift #2: FROM transmitting meaning TO constructing meaning. Meaning making is not a spectator sport. Knowledge is a constructive process rather than a finding. It is not the content that is stored in memory but the activity of constructing it that gets stored. Humans don't *get* ideas; they *make* ideas. German philosopher Martin Heidegger put it well when he said, "Learning is an engagement of the mind that changes the mind."

As scientists study the processes of learning, they are realizing that a constructivist model of learning reflects their best understanding of the brain's natural way of making sense of the world. Constructivism holds that learning is essentially active. A person learning something new brings to that experience all of her previous knowledge and present mental patterns. Each new fact or experience is assimilated into a living web of understanding that already exists in that person's mind. As a result, learning is neither passive nor simply objective (Abbott & Ryan, 2006).

Furthermore, meaning making is not just an individual operation. The individual interacts with others to construct shared knowledge. There is a cycle of internalization of what is socially constructed as shared meaning, which is then externalized to affect the learner's social participation. Constructivist learning, therefore, is viewed as a reciprocal process in that the individual influences the group, and the group influences the individual (Vygotsky, 1978).

Our perceptions of learning need to shift from educational outcomes that are primarily an individual's collections of subskills to include successful participation in socially organized activities and the development of students' identities as conscious, flexible, efficacious, and interdependent meaning makers. We must let go of having learners acquire *our* meanings and have faith in the processes of individuals' construction of their own and shared meanings through individual activity and social interaction. That's scary because the individual and the group may *not* construct the meaning we want them to: a real challenge to the basic educational framework with which most schools are comfortable.

Mind shift #3: FROM external evaluation TO self-assessment. We must ask ourselves, are we educating students for a life of tests or for the tests of life? Evaluation of learning has been viewed as summative measures of how much content a student has retained. It is useful for grading and segregating students into ability groups. It serves real estate agents in fixing home prices in relationship to published test scores from local schools.

Because process-oriented goals cannot be assessed using product-oriented measurement techniques, our existing evaluation paradigm must shift as well. Assessment should be neither summative nor punitive. Rather, assessment should be a mechanism for providing ongoing feedback to the learner and to the organization as a necessary part of the spiraling processes of continuous renewal: self-managing, self-monitoring, and self-modifying. We must constantly remind ourselves that the ultimate purpose of evaluation is to have students learn to become self-evaluative. If students graduate from our schools still dependent upon others to tell them when they are adequate, good, or excellent, then we've missed the whole point of what self-directed learning is about.

Evaluation, the highest level of Bloom's taxonomy (Bloom & Krathwohl, 1956), means generating, holding in your head, and applying a set of internal and external criteria. For too long, adults alone have been practicing that skill. We need to shift that responsibility to students—to help them develop the capacity for self-analysis, self-referencing, and self-modification. We should make student self-evaluation as significant an influence as external evaluations (Costa & Kallick, 1995).

In Summary

If we accept that we need to prepare students for a vastly different future than we have known, then our understanding of the focus of education also needs to shift. This change will require a curriculum that provides individuals with the dispositions necessary to engage in lifelong learning. Simultaneously, our vision of the teacher's role needs to shift from that of the information provider to one of a catalyst, model, coach, innovator, researcher, and collaborator with the learner throughout the learning process. Furthermore, the notion of assessment needs to shift toward having students learn to value feedback, to gather data about their own performance, and to become self-modifying in a journey of continuous learning.

Mind shifts do not come easily, as they require letting go of old habits, old beliefs, and old traditions. There is a necessary disruption when we shift mental models. If there is not, we are probably not shifting. Growth and change are found in disequilibrium, not balance. It takes some getting used to.

REFERENCES
AND RESOURCES

....

Abbott, J., & Ryan, T. (2006). *The unfinished revolution: Learning, human behavior, community, and political paradox.* Alexandria, VA: ASCD.

AFS Intercultural Programs. (2008). *AFS long-term impact study.* Available: www. afs.org

Asia Society. (2008). *Going global: Preparing our students for an interconnected world.* New York: Author.

Asia Society. (2009a). *Expanding horizons: Building global literacy in afterschool programs.* New York: Author.

Asia Society. (2009b). *Putting the world into world-class education: A national imperative and a state and local responsibility.* New York: Author.

Asia Society and College Board. (2008). *Chinese in 2008: An expanding field.* New York: Author.

Benyus, J. (1997). *Biomimicry: Innovation inspired by nature.* New York: Morrow.

Berger, J. (2008, March 9). A science prodigy in an unlikely place. *New York Times.* Available: www.nytimes.com/2008/03/09/nyregion/nyregionspecial2/09Rintel.html

Bloom, B., & Krathwohl, D. R. (1956). *Taxonomy of educational objectives. Handbook I. Cognitive domain.* New York: David McKay.

Bowser, J. (n.d.). *Strategic co-opetition: The value of relationships in the networked economy.* Available: www-935.ibm.com/services/uk/index.wss/multipage/igs/ibvstudy/a1008082?cntxt=a1006870

Boyd, D. M., & Ellison, N. B. (2007). Social network sites: Definition, history, and scholarship. *Journal of Computer-Mediated Communication, 13*(1). Available: http://jcmc.indiana.edu/vol13/issue1/boyd.ellison.html

Burke, J. (2003). *The English teacher's companion: A complete guide to classroom, curriculum, and the profession.* Portsmouth, NH: Heinemann.

Carpenter, E. S., & McLuhan, M. (1960). *Explorations in communication: An anthology.* Boston: Beacon Press.

Central Intelligence Agency. (2008). *The 2008 world factbook.* Washington, DC: Author. Available: www.cia.gov/library/publications/the-world-factbook/

Christel, M. T., & Sullivan, S. (2007). *Lesson plans for creating media-rich classrooms.* Urbana, IL: National Council of Teachers of English.

Cody, E. (2006, February 15). The NBA has become a leading export to China. *Washington Post,* p. E-1. Available: www.washingtonpost.com/wp-dyn/content/article/2006/02/14/AR2006021401827.html

Committee for Economic Development. (2006). *Education for global leadership: The importance of international studies and foreign language education for U.S. economic and national security.* Washington, DC: Author.

Committee to Review the Title VI and Fulbright-Hays International Education Programs. (2007). *International education and foreign languages: Keys to securing America's future.* Washington, DC: National Academies Press.

Conley, D. T. (2005). *College knowledge: What it really takes for students to succeed and what we can do to get them ready.* San Francisco: Jossey-Bass.

Considine, D. (2002, March). National developments and international origins (Media Literacy). *Journal of Popular Film and Television, 30*(1), 5.

Costa, A. (2001). Mediating the metacognitive. In A. Costa (Ed.), *Developing minds: A resource book for teaching thinking* (pp. 408–412). Alexandria, VA: ASCD.

Costa, A., & Kallick, B. (1995). *Assessment in the learning organization.* Alexandria, VA: ASCD.

Costa, A., & Kallick, B. (2000). *Habits of mind: A developmental series.* Book I: *Discovering and exploring habits of mind.* Book II: *Activating and engaging habits of mind.* Book III: *Assessing and reporting on habits of mind.* Book IV: *Integrating and sustaining habits of mind.* Alexandria, VA: ASCD.

Costa, A., & Kallick, B. (2004). *Assessment strategies for self-directed learning.* Thousand Oaks, CA: Corwin.

Costa, A., & Kallick, B. (2009). *Learning and leading with habits of mind: Sixteen dispositions of success.* Alexandria, VA: ASCD.

Council of Chief State School Officers. (2008). *Putting the world into world-class education: State innovations and opportunities* Washington, DC: Author.

Curriculum Standing Committee of National Education Professional Associations (CSCNEPA). (2007). Developing a twenty-first century school

curriculum for all Australian students [Working paper]. Available: www.acsa.
edu.au/pages/images/CSCNEPA_paper_June087.pdf

Daggett, W. (2005). *Achieving academic excellence through rigor and relevance* [White paper]. Rexford, NY: International Center for Leadership in Education.

Daly, J. (2004, September). Life on the screen: Visual literacy in education. *Edutopia*. Available: www.edutopia.org/life-screen

Darling-Hammond, L., Ancess, J., & Falk, B. (1995). *Authentic assessment in action: Studies of schools and students at work*. New York: Teachers College Press.

Dernbach, J. C. (Ed.). (2002). *Stumbling toward sustainability*. Washington, DC: Environmental Law Institute.

Dernbach, J. C. (Ed.). (2009). *Agenda for a sustainable America*. Washington, DC: Environmental Law Institute.

DiMarco, J. (2005). *Web portfolio design and application*. Hershey, PA: Idea Group.

Dubner, S. J. (2007, December 27). Is the U.S. graduation rate worse than we thought? [Blog entry]. Available: http://freakonomics.blogs.nytimes.com/2007/12/27/is-the-us-high-school-graduation-rate-worse-than-we-thought/

Dyson, F. (2005, March). The Darwinian interlude. *Technology Review*. Available: www.technologyreview.com/read_article.aspx?ch=specialsections&sc=stemcell&id=16368

Edelman, G. M. (2006). *Second nature: Brain science and human knowledge*. New Haven, CT: Yale University Press.

Ericksen, L. (2002). *Concept-based curriculum: Teaching beyond the facts*. Thousand Oaks, CA: Corwin.

Exemplars. (2008). *NCTM standard rubric*. Retrieved August 1, 2008, from www.exemplars.com/media/pdf/rubrics/nctm.pdf

Fanton, J. (2007, June 19). New generations, new media challenges. *St. Louis Dispatch*. Accessed at www.macfound.org/site/apps/nlnet/content2.aspx?c=lkLXJ8MQKrH&b=1137397&ct=3970699

Federico, C. M., Cloud, J. P., Byrne, J., & Wheeler, K. (2002). Education for sustainability: Kindergarten through 12th grade. In J. C. Dernbach (Ed.), *Stumbling toward sustainability* (pp. 607–624). Washington, DC: Environmental Law Institute. Available: www.sustainabilityed.org/what/education_for_sustainability/documents/K12Chapter.PDF

Feldman, D. (1999, Fall). National policy, local interpretation: The American rural curriculum, 1897–1921. *Rural Educator, 21*(1), 8–14.

Fernandez-Armesto, F. (2003). *Ideas that changed the world*. London: DK.

Friedman, T. L. (2005). *The world is flat: A brief history of the twenty-first century*. New York: Farrar, Straus, & Giroux.

Gardner, H. (2007). *Five minds for the future*. Boston: Harvard Business School Press.

Gardner, M. (1999, November 24). Body by Madison Avenue. *Christian Science Monitor*. Available: www.csmonitor.com/1999/1124/p18s1.html

Goodlad, J. (2004). *A place called school.* New York: McGraw-Hill.

Greene, J. P. (2002). *High school graduation rates in the United States.* New York: Manhattan Institute for Policy Research.

Greene, M. (1989). Art worlds in schools. In P. Abbs (Ed.), *The symbolic order.* London: Falmer.

Grunwald Associates. (2006, November). CIC survey shows media literacy a vital and underserved need in schools. *Cable in the Classroom.* Available: http://i.ciconline.org/docs/CICmedialitreport11-2006.pdf

Haythornthwaite, C. (2005). Social networks and Internet connectivity effects. *Information, Communication & Society, 8*(2), 125–147. Available: www2.scedu. unibo.it/roversi/SocioNet/114601.pdf

Hobbs, R. (1998). Literacy in the information age. In J. Flood, D. Lapp, & S. B. Heath (Eds.), *Handbook of research on teaching literacy through the communicative and visual arts* (pp. 7–14). New York: Macmillan.

Hyerle, D. (2008). *Visual tools for transforming information into knowledge.* Thousand Oaks, CA: Corwin.

Jackson, A. (2008, May). High schools in the global age. *Educational Leadership, 65*(8), 58–62.

Jacobs, H. H. (1989). *Interdisciplinary curriculum: Design and implementation.* Alexandria, VA: ASCD.

Jacobs, H. H. (1997). *Mapping the big picture: Integrating curriculum and assessment K–12.* Alexandria, VA: ASCD.

Jacobs, H. H. (2004). *Getting results with curriculum mapping.* Alexandria, VA: ASCD.

Jacobs, H. H. (2006). *Active literacy across the curriculum: Strategies for reading, writing, speaking, and listening.* Larchmont, NY: Eye on Education.

Jacobs H. H., & Johnson, A. W. (2009). *The curriculum mapping planner: Templates, tools and resources.* Alexandria, VA: ASCD.

Jacoby, S. (2008). *The age of American unreason.* New York: Pantheon Books.

Jenkins, H. (2006a). *Confronting the challenges of participatory culture: Media education for the 21st century* [Occasional paper]. Chicago: MacArthur Foundation.

Jenkins, H. (2006b). *Convergence culture: Where old and new media collide.* New York: New York University Press.

Jensen, E. (2005). *Teaching with the brain in mind* (2nd ed.). Alexandria, VA: ASCD.

Johnson, E. (2008). *Brain-based learning: How does what we know about the brain inform us about student learning?* [Keynote address]. Creative Learning Exchange conference.

Johnson-Towles, L., & Shessler, T. (2005, March). Media matters: The critical role of library media specialists in making media literacy happen in your school. *Access Learning,* 10–11.

Just Think Foundation. (2007, December 4). *Groundbreaking study proves quantifiable benefits of media literacy education*. [Press release]. Available: www.reuters.com/article/pressRelease/idUS203276+04-Dec-2007+PRN20071204

Kaiser Family Foundation. (2003, Fall). *Key facts: Media literacy* [Publication #3383]. Available: www.kff.org/entmedia/upload/Key-Facts-Media-Literacy.pdf

Kaiser Family Foundation. (2006, May 24). *New study shows how kids' media use helps parents cope*. Available: www.kff.org/entmedia/entmedia052406nr.cfm

Kallick, B., & Colosimo, J. (2009). *Using curriculum mapping and assessment data to improve learning*. Thousand Oaks, CA: Corwin.

Kamana, K., & Wilson, W. H. (1996). Hawaiian language programs. In G. Cantoni (Ed.), *Stabilizing indigenous languages*. Flagstaff, AZ: Center for Excellence in Education, Northern Arizona University.

Koppel, L. (2005, January 27). New York students dominate Intel science contest. Again. *New York Times*. Available: www.nytimes.com/2005/01/27/nyregion/27intel.html

Kraft, S. (2006, February). Digital storytelling. *Learning and leading with technology, 33*(5), 45–46.

Kubey, R., & Baker, F. (1999, October 27). Has media literacy found a curricular foothold? *Education Week, 19*(9)56.

Lappe, F. M. (with Joseph Collins). (1977). *Food first: Beyond the myth of scarcity*. New York: Houghton Mifflin.

Lappe, F. M. (1991). *Diet for a small planet*. New York: Ballantine Books.

Link, M. (2008, May 19). Introducing McCainpedia. In *Kicking ass: The Democratic party's blog*. Available: www.democrats.org/a/2008/05/introducing_mcc.php

Littky, D., & Grabelle, S. (2004). *The big picture: Education is everyone's business*. Alexandria, VA: ASCD.

Longview Foundation. (2008). *Report on internationalizing teacher preparation*. Silver Spring, MD: Author.

Martin-Kniep, G. O. (2008). *Communities that learn, lead, and last: Building and sustaining educational expertise*. San Francisco: Jossey-Bass.

Mathews, J. (2009, January 5). The latest doomed pedagogical fad: 21st-century skills. *Washington Post*, p. B2. Available: www.washingtonpost.com/wp-dyn/content/article/2009/01/04/AR2009010401532.html

Mertz, J. E., Andreescu, T., Gallian, J. A., & Kane, J. M. (2008). Cross-cultural analysis of students with exceptional talent in mathematical problem solving. *Notices of the AMS, 55*(10), 1248–1260.

Miller, M. (2005, April 1). A history of home video game consoles. *InformIT*. Available: www.informit.com/articles/article.aspx?p=378141

Ministry of Education. (2007). *The New Zealand curriculum*. Wellington, NZ: Author.

Nair, P. (2009, April 6). Don't just rebuild schools—reinvent them. *Education Week.* Available: www.edweek.org

National Center for Education Statistics, U.S. Department of Education. (2007, June). *Mapping 2005 state proficiency standards onto NAEP scales.* Author.

National Education Association. (1893). *Report of the Committee on Secondary School Studies* [commonly known as *The Committee of Ten report*]. Washington, DC: Government Printing Office

NCTE Passes Visual Literacy Resolution. (1997, Spring). *Kairos: A Journal for Teachers of Writing in Webbed Environments, 2*(1). Available: http://english.ttu.edu/Kairos/2.1/news/briefs/nctevis.html

Negroponte, N. (1995). *Being digital.* New York: Knopf.

Niguidula, D. (1993). *The digital portfolio: A richer picture of student performance* (Studies on Exhibitions, No. 13). Providence, RI: Coalition of Essential Schools.

Niguidula, D. (1997, November). Picturing performance with digital portfolios. *Educational Leadership, 55*(3), 26–29.

Niguidula, D. (2005, November). Documenting learning with digital portfolios. *Educational Leadership, 63*(3), 44–47.

Ohler, J. (2006). The world of digital storytelling. *Educational Leadership, 63*(4), 44–47.

Ontario Ministry of Education. (1989). *Media literacy resource guide: Intermediate and senior divisions.* Toronto: Queen's Printer for Ontario.

Oppenheimer, T. (2003). *Flickering mind: The false promise of technology in the classroom and how learning can be saved.* Westminster, MD: Random House.

O'Reilly, T. (2005, September 30). *What is Web 2.0: Design patterns and business models for the next generation of software.* Available: www.oreillynet.com/pub/a/oreilly/tim/news/2005/09/30/what-is-web-20.html

Organisation for Economic Co-operation and Development (OECD). (2008). *Education at a glance: OECD indicators.* Paris: Author.

Partnership for 21st Century Skills. (n.d.). *Framework for 21st century learning.* Tucson, AZ: Author. Available: www.21stcenturyskills.org/index.php?option=com_content&task=view&id=254&Itemid=120

Partnership for 21st Century Skills. (n.d.). *Media literacy* [Web page]. Available: www.21stcenturyskills.org/index.php?option=com_content&task=view&id=349&Itemid=120

Perez, J. C. (2008, July 25). Google counts more than 1 trillion unique Web URLs. *PC World.* Available: www.pcworld.com/businesscenter/article/148964/google_counts_more_than_1_trillion_unique_web_urls.html

Pink, D. H. (2006). *A whole new mind: Why right-brainers will rule the world.* New York: Riverhead Books.

Prensky, M. (2005, December/2006, January). Listen to the natives. *Educational Leadership, 63*(4), 9.

PRWeb. (2008, April 8). Students want the 21st century classroom, but schools not meeting student expectations, according to latest national study [Press release]. Available: www.prweb.com/releases/2008/04/prweb840274.htm

Pufahl, I., Rhodes, N. C., & Christian, N. (2001). *What we can learn from foreign language teaching in other countries.* Washington, DC: Center for Applied Linguistics.

Richardson, W. (2005, December/2006, January). The educator's guide to the read/write web. *Educational Leadership, 63*(4), 24.

Rimer, S. (2008, October 10). Math skills suffer in U.S., study finds. *New York Times.* Available: www.nytimes.com/2008/10/10/education/10math.html

Rose, L., & Gallup, A. M. (2007, September). The 39th annual Phi Delta Kappa/ Gallup poll of the public's attitudes toward the public schools. *Phi Delta Kappan, 89*(1), 33–48.

Saulny, S. (2005, January 19). State to state: Varied ideas about "proficient." *New York Times.*

Schank, R. C. (2002). Are we going to get smarter? In J. Brockman (Ed.), *The next fifty years: Science in the first half of the twenty-first century* (pp. 206–215). New York: Vintage Books.

Schlechty, P. C. (2002). *Working on the work: An action plan for teachers, principals, and superintendents.* San Francisco: Jossey-Bass.

Schleicher, A., & Stewart, V. (2008, October). Learning from world-class schools. *Educational Leadership, 66*(2), 44–51.

Schwarz, G. (2001, Spring). Literacy expanded: The role of media literacy in teacher education. *Teacher Education Quarterly, 28*(2), 111–119. Available: http://findarticles.com/p/articles/mi_qa3960/is_200104/ai_n8950119/pg_1

Senge, P. (1990). *The fifth discipline: The art and practice of the learning organization.* New York: Doubleday.

Senge, P. (2000). *Schools that learn: A fifth discipline fieldbook for educators, parents, and everyone who cares about education.* New York: Doubleday.

Shirky, C. (2008). *Here comes everybody: How digital networks transform our ability to gather and cooperate.* New York: Penguin Press.

Snyder, J. (1993). *Flattening the earth: Two thousand years of map projections.* Chicago: University of Chicago Press.

Stiggins, R. (2005, December). From formative assessment to assessment FOR learning: A path to success in standards-based schools. *Phi Delta Kappan, 87*(4), 324–328.

Surowiecki, J. (2004). *The wisdom of crowds: Why the many are smarter than the few and how collective wisdom shapes business, societies, economies, and nations.* New York: Doubleday.

Swaim, S. (2002, Fall). Media literacy in middle school: An important curriculum component. *Telemedium: The Journal of Media Literacy, 48*(2). Available: www.medialit.org/reading_room/article562.html

Tapscott D., & Williams, A. D. (2008). *Wikinomics: How mass collaboration changes everything*. New York: Portfolio.

Thoman, E. (n.d.). *Skills and strategies for media education*. Malibu, CA: Center for Media Literacy.

Totty, M. (2006, June 19). Business solutions: How to decide? Create a market. *Wall Street Journal*. Available: http://online.wsj.com/article/SB115073365085184192.html

U.S. Census Bureau. (2004a). Table 2. In *Exports from manufacturing establishments: 2001*. Washington, DC: U.S. Department of Commerce.

U.S. Census Bureau. (2004b). Population projections. Available: http://www.census.gov.

U.S. Census Bureau. (2009, March 19). *Population* [Press release]. Washington, DC: U.S. Department of Commerce.

Vygotsky, L. (1978). *Mind in society*. Cambridge, MA: Harvard University Press.

Wackernagel, M. (2008). *Living planet report*. Accessed: www.footprintnetwork.org. Washington, DC: WWF.

Wagner, T. (2008). *The global achievement gap*. New York: Basic Books.

Wagner, T. (2008, October). Rigor redefined. *Educational Leadership*, 66(2), 20–25.

Weinberger, D. (2007). *Everything is miscellaneous: The power of the new digital disorder*. New York: Times Books.

Wheeler, K. A., & Bijur, A. P. (Eds.). (2000). *Education for a sustainable future: A paradigm of hope for the 21st century*. New York: Kluwer Adademic/Plenum.

Wiggins, G. (1998). *Educative assessment*. San Francisco: Jossey-Bass.

Wiggins, G., & McTighe, J. (2005). *Understanding by design*. Alexandria, VA: ASCD.

Wilson, W. T. (2005). *The dawn of the India country: Why India is poised to challenge China and the United States for global economic hegemony in the 21st century*. Chicago: Keystone India.

Woese, C. R. (2004, June). A new biology for a new century. *Microbiology and Molecular Biology Reviews*, 68(2), 1092–2172.

Zakaria, F. (2008). *The post-American world*. New York: W. W. Norton.

Resources

Web Sites

Center for Eco Literacy—www.ecoliteracy.org

Center for Food & Environment at Teachers College Columbia University, New York—www.tc.columbia.edu/LIFE/

Center for Media Literacy—www.medialit.org

Cloud Institute for Sustainability Education—www.cloudinstitute.org

Council of Chief State School Officers (CCSSO)—www.ccsso.org
Creative Learning Exchange—www.clexchange.org
Curriculum 21—www.curriculum21.com
DesignShare—www.designshare.com
Facing the Future—www.facingthefuture.org
Lawrence Hall of Science at UC Berkeley—www.lhs.berkeley.edu
Media Awareness Network—www.media-awareness.ca/
Media Literacy Clearinghouse—www.frankwbaker.com
Met Schools—www.themetschool.org/Metcenter/The_Education.html
November Learning—www.novemberlearning.com
ODT Maps—www.ODTmaps.com
Read-Write-Think—www.readwritethink.org/lessons
Shelburne Farms Sustainable Schools Project—www.sustainableschoolsproject.
  org
TeachingMediaLiteracy.com—www.teachingmmedialiteracy.com

Books and Articles

Help your kids see through the media-peddled culture of celebrity. (2006, March 14). *Kansas City (MO) Star*. Available: www.frankwbaker.com/kids_media_celebrity.htm

Jakes, D. (2007, April 20). Web 2.0 and the new visual literacy. *Tech & Learning*. Available: www.techlearning.com/article/7236

Mustacchi, J. (2008, March). What's relevant for YouTubers? *Educational Leadership, 65*(6).

Stansbury, M. (2008, March 10). Schools add digital arts to the curriculum. *eSchool News*. Available: www.eschoolnews.com/news/top-news/index.cfm?i=52989

Stansbury, M. (2008, March 26). Analysis: How multimedia can improve learning. *eSchool News*. Available: www.eschoolnews.com/news/top-news/?i=53243

Sussman, A. (2000). *Dr. Art's Guide to Planet Earth: For Earthlings ages 12 to 120*. White River Junction, VT: Chelsea Green.

Zeeck, D. (2008, March 2). Media literacy crucial in the age of Internet news. *Tacoma News Tribune*. Available: www.thenewstribune.com/news/columnists/zeeck/story/298285.html

Sources for Media Literacy Curriculum Materials

First Light Video Publishing—www.firstlightvideo.com/
Media Education Foundation—www.mediaed.org/
NAMLE Marketplace—http://shopdei.com/namle/index.php
New Mexico Media Literacy Project—www.nmmlp.org/
Theatre Books—www.theatrebooks.com/

Organizations Offering Media Literacy Teacher Institutes

American Film Institute—www.afi.com/
. Educational Video Center—www.evc.org/
Jacob Burns Film Center—www.burnsfilmcenter.org/
Media Education Lab at Temple University—www.mediaeducationlab.com/
Media Literacy Graduate Program at Appalachian State University—www.ced.
    appstate.edu/departments/ci/programs/edmedia/medialit/
New Mexico Media Literacy Project—www.nmmlp.org/
Project Look Sharp at Ithaca College—www.ithaca.edu/looksharp/

INDEX

....

The letter *f* following a page number denotes a figure.

Media Sharp: Analyzing Tobacco and Alcohol Messages (Kaiser Family Foundation), 149
media violence, aggression, and antisocial behavior, 144
Mercator projection map, 36–38, 37f
Mertz, Janet E., 54
metacognition, 214–215
Metropolitan Regional Career and Technical Center, 67
migration, domestic, 40
moral dilemmas in science education, 43–44
MP3 players, 25, 205–207
Mt Hope High School, 156–157
Mulready, Thomas, 57
MySpace, 204

Nair, Prakash, 74–75
National Assessment of Education Progress (NAEP), 10
National Association for Media Literacy Education, 138
National Association of Independent Schools, 180–181
National Basketball Association, 47
National Center for Research Resources, 41
National Council of Teachers of English (NCTE), 136, 137, 146
National Eating Disorders Association, 144
National Institutes of Health, 41, 149
National Science Foundation, 43
National Telemedia Council, 137
New Jersey, 12
New Mexico Literacy Project, 138
New York state, 42, 54
New Zealand, 41, 51
Niguidula, David, 64
No Child Left Behind (NCLB), 10, 136
nostalgia in limiting change, 15
nutrition, effect of media literacy on, 144
NYC Public Schools, 176–177

on-demand educational video, 200–201
"One Laptop per Child" project, 199
online games, 91–93
open-source social production, 84

open-source software movement, 84
Organization for Economic Cooperation and Development (OECD), 100–101

Papahana Kaipuni Hawai'i (Public School Hawaiian Immersion Program), 51
Partnership for 21st Century Skills, 26–28, 135–136, 141–142, 211
Partnership for Global Learning, 110
Partnership for Media Education, 138
Penn LPS Commons, 74
Peters, Arno, 36–38
Photosynth, 89–90
physical education curriculum, 45–47
physical fitness, effect of media literacy on, 144
Piaget, Jean, 9
Plato, 27
podcasts, audio and video, 205–207
portfolios, Web-based, 204–205. *See also* digital portfolios
The Post-American World (Zakaria), 38
prediction markets, 83–84
Prensky, Marc, 134
Princeton University, 41
printing press, 207
problem-solving methods, 208, 223–224
professional development, 59, 112
professionals, grouping of, 71–74
Proxmire, William, 137
Public Broadcasting Service (PBS), 137, 148
Public School Hawaiian Immersion Program (Papahana Kaipuni Hawai'i), 51
Putnam/Northern Westchester BOCES, 174–175
Putting the World into World-Class Education (CCSSO), 110

Read-Write-Think Web site, 146
religion, science education and, 43–44
researchers, students as, 190–191
Rhode Island, 12, 64, 67, 156
Richer Picture portfolio tool, 155
right-brained thinkers, 17, 55–58
Rio Summit, UN, 171

Scene Smoking (CDC), 149
schedules, the structure of time, 63–69, 103, 109–110

ABOUT THE EDITOR AND CONTRIBUTING AUTHORS

About the Editor

Heidi Hayes Jacobs is founder and president of Curriculum Designers Inc., consults to schools nationally and internationally, and is executive director of the Curriculum Mapping Institute. She has taught courses at Columbia University's Teachers College in New York City since 1981. Among Jacobs's books are *Interdisciplinary Curriculum: Design and Implementation; Mapping the Big Picture: Integrating Curriculum and Assessment K–12; Getting Results with Curriculum Mapping;* and is coauthor with Ann Johnson of *The Curriculum Mapping Planner: Templates, Tools, and Resources for Effective Professional Development,* all published by ASCD. *Active Literacy Across the Curriculum: Strategies for Reading, Writing, Speaking and Listening* is published by Eye on Education. Her online courses appear with PBS Teacherline. Working with a wide range of organizations, Jacobs has consulted to the College Board,

NBC *Sunday Today* show, the Peace Corps, the Discovery Channel, Children's Television Workshop, the Kennedy Center, Carnegie Hall, New York City Ballet Education, the International Baccalaureate, and state education departments. Her doctoral work was completed at Columbia University's Teachers College in 1981, studying under a national Graduate Leadership Fellowship from the Utah State Office of Education. Jacobs earned a master's degree at UMass at Amherst; her undergraduate studies were at the University of Utah in her birthplace, Salt Lake City. The fundamental backbone of Jacobs's experience comes from years as a teacher of high school, junior high school, and elementary children in Utah, Massachusetts, and New York. She is married with two adult children and lives in Westchester County. Contact Jacobs through www.curriculumdesigners.com or www.curriculum21.com.

About the Contributing Authors

Frank W. Baker is a graduate of the University of Georgia (ABJ, Journalism). He has worked in both broadcast journalism and public education. In 1997, Baker taught a college-level media literacy course for educators and developed a nationally recognized media literacy resource Web site. In 1999, his content analysis of teaching standards in all 50 states revealed that almost all include elements of media literacy. Baker has presented at the national conferences of the International Reading Association, the National Middle Schools Association, and the National Council of Teachers of English (NCTE). He served on the NCTE's Commission on Media from 2005 to 2008. Baker assisted the South Carolina State Department of Education's English Language Arts team in revising the state teaching standards to include elements of media literacy. His first book, *Coming Distractions: Questioning Movies*, was published in 2007 by Capstone Press. In June 2007, Baker's work was recognized by the National PTA and the National Cable TV Association with the national Leaders in Learning award. He contributed a lesson plan to the NCTE text "Lesson Plans for Creating Media-Rich Classrooms." Baker's second book, *Political Campaigns & Political Advertising: A Media Literacy Guide*, was published in 2009 by Greenwood Press. Baker is an educational consultant and can be reached at FBaker1346@aol.com.

Jaimie P. Cloud is the founder and president of the Cloud Institute for Sustainability Education in New York City. The Cloud Institute monitors the evolving thinking and skills of the most important champions of sustainability, and transforms them into educational materials and a pedagogical system that inspire young people to think about the world, their relationship to it, and their ability to influence it in an entirely new way.

Cloud is one of the pioneers of Education for Sustainability (EfS) in the United States. She writes and publishes extensively, and consults, coaches, and teaches in schools and school districts around the country and in other parts of the world. Cloud has developed exemplary curriculum units and full courses of study, and has produced a set of EfS Standards and Performance Indicators that schools are using to innovate their own curricula to educate for sustainability. Cloud also serves as chair of Communities for Learning Inc., a member of the Advisory Committee of The Buckminster Fuller Institute, and a member of the Editorial Board of the International Journal of Education for Sustainable Development. You may contact Cloud at Jaimie@cloudinstitute.org.

Arthur L. Costa is emeritus professor of education at California State University, Sacramento, and cofounder of the Institute for Intelligent Behavior in El Dorado Hills, California. He has served as a classroom teacher, a curriculum consultant, and an assistant superintendent for instruction and as the director of educational programs for the National Aeronautics and Space Administration. Costa has made presentations and conducted workshops in all 50 states as well as Mexico, Central and South America, Canada, Australia, New Zealand, Africa, Europe, Asia, and the Islands of the South Pacific.

Costa has written and edited numerous books, including *Techniques for Teaching Thinking*, *The School as a Home for the Mind*, and *Cognitive Coaching*. He is editor of *Developing Minds: A Resource Book for Teaching Thinking* and coeditor of the *Process as Content* trilogy; Costa is the co-author (with Bena Kallick) of the four-book developmental series, *Habits of Mind*, along with *Learning and Leading with Habits of Mind*, and *Habits of Mind Across the Curriculum*. His books have been translated into Arabic, Chinese, Italian, Spanish, and Dutch.

Active in many professional organizations, Costa served as president of the California Association for Supervision and Curriculum Development; he was the president of the Association for Supervision and Curriculum Development from 1988 to 1989.

Bena Kallick is a private consultant providing services to school districts, state departments of education, professional organizations, and public agencies throughout the United States and internationally. Kallick received her doctorate in educational evaluation from Union Graduate School. Her areas of focus include group dynamics, creative and critical thinking, curriculum mapping, and assessment strategies for the classroom. Her written work includes *Assessment in the Learning Organization, Learning and Leading with Habits of Mind,* and *Habits of Mind Across the Curriculum* (the latter two coauthored with Art Costa) and *Curriculum Mapping and Assessment to Improve Student Learning* (coauthored with Jeff Colosimo).

Formerly a teachers' center director, Kallick also created a children's museum based on problem solving and invention. She was the coordinator of a high school alternative designed for at-risk students. She is cofounder of Performance Pathways, a company dedicated to providing easy-to-use software that helps integrate and make sense of data from curriculum, instruction, and assessment. Kallick has taught at Yale University School of Organization and Management, University of Massachusetts Center for Creative and Critical Thinking, and Union Graduate School. She is on the board of Communities for Learning. Kallick can be reached at 12 Crooked Mile Road, Westport, CT 06880. Phone or fax: 203-227-7261. E-mail: bkallick@aol.com.

Alan November is an international leader in education technology. His team at November Learning works with educators at all levels who strive to expand the boundaries of learning and bring authenticity and rigor into their classrooms. Visit www.novemberlearning.com to learn more about November's work and to gain access to a variety of useful resources. You may contact November at alan@novemberlearning.com or 781-631-4333.

David Niguidula is founder of Ideas Consulting, an educational technology and consulting firm based in Providence, Rhode Island. Niguidula led the first research project on digital portfolios while at the Coalition of Essential Schools and Annenberg Institute for School Reform at Brown University. Through Ideas Consulting, Niguidula has developed the *Richer Picture* digital portfolio software tools and professional development workshops to help schools successfully implement portfolios in their own settings. Niguidula worked with policymakers and educators on statewide implementation of portfolios, including the use of portfolios as a graduation requirement. His most recent work helps schools connect portfolios to other initiatives, including curriculum mapping, individual learning plans, and personal literacy plans.

Niguidula has served on numerous national advisory boards and has presented his work on educational technology to groups including the U.S. Department of Education, the National Governors' Association, ASCD, the National Science Foundation, and the International Society for Technology in Education, and the European Institute for E-Learning.

Niguidula received two bachelor's degrees (in computer science and education) from Brown University and his doctorate in instructional technology and media from Teachers College, Columbia University.

Bill Sheskey is a lifetime educator with experience as a public school instructional technology specialist, classroom teacher, athletic coach, and is now affiliated with Heidi Hayes Jacobs's Curriculum Designers Inc. as a faculty member. Sheskey designed and facilitates a series of engaging workshops for educators at national, state, and local education conferences where participants leave the workshop with multimedia tools to immediately engage their students. These dynamic experiences for all levels of educators provide hands-on experience in the development of authentic assessment strategies, essential question writing, and digital literacy tools for the classroom. These multimedia and Web-based applications guide educators in creating learning environments where student achievement is the number one goal. Web site: http://sheskeylearning.com. E-mail: bill@sheskeylearning.com.

Vivien Stewart is senior advisor for education at Asia Society, where she has been leading a national effort to prepare American students and educators for the interconnected world of the 21st century. Stewart's position includes working with a network of state leaders to promote international education; developing a national initiative to expand the teaching of Chinese; creating a prizes program to recognize excellence in international education; providing publications and Web resources for teachers and students; and developing a model network of internationally oriented schools in inner cities around the United States. Internationally, Stewart has developed a series of international benchmarking exchanges to share expertise between American and Asian education, business, and policy leaders on how to improve education to meet the demands of globalization. Prior to Asia Society, she was the director of education programs at Carnegie Corporation of New York, where Stewart developed grant making and reform agendas on child and youth development issues and managed a series of influential education task forces. She has also been a senior advisor at the United Nations on refugee education. Stewart has undergraduate and graduate degrees from Oxford University. In 2007, she was awarded the Harold McGraw Prize for national contributions to education. E-mail: vstewart@asiasoc.org.

Tim Tyson has been called the Pied Piper of Educational Technology by *The School Library Journal.* Tyson has worked in the field of education for nearly 30 years as a teacher (in middle school, high school, and college) and an administrator. He served the students in the Cobb County School District for about 20 years and was principal of Mabry Middle School before retiring. Tyson was named one of Georgia's High Performance Principals by Governor Sonny Purdue.

Tyson has a passion for meaningful, authentic student engagement and envisions technology as a centerpiece for irresistible academic achievement through creative, global, project-based learning activities. Tyson is now supporting the education profession on a national and international level by sharing his passion for and practical expertise in integrating technology into the entire school plan—a vision that works. E-mail: tim@drtimtyson.com, Web site: drtimtyson.com.

Stephen Wilmarth is an education futurist and social entrepreneur who brings innovative thinking to curriculum design issues arising out of rapidly changing workforce needs in a global knowledge economy. In 2008, he founded New School Student Ambassadors Inc., a nonprofit organization developing model private schools in northwest China that facilitate participatory learning programs using project-based curriculum and rapidly evolving social media technologies.

Wilmarth is a visiting lecturer at Ningxia Polytechnic University and Ningxia Teachers University in northwest China, and a featured speaker at several international conferences on curriculum reform and design. He serves as a consultant to the software developer for the Hanban, the official Chinese agency charged with developing language learning and cultural export programs for the Chinese government through worldwide Confucius Institutes.

Wilmarth is a former classroom teacher and a guest lecturer at MIT's Sloan School of Management, the London Business School, and University of Connecticut's Graduate School of Business. He is an active proponent of participatory learning through membership in the Action Coalition for Media Education and the MIT Center for Future Civic Media, and as a friend of the Information Society Project at Yale Law School. Contact Wilmarth by e-mail at Stephen.Wilmarth@Gmail.com.